HYLO NARRANS

Hylo Narrans

Echoes of Material Marronage

Kevin Toksöz Fairbairn

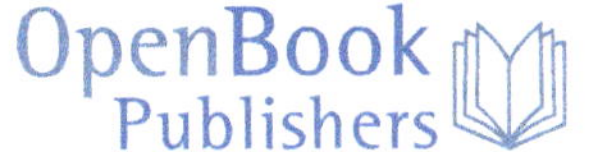

https://www.openbookpublishers.com

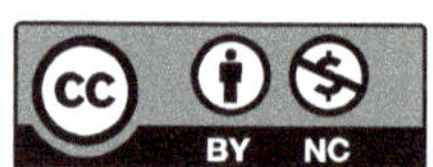

All external links were active at the time of publication unless otherwise stated and have been archived via the Internet Archive Wayback Machine at https://archive.org/web

Digital material and resources associated with this volume are available at https://doi.org/10.11647/OBP.0476#resources

ISBN Paperback: 978-1-80511-643-1
ISBN Hardback: 978-1-80511-644-8
ISBN Digital (PDF): 978-1-80511-645-5
ISBN HTML: 978-1-80511-647-9
ISBN Digital ebook (epub): 978-1-80511-646-2

DOI: 10.11647/OBP.0476

Cover image: Kevin Toksöz Fairbairn, CC BY-NC
Cover design: Jeevanjot Kaur Nagpal

Table of Contents

List of Figures

List of Audio Recordings

The audio recordings are also available on the OBP Zenodo Community (https://zenodo.org/communities/openbookpublishers/records): https://doi.org/10.5281/zenodo.17035742

Audio and video recordings with the same number/title are the same session.

List of Video Recordings

The video recordings are also available on the OBP Zenodo Community (https://zenodo.org/communities/openbookpublishers/records): https://doi.org/10.5281/zenodo.17035742

Audio and video recordings with the same number/title are the same session.

Preface

Figs. 1-3 Annealing brass. Photos by author (2024).

Audio Recording 1 *Thermoform*. Recording by author (2024), http://hdl.handle.net/20.500.12434/0ede767b

Video Recording 1 *Thermoform*. Recording by author (2024), http://hdl.handle.net/20.500.12434/1d61fd87

George McCracken opened his brass instrument workshop in Barhamsville, Virginia, in 1980, after leaving a position as chief designer at King Musical Instruments following an argument over the soldering of a single joint on a commercial line of sousaphones. As in many previous situations, the company had opted for a cost-effective solution despite the obvious flaws it would introduce into the instrument, which would inevitably break more frequently and require extra repairs. Exhausted by years spent battling such planned obsolescence, George moved to Barhamsville and opened his own small business making custom brass instruments. In a repurposed garage, he assembled a workshop and began fabricating just about any traditional brass instrument you might imagine. Specialized primarily in French horns—George's own instrument and first love—he would also create unique new models of tuba, trombone, trumpet, and many other instruments.

I met George as a teenager when I brought him my trombone for some basic repair work. I was as intrigued by George himself as I was by the surrounding machines, tools, and assorted collections of raw brass, unfinished new instruments, and disassembled old ones. He was a treasure trove of information about brass instruments and stories about the famous performers who had played them. Shortly afterwards I approached him about starting as an apprentice in the trade. Happy for the extra pair of hands, he took me on, and my long relationship with metalworking commenced in earnest.

In the early days, I would alternate between grunt labor (endless hours annealing, bending, sanding, and polishing), studying old design drawings from his collection, and listening to George's endless stream of recollections about the business, pointers on working with brass, and commentary on the local classical radio station's programming. Over the years I spent there, I would eventually learn every aspect of the trade, from the most basic forms of manipulating raw brass to more specialized skills in manual machining and the design process itself. I learned how to transform raw metal stock into world-class boutique instruments, many of which are still being played in famous concert halls around the world. But the most enduring habits I picked up from George were not the basics of metallurgy but rather his personal commitment to evolving with and alongside his instruments. Despite his ability to produce some of the finest instruments in the world, many of which could have been marketed to relatively high demand, I would come to learn that he was more or less constitutionally incapable of building the same instrument twice. It didn't matter how elegantly a new horn played or how many performers were interested in getting their hands on it, he simply had no interest in replicating these projects. Indeed, even before a new model was finished, he was normally already drawing up plans for the next one, and if a customer called to request an older model, he would instead try to talk them into ordering whatever crazy new ideas he'd recently dreamt up.

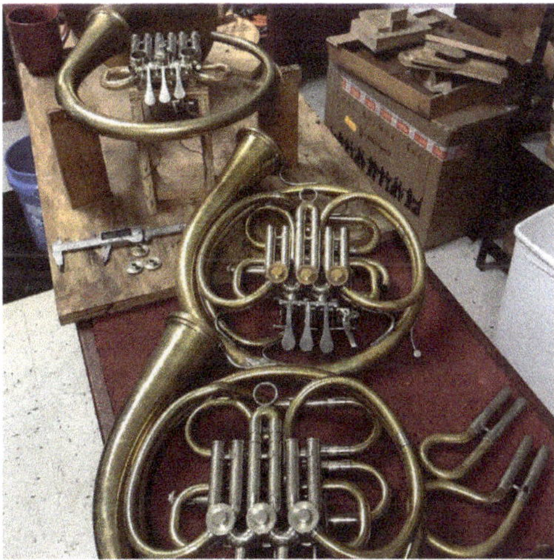

Fig. 4 George McCracken's workshop, featuring three unique French horn models in various stages of completion. Photo by George McCracken (date unknown).

He relished the puzzles and the problem solving, and every new instrument was another opportunity to scratch that itch, a chance to quite literally return to the drawing board, charting new trajectories of research and design. For years, I didn't even realize quite how unusual this was. As an apprentice in his shop, it was the only thing I knew, and just as I learned and internalized a million other embodied tricks and tics while observing and imitating George, I had similarly internalized these ceaseless drives of curiosity and creativity. Unwittingly, I had learned not only how to solder, how to machine, and how to buff, but also how to transform daydreams into elegant designs and, eventually, beautiful new material objects in the world. George showed me how to cultivate the inquisitive dimension of craft, how to appraise a pile of scrap brass and rotate it in my mind until it bore some new tool or valve design.

Since that time I have also worked in commercial production and on factory floors. I've learned how to bring my skills to bear on production line tasks and carbon copy instruments, funneling my creativity into efficiency rather than acoustic innovation. But those endeavors never really scratch the itch, and so it is perhaps little surprise that I ended up cultivating space for fantasy both within and outside those confines. I have never been able to stop whittling away at ideas first hatched during my apprenticeship, sometimes honing my own designs for years before finally producing a new instrument that I'd first hypothesized while sitting with George and a cup of herbal tea. Although I had embarked on my apprenticeship with the vague notion of 'getting more in touch' with the instruments that at that time I was studying, and which I now perform professionally, I was lucky that George didn't practice his trade as something purely practical or logistical. Rather, he inculcated principles of introspection and experimentation, such that I never learned to manipulate a piece of brass without already being aware of that metal as a clue, as a stepping stone, or as a portal into some new acoustic register or musical dimension.

Ultimately, I followed this path further than I think George could have ever imagined. As the ensuing pages will demonstrate, I have spent years developing an experimental craft practice that, after recovering rejected brass from industrial instrument manufacturing, then approaches these metals as affordances, as agencies, and even as animacies, in and of themselves. As collaborators in the workshop, these metals hijack the trajectory of their own construction, and in so doing, also reorient my own metallurgical training towards new acoustic topologies that I could never have dreamt up alone. George taught me that building an instrument was an act of care, a way of cultivating both communication and community. He demonstrated how metal could be addressed with compassion, neither in a metaphorical sense nor in a purely practical way, but as a genre of care that attends not only to the task at hand but also to its echoes in other hands and spaces in the future. He taught me to treat metal with the kind of tenderness that you show to something or someone that will outgrow your attention, whose story your attentiveness charts and propels. It was the same care that he showed me, for example, as an apprentice, a collaborator, and a friend. And it has become the foundation beneath my own creative practice rooted in materiality, investigating not only the limits of human organological imagination, but also the histories, qualities, and still-unfolding stories that these brasses themselves articulate.

Introduction

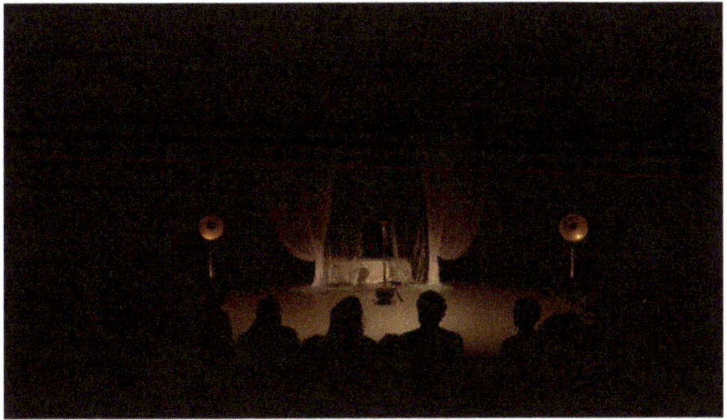

Fig. 5 Chimeracord installation: *Funeous*. Photo by Davids Danoss (2025).

Audio Recording 2 *Funeous*. Recording by author (2025), http://hdl.handle.net/20.500.12434/a84da447

Video Recording 2 *Funeous*. Recording by Siamak Anvari (2025), http://hdl.handle.net/20.500.12434/47b5ff7b

This book cannot claim to tell the stories of brass, but it nonetheless aspires to help make them audible. It aims to reorient readers' senses towards the narrative agencies in brass's molecular latticework, both those long since etched and those still ineluctably evolving. Their

 https://doi.org/10.11647/OBP.0476.00

material ontogenies articulate histories of sedimentation and subsidence, of geological transformations and chemical metamorphoses; but they also record histories of extraction, and displacement through capitalist industry, subjected to mutilation and exploitation at the hands of those humans who mold their stories into new shapes—including my own. Although this book attempts to render non-metaphorical material voices and stories decipherable, it can only do so by documenting the relationships that I have personally and physically formed with brass over the last decades, ranging from music to metallurgy, and from coercion to complicity. It is an attempt to make audible voices of material agency that might otherwise remain unnoticed, obscured by the overbearing soundscapes of the human societies in which they are embedded, from the realms of industrial production, to concert halls full of music, and through all the intervening spaces that connect them. In attuning to the frequencies of brass that suffuse contemporary life, this book seeks to reveal not only how materials are already enlisted into practices of cultural production, but also how their capacities for creative expression and narrative agency can exceed that utilitarian debasement. In questioning how material voices might not only contribute to but even direct conversations about our entangled human and more-than-human futures, this book revolves around the question: how do material voices become both audible and instrumental within our collective imaginary?

Brass itself is a figment. Like many of the materials that populate contemporary cities and the plantation infrastructures that sustain them (from steel to concrete to glass to plastic), brass is a product of extraction and refining, a distillation of naturally-occurring substances into domesticated 'raw' materials. Some metals do occur naturally, of course—most famously gold and silver, and most influentially copper and iron. But even these materials derive their value from how they are treated, shaped, and molded. Whether carved, melted, or cast, these metals' utility has always been defined by their compliance to human artifice. Like most metals that surround us, brass is an alloy comprising multiple metals smelted together and bonded. These alloys reify superficially idealized forms of regularity and consistency: isotropic blocks of lustrous, resilient, malleable metal. At the molecular level, though, they are anything but uniform. Beneath their deceptively stable facade, their crystallized metallic lattices are fragmented, irregularly bonded, and incorrigibly reactive to their environment. Like many metals, their utility must be sustained through careful isolation, such as with brass musical instruments, which are coated in blankets of clear enamel in order to preserve the momentary sheen that emerges once polished. In other words, brass is a carefully concocted illusion of momentary molecular bonding, lovingly preserved, but which invariably leeches and corrodes and degrades if left exposed. Although this molecular motility occurs in material timeframes more aligned with geological sedimentation than capitalist industry, there is never any single instant within the subdual of brass when it is not already in flight.

This book seeks to attune to these fugitive materials as they wriggle and writhe out of the grasp of industrial capitalism. Material marronage describes materials-in-flight; it catalogs forms of molecular dynamism or rebellious irrecuperability through which materials resist their absorption into cycles of extraction, industry, and utility. But like all maroons, their stories don't commence with flight, but radiate outwards from these moments of resistance in intricate webs of past and future storylines. Aimé Césaire challenged the grammatical "thingification" (Césaire 1950/2000: 42) enacted by the noun marronage, in which vital assertions of motility are recast as static states of being—as though maroons exist detached from any previous or future modes of living. In its place, Césaire crafted the verb *marronner* (Césaire 1955/1983: 368-369) in order to articulate the intransitive nature of fugitivity amid the pulsing energies that drive and sustain it. For while these energies may pool and concentrate in punctuating bursts of flight or revolt, they are outgrowths of wider networks of agency through which they are invariably threaded. Every marronage implicates the stories and histories that flow into its kinetic outburst, with each flight an evocation of the energies that bore it to that moment.

Scholars of marronage and the African diaspora document the "dehiscent anterior" (Bradley 2023: 11) that marks these passages from captivity to fugitivity. The freedom that maroons wrest from the world embodies both a rupture from and suture to the lineages and histories that flow into their confluence. And while marronage carves new spaces out of a landscape that is itself wounded by the same settler plantation infrastructures that swallowed their Black bodies, those spaces retain a "*cultural* vestibularity" (Spillers 1987) that echoes the old world even as it crafts new collective futures within a new one. From the depths of this displacement, maroon voices amplify the "sea-changed song [...] of exile[,...] the worldwide beat and sound and pressure of humiliated, degraded, disrupted, abandoned man," that emerged from this "new and alien *rite de passage*" (Wynter n.d.: 55). Césaire's insistence on the intransitive agency of *marronner* exposes the deep resonating echoes that bridge these ongoing stories of captivity, displacement, marronage, and resistance—stories that are not inhabited by maroons, but which are rather seized by them, re-narrating collective futures that still bear traces of the lacerations from which they sprang.

Material marronage is a complicated cousin of these maroons, occupying radically different registers of time and space while still flowing through kindred channels of flight. Metallic distortions, fractures, and corrodings are direct reactions to the operations that seek to 'break' and domesticate them. Each single instance in which they warp is a uniquely individual and unpredictable act of disobedience, rejecting the yoke of molecular metallicity in which they have been quite literally cast. They enact different genres of resilience than the human maroons that came before them, but both embody resistance to the same extractive drive—that deep-rooted Western compulsion to subjugate the entire Earth *propter nos homines*, for the sake of (a normative, hegemonic definition of white Western) man. As this book dives into the history of brass extraction, refining, and manufacture, I will explore how the plantation dogmas of purity and profit that maroons fled are entangled in the ontogenies of these metals, as well. And just as human and metallic bodies mingled in the early copper mines where brass was produced by slaves "doomed to a quick death[,...] continually spent by disease" (Strabo 1961: 451), they also converge in the sites of collective resistance and sustenance that Sylvia Wynter theorizes as the *plot* (Wynter 1971). Evoking both "material site and narrative mode" (Moulton 2024: 271), these tracts of land allow the interscalar trajectories of terrestrial, material, organic, and human rebellion to take root in each other, shaping fecund new futures out of transplanted maroon ecosystems. It is within these spaces that the seemingly incompatible modalities of anterior human and material histories intertwine in new forms of collective narrative agency.

These *plots* are the soil in which collective narratives take root, in which bodies subjugated to the inertia of the capitalist origin myth of economic productivity can not only imagine alternative modes of existence but can also collectively cultivate them, speaking new versions of the world into existence. Wynter notes how collective storytelling shapes the world around us, determining not only our metaphorical understanding of our situated reality, but also its very material affordances. As a species whose biological reality is tethered to these mythological dimensions, Wynter formulates the concept of *homo narrans*—not only the human as storyteller, but being human as storytelling, a hybridly biological and cultural praxis—in part to assert how collective resistance emerges from intergenerational networks of cultural creativity that ultimately define which acts of resistance, rebellion, or marronage might become possible. The *plot* demarcates not only a tract of communal cultivation and practical nourishment but also the narrative agency that sprouts within these sites of mutual care, which in turn sustain the conditions for intergenerational and interspecies resilience. The stories that germinate in these *plots* enact cycles of communal self-re/generation, with each song and each speech channeling histories of displacement and oppression into the re/invention of new origin myths and the futures they bring into focus.

In turning to the soil in these *plots*, and to the tools and utensils that help till it, this book attempts to trace the threads of materiality woven into the narrative arcs that maroons follow outwards from these sites. I posit that the storytelling agency of *homo narrans* is accompanied by a material *hylo narrans* (after the Greek *hylē*, meaning matter), whose voices sprout forth from the decomposing molds of a Western hylomorphic ideology. *Hylo narrans* embodies both the pulsating acoustic presence of materials-in-flight as well as their structural support to the lattice of interwoven agencies that constitute the collective cultural re/invention of *homo narrans*. I propose to approach the leakage and slippage of materials that resist the disciplining of industrial production as they whisper, murmur, and indeed often shriek, shout, or sing under the duress of industrial manipulation and mutilation. In their visceral resistance to commodification, their voices breach the barriers between the seemingly incommensurate narrative scales that they occupy as mineral ores in the sedimented strata of the Earth's crust and the scales of extraction and consumption into which they have been absorbed by capitalist enterprise. They shift obliquely, disengaging at a molecular level from their prospective utilitarian futures and swerving towards other potential valences. This book focuses on particular pieces of metal as they grasp this obliquity. These fragments of brass were conscripted into factories to be formed into carefully precise forms—in this case, as musical instruments intended for the concert stage. But as these metals deform and corrode on the factory floor, slipping from the craftsperson's grasping clutch, they audibly voice their fugitive agency against the tools and machines that would subdue their resounding insubordination.

Their acoustic interpellations invite us to recalibrate, to build differently, and to listen otherwise, finding alternative trajectories from the maps that their scars render intelligible. Through their mediation, our material and human agencies can collectively generate new forms of propulsive deterioration, reorienting our perception towards forms of relation and community that suture these material voices to the collective imaginaries of the *plot*. Their resilience in the face of industrial exploitation invites not only our responsivity, but also our complicity. Like any marronage, material marronage can take many forms, from fleeting to epochal, from singular to communal, but in every case relies on the networks of complicity in which it might emerge, survive, or thrive (Diouf 2014). The voicings of materials-in-flight are outgrowths of other stories, songs, and invocations that came before, and which depend on the platform of other sounding agencies that buttress their impulse towards obliquity. The syllables that their bodies shape implicate the interscalar histories of their material dehiscence, but are also inextricably entangled in the specific forms and operations of the workshop from the moment of their flight.

Brass records and remembers every intervention, from mining to smelting to casting and fabrication. It retains a memory and an imprint of everything that's been done to it. And while it can undergo a theoretically infinite amount of heating, cooling, and molding, it always retains a memory of each tiny molecular modification it has undergone. Every time it is heated red hot, it builds a relationship to that moment, and each time it is bent or straightened, its body records that molecular motion, absorbing each inscription into increasingly intricate patterns of internal tension and release. It is impossible to predict precisely at what stage of working a piece of metal will suddenly react to a tool or a machine, or simply to the oxygen in the air. Some brass takes flight while still a raw piece of stock, while some will flee after having already been molded into intricate new instrumental forms. Each piece of marooning brass holds not only an archive of its history in becoming brass, but also a core-sample of the workflow precisely when it rebels. Each of these pieces of metal holds a freezeframe of the moment when it escapes as a tube, as a flare, as a rod, or a cord, and retains within its ongoing narration all of the energies and agencies that congealed in that moment. In their implacable, rebellious deformation, their metal voicings echo and transpose the needling interjections of the torches, hammers, and human bodies that address them.

And so this book begins—has already begun—in the workshop. As these reflections have helped to show, the workshop is not an idealized, neutral space. It is a space for work; its most intimate relations are not physical but economic and extractive, and my own involvement in these relations of productivity cannot be overlooked. In drawing my research out of the workshop, I am relying on decades of experience, ranging from the artisanal workshop where I did my apprenticeship to more recent atelier spaces where I work as an artist; but in between these two ends of the spectrum lie years spent working for capital, years on factory floors contributing my craft expertise to the demands of the market. And while the workshop floor contains all of the requisite conditions to foster intermedial intimacy in theory, in practice it is most often oriented towards diametrically different outcomes—iterative practices of discipline, manufacture, and profit, which I have personally executed countless times with my own two hands. The workshop is fundamentally conceived as a space for material to be invested with form, embodying the continuity of the grand Aristotelian tradition of hylomorphism. Material here is something raw, something to be processed and manipulated, coaxed into new forms that reflect the ingenuity of (implicitly human) design. The workshop could theoretically become a space that encourages other forms of innovation, or even fantasy, but there are very strict ideological guardrails constricting those trajectories of speculation and invention. My entire career—from trade to performance to research—has been built around this scaffolding of control and manufacture, and so while this book focuses primarily on the amplification of material voices and the propagation of material agencies, it also charts my own attempts to fracture the inertia of workshop production and to divert my own complicity away from manufacturing profit and towards the enabling and sustaining of these material marronages.

Because this research is so intimately tied to my own metalworking experience, it adheres closely to the specific history of brass musical instruments, addressing their material and construction as a crucible for examining broader infrastructures of material extraction and exploitation. But the material history of brass musical instruments is also deeply embedded in musical and cultural history; more than just physical artifacts, they are inextricably entangled in Western ideological systems and the evolutions of artistic practice and creative expression that have reinforced their hegemony. Brass instruments help expose the consubstantiality of material extraction, industrial production, and cultural creativity, and so this research embarks from a particularly salient confluence of metalworking and music at the heart of the Western cultural imagination: the forge where Pythagoras first discovered the laws of harmony that would go on to shape Western philosophical and musical discourse for millennia. As the legend goes, while simply wandering by one day, Pythagoras's attention was grabbed by a startling consonance of blacksmithing hammers sounding in unison, which, upon closer inspection by the renowned philosopher, revealed the germs of a harmonic law of universal proportion that would eventually exert an overbearing influence on Western—and indeed global—history. Though sparked by the hammers and their forge, Pythagorean harmony found its ultimate expression in the monochord. Pythagoras's monochord was an extremely simple instrument, just a single string stretched across a wooden box. As an organological design, it was hardly unique to Western culture, and in fact many other cultures have developed versions of the monochord that are considerably more inventive and expressive.[1]

1 There are several varieties of monochord prevalent in various cultures. Most similar to Pythagoras's monochord are the plucked zither monochords, such as the *đàn bầu* from Vietnam, the Chinese *duxianqin*, and the Japanese *ichigenkin*. There are also a variety of held monochords, which are normally bowed or plucked, such as the Thai *phin pia*, the Khmer *kse diev*, the Vietnamese *dan k'ni*, the Indian *ektara*, and the American *Diddley bow*. Also bowed is the European *tromba marina* (or *Trumscheit*), a curious alternative to the natural trumpet. Monochord musical bows are quite common among cultures in Africa and the African diaspora, comprising two distinct morphologies and performance practices: held and struck musical

Nonetheless, Pythagoras's stubbornly simplistic monochord would still be deployed as the tangible, concrete foundation of Pythagorean rationalism, and over the ensuing centuries it would be repeatedly invoked in the history of Western music to support claims to harmonic truth and objectivity.

My concern in these pages is less Pythagoras's monochord itself than the hammers that first hinted at its possibility. As others before me have shown in more detail (particularly Daniel Heller-Roazen and Frances Dyson, whose work occupies much of Chapter 1), Pythagorean claims to rational elegance are largely spurious; in fact (as has been repeatedly rediscovered throughout the centuries since Pythagoras's experiments), the proportions of mass in objects such as hammers do not correspond to the supposedly immutable ratios in Pythagorean texts. Instead, these hammers help reveal a variability and diversity in the world of material relation that bely Pythagorean dreams of an elegant, rational universe. By representing these hammers as an idealized version of their uncooperative material reality, though, Pythagoreanism instigated a normative rationalism whose distortion of reality would come to dominate entire centuries and continents. In the Pythagorean blacksmithing workshop, materials and tools were accorded no voice—their reality was disregarded and their consonances misattributed. As a workspace, this forge was oriented not around material potential, but around a compulsion to manifest a reality in which matter serves design and where human assumption supersedes material reality. Pythagoreanism's simplistic reduction of the laws governing the universe were facilitated by a workshop hierarchy that allowed hammers to be discarded or disregarded at will, and which misrepresented materials in order to support preordained theoretical narratives. And so, by establishing this particular frame around the material reality of the hammers and their resonance, the workshop floor

---

bows, such as the *berimbau,* which typically use either the mouth or a gourd as a resonator; and ground bows, which use the ground itself as a resonator. Musical bows from other cultures include the *onavillu* of India, the Maori *ku,* mouth bows known by many names among Indigenous peoples of the Americas (particularly around the Andes mountains), and the *Appalachian mouth bow* of North America. There are also more recent innovations such as the *sledgehammer dulcimer* of the Sleepytime Gorilla Museum or some of Görkem Şen's *yaybahars,* not to mention the amazing wind-powered monochords under development by the *World Wide Wind* project's *Triple Instruments.*

effectively fabricated not only physical objects, but also the normative ideology of Pythagorean purity that would infect Western culture, itself hammered into form like just one more piece of iron.

With that in mind, this research turns back to the workshop where hammers and metals commingle in cacophony, attempting to reinitiate that interaction upstream from Pythagorean intervention. I wondered what sort of instrument might emerge from an inquiry made to the materials themselves, one attending to their diversity, inconsistency, and mutability. Returning to the metallurgical workshop, I did not know what I would find. As the following chapters will relate in more detail, I trusted the materials—brass, bronze, copper, steel—to have their own sounds and stories to tell. I did not want to self-consciously design a new monochord as just one more punctuating gesture, like Pythagoras's; I strove instead to pose questions to these materials in the hopes that their own acoustic inclinations or predilections might surface, might grow, might slowly seep into sounding. In following these lines of inquiry, new instruments began to take shape. Their plurality was important to me: I did not intend to craft a single instrument representative of all these endeavors. Instead, I allowed varied possibilities to sprout collectively, experimenting with multiple vectors and iterations of instruments that shared components and sound-worlds, tracing unpredictably flickering configurations of convergence and divergence.

Although these experiments began by simply mounting strings on brass and testing how they resonated, I quickly found that these various materials amplified their respective acoustic potential, and that their threads of agency diffracted through one another to illuminate even further possibilities. What began as an experiment in superposing different instrumental consorts (e.g. string and brass) evolved instead into a prismatic spectrum of acoustic material hybridity. Although always rooted in a single string mounted directly into the brass, these instruments grew into wilder, denser thickets of sounding activity: the brass that amplified the string could also be bowed, producing a whole new order of harmonic spectra; the volume of air inside this resonating chamber could be activated, as well, inviting reeds and other mouthpieces to branch off from this central organ; the string itself could be strung taut through multiple passages within the brass, refracting its single cord into myriad spectra of harmonic interactivity. Far removed from the austere single-mindedness of Pythagoras's iconic monochord, these confluences of brass, copper, steel, cane, and other membranes were less instruments than budding acoustic ecosystems, inhabiting the workshop space rather than being subjected to it. As this multifaceted polyvocality coalesced, I began to think of these instruments as *chimeracords*, voicing their hybrid organologies as they slowly sounded their collective creative agency.

As I learned to reorient myself to these genres of material motility, I strove to facilitate these agencies rather than subdue them. I sought to liberate materials that managed to flee from the trajectories of industrial production, helping them escape from inevitable cycles of recycling and reconstitution, and instead welcoming them into an alternative workshop space where they could determine their own future stories. Already transformed beyond the point of returning to their naturally-occurring forms, and yet in flight from the designs in which they were ordained to be cast, these materials inhabit liminal states of material marronage. And just as human maroon communities do, they carve out pockets of inhabitability within the oppressive infrastructures that surround them on all sides. Indeed, many of the workshop spaces in which I tended them were under the same roof as the workshop spaces that subjugated them: hidden, secret, and at constant risk of discovery, materializing at times of day when the industrial gaze was shuttered, before fading back into ephemeral border spaces when those spaces opened back up to business. They survived within and in spite of the systems of extraction that created them, crafting alternative destinies out of the very tools that were designed to break their resistance.

These metals are united in collective fugitivity, and the instruments towards which they coalesce in these states articulate just a few of the many possible voicings that such material agency can take. Following Sylvia Wynter's understanding of marronage as an outgrowth of collective narrative agency, I propose analogous readings of these materials as agencies capable of singing their own spacetimes of resistance into reality. I seek to uncover new means by which a workshop can come to embody Wynter's conceptualization of the *plot*, becoming simultaneously a physical space and a creative instrument for cultivating collective resistance, marronage, and re/invention. And while this research took initial form as a means to understand and then describe the material agencies I was encountering in this brass, it gradually accumulated other genres of complicity, informing and guiding physical interactions with material on the workshop floor where these instruments took shape and voice.

Throughout this book, I will turn always to the materials themselves to make audible their own contentions and interpolations. Although diffracted through my own artistic practice, these recordings hope to platform these voices, providing a background to their instrumental materialization that helps render their storytelling more intelligible. This book ranges from the history of the monochord through Indigenous philosophical alternatives to Pythagoreanism, and from histories of metallurgy, mining, and refining through philosophies of marronage and fugitivity that attend to the spacetimes of collective creativity and complicity necessary to sustain them. These strands of philosophical speculation are intimately entangled with the material realities of the brass they describe, the instruments they form, and the auralities that those instruments voice. The recordings that accompany each chapter will seek to suture these pages to the material soundwaves that call your attention beyond them, offering their own more radical reorientations to the hybrid collective imaginary of material agencies in our lives, in our societies, and in the fabric of the world that we share.

Chapter Summary

Following Heller-Roazen's evocative retelling of the monochord's origins (Heller-Roazen 2011), Chapter 1 opens with a closer look at the situations that prompted Pythagoras's famous acoustic experiments. Provoked by the consonances created by the ringing of four hammers used simultaneously in a forge, Pythagoras extrapolated the rules of proportion that dictated their degree of consonance and dissonance, which he then extended to a number of different acoustic experiments including, most famously, the monochord. Resurrected centuries later by Boethius, the harmonic phenomena inherent in a single string divided into specific proportions provided the theoretical grounding for Western tonal harmony. The evolution of that musical practice, though, departed in significant ways from the actual acoustic phenomena of Pythagorean harmony, mirroring the distortions and contortions of Pythagoras's original experiments. In Heller-Roazen's reading, Pythagoras's choice to ignore the fifth, dissonant hammer embodies dramatic symbolism of a more complex paradox at the heart of Pythagoreanism: the coexistence of an irreducible incompleteness alongside the compulsion to elide that deficiency. Frances Dyson expands on Heller-Roazen's reflections in order to explore how this foundational "glitch" within Western culture supported a philosophical grounding for contemporary capitalism's penchant for coercing irreducible multiplicity into an illusory unity of thought, purpose, and practice (Dyson 2014: 4). Dyson's call for "resistive echo-ing, or echopraxia" embraces acoustic decay as a template for cultivating multiplicity and divergence, sown from "[t]he echoes of corporeal communication [that] rebind as they rebound" (Dyson 2014: 152-153). In turn, Annie Goh turns to the mythical character of Echo to indicate how "sounding situated knowledges" carry the imprinted traces of the myriad agencies and spaces that converge in their messy coalescence (2017: 4-5). Drawing on Goh's Echo alongside Dyson's echographic (Voegelin 2019: 21) critique of capitalist hegemony, I relate how the conception and construction of an alternative monochord from the chaff of industrial capitalism can craft an alternative narrative wherein the single string of the monochord braids together hybridity, relationality, and cacophony.

Despite its intricate entanglement with the history of Western music, tonality, and culture, the monochord is still an instrument: a string stretched in space. Before its divisions and proportions could support the millennia of cultural baggage that has since accrued, it was a construction of string, wood, or metal, assembled from materials at hand and intimately connected to the physical and artisanal spaces in which it was developed. By looking closely at the monochord's roots in craft and materiality—and by comparing them to the genesis of its doppelgänger in these pages, the chimeracord—Chapter 2 proposes that the sound it produces is a complex synthesis of the workshop, the hands, and the materials that commingled in its fabrication. By refusing to see its voice as an isolated physical vibration in a particular time and space, this chapter asserts that the sonic presence of an instrument inheres not only in its physical vibration, but also in the threads of activity and materiality that run through its construction to its sounding form. Drawing on non-Western traditions of thought, and with a particular focus on orality and sound in the works of Indigenous philosophers from North America (Cordova 2007, Deloria 1973/2003, Deloria 1999, Simpson 2014, Borrows 2018, Watts 2015, Todd 2016, among others), I introduce conceptions of sound that center duration, entanglement, and emplacement. These engagements will reveal sound as a form of thinking and living within an ongoing continuity, inseparable from its surrounding community, ecosystem, and environment. I propose that they can be interpreted through a lens of sonic materialism, embedding sound in the site of its material fabrication through a dynamic form of "Place-Thought" (Watts 2015).

This discussion of place in turn draws attention to the landscapes from which these materials were extracted. Beginning from the early history of mining and metallurgy, Chapter 3 turns its attention towards developments in smelting and casting that allowed for increasingly toxic methods of extraction to become standard in copper and zinc mining over the course of the industrial age. The environmental costs of large-scale open pit copper and zinc mining are severe, as they regularly (and arguably invariably) contaminate groundwater for generations or, in some cases, in perpetuity (Gestring 2012). Mark Jarzombek addresses these symptoms of overgrowth in his "Quadrivium Industrial Complex" (Jarzombek 2019), referencing the relationship between exploding material production (most notably the quadrivium of concrete, steel, glass, and plastic) and waste, pollution, and overconsumption. By tracing their roots in toxic extraction methods, the sonic materiality voiced by modern brass instruments becomes increasingly problematic. Referencing recent literature on the practice of field recording and its complicated relationship to colonialism and extractive logics (e.g., Kanngieser 2023; Wright 2022; Ouzounian 2017), I will suggest that the building materials of our instruments and even of our cities give voice to their extraction and manufacture. The quadrivium of materials that surround us in contemporary urban life echo the traumas of their production, enacting a form of acoustic filtration of the urban acoustic soundscape. In returning to this troubling realization at the smaller scale of modern brass instruments, this chapter will close by suggesting that material complicity in our sounding environment is not an entirely innocent activity, and that any attempt to address material agency in sound must also account for the extractive violence in which these materials' ontogenies are rooted.

Chapter 4 examines the production of material after extraction as both a practical and an ideological process. Although mineral ores are inorganic and ostensibly inert, industrial designations of purity and impurity shape their refining. These "dreams of purity" correspond to normative delineations of normal/deviant, white/Black, civilized/native, etc., that prop up the hegemonic "vision of homogeneity, order, and discipline" that haunts "the plantation regime as industrial formation and enduring logic" (Chao 2023: 184). As Manuel DeLanda notes, "both human workers and the materials they used needed to be disciplined and their behavior made predictable" (DeLanda 2004: 20). Delving into the processes of smelting and casting, I will outline how the disciplining order of refining introduces both the qualities that make metal valuable (malleability married to resilience; luster accompanied by durability) as well as numerous lurking molecular instabilities. Drawing on Simondon's influential discussion of clay bricks in *L'individu et sa gènese physico-biologique*, I turn to Katie Lloyd Thomas's attentive study of industrial building materials, which help us observe the complex latticeworks of commingling energy exchange that animate these seemingly inert blocks of raw material (Lloyd Thomas 2022). Although harnessed by industrial production in search of isotropically utilitarian materials, refining and purification rely on intervening stages of energetic "metastability" (Simondon 2005/2020). Even within the rigidly controlled conditions of industry, close examination of these materials reveal complex behaviors of bonding and, consequently, metamorphosis. The history of metallurgy reveals a complicated dance between disciplined materials and those that resist—corroding and reacting in unpredictable chemical choreographies. Ironically, the conditions in which this material disobedience thrives have flourished under the regime of late capitalism, as the drive for cheap, unregulated production allows ever more materials to slip through the cracks. These materials—corroded, distorted, and expelled from the industrial pipeline—defy the disciplining grasp of plantation capitalism and take flight through the molecular percolations of their own chemical agency. Inspired by speculative "chemo-ethnography," I will trace these "molecular dreamworlds" (Shapiro and Kirksey: 2017:

481) as their corrosive assertions of self-determination evoke alternative configurations of animacy, communalism, and the resultant potential for "'care' across the realm of animacy [...] as a means of unlikely cross-affiliation" (Chen 2012). In attending to these networks of agency and animacy, I join Mel Y. Chen as they ask: "what are the possibilities of rejoinder, of response, for those considered nonsubjects or errant subjects?" (Chen 2012: 212).

This capacity for rejoinder derives in part from the many diverse layers of space and time that congeal in metallic nucleation. Although superficially uniform, the lattice of metallic molecular structure is in fact quite irregular. One of the most valuable traits of metal is its ability to react to manipulation, often using heat, transforming under pressure before reforming. But all of these processes—from refining to annealing to contorting—are recorded in a piece of metal's granular structure, each of which is as diverse as a snowflake, a detailed body archive illegible to the human gaze. Influential historian of metallurgy Cyril Stanley Smith named this specifically material form of memory "funicity," after Jorge Luis Borges's famous character Funes the Memorious. Like Funes, who is unable to forget a single moment or detail, these funeous metals persist in the world beneath innumerable layers of accreted memory, kneading together wholly disparate scales of time and space. Recalling their extraction and subjection under the regime of plantation capitalism, I turn to theorizations of cultural memory within the African diaspora to help understand these complex material memories and the agencies that germinate within them. Departing from Jared Sexton's use of "dehiscence" to articulate the overlapping, ongoing ruptures and sutures of Black bodies and cultures from the Middle Passage (Sexton 2011), Chapter 5 addresses forms of collective agency that enable survival and ongoing resistance. Sylvia Wynter invokes the idea of "transplantation" (Wynter n.d.) to help explain the commingling of old traditions carried over and new ones reinvented. She identifies *cultural* creativity as a primary agent of suture, preserving memories while grafting them onto newly germinated seeds of survival and resistance. Hortense J. Spillers echoes this conviction, noting that spaces of "*cultural* vestibularity" (Spillers 1987) emerge from the lacerations of plantocratic oppression, and Rizvana Bradley similarly responds by invoking the enmeshed and unfolding *before* that is inseparable from black aesthesis—which she aptly names anteaesthetics (Bradley 2023). I read Bradley's concept of *ante* through material funicity, examining how untreated lesions of extraction are retained in the voices of the bodies that bear them. Following Wynter's insistence on the collectivity of this voice, I turn to her concept of the *plot* as both narrative device and cultivation site. Slave plots served as spaces of cultural resilience and resistance, occupying liminal spots of untameable land simultaneously engulfed by and isolated from the surrounding plantation landscape. As a space of material support for Black culture as well as for the concrete actions of marronage or revolt, Wynter embraces the *plot* as a means to conceptualize the multi-generational enactment of cultural creativity that preserves the conditions and means for resistance. She extrapolates the *plot* further as a form of narrative agency—which she terms a science of the Word—in which she outlines a conceptualization of human hybridity establishing "narration as a pillar of an alternate, non-Eurocentric genre of the human. This human as storytelling, or *homo narrans*, recognizes that in generating stories, humans are also generating themselves" (Alagraa 2018: 166-167). Wynter roots this autopoietic narrative agency in material declamation, revealing how the musical, dance, and religious traditions of the Black diaspora excite the driving pulse of *homo narrans* and the drum it beats. Positing a kinship between the *plot* and the workshop's bounded spaces of material fugitivity, I highlight the material strands that are threaded through the dehiscent creativity of the *plot* and propose a *hylo narrans* complementary to Wynter's *homo narrans*. *Hylo narrans* asserts that material agency is a question not of reality but of awareness; it does not depend on our acknowledgment in order to voice its own story, but on our ability to assimilate that voice into the ongoing autopoietic narrative of *homo narrans*.

The final chapter addresses how this material voice might become intelligible within our communities, and how it might then contribute to our collective narration of the worlds we hope to create. As the book progresses, it follows the brass of the chimeracord from its dispersal in mineral ore through its extraction, refining, and distribution. At this point, I look more closely at its fabrication, through which it is transformed from cast sheets, rods, and tubes into finished musical instruments. I borrow from Sylvia Wynter's framework of the overrepresentation of Man and Annie Goh's recent application of Wynter's work in sound studies to address the complementary ideological and acoustic overrepresentations of brass instruments (Goh 2019). Following Goh's contestation of Western acoustemological hegemonies, I compare the finely-tuned acoustic profiles of finished brass instruments to the starkly visceral soundscapes of the workshop, replete with the shuddering, shrieking rejoinders of brass not-yet-tamed. In turning an ear to the sound of these materials-in-flight, I return to the concept of marronage and the role of the *plot* as both vector of escape and network of complicity (Diouf 2014). I ask how we might attune ourselves to these voices of material marronage, reorienting our workshop, community, and performance spaces towards the "waveforms" of their "reparative rebellious inventions" (McKittrick 2016: 88). In considering how the concept of voice can be returned to its sonic materiality from discourses that have overrepresented it as political agency, I build on Zeynep Bulut's reconception of "voice-as-skin" (Bulut 2025: 6): "a shared surface, a multisensory interface that behaves both as a boundary and as a web of connection across various bodies and environments" (Bulut 2025: 1). Drawing on my previous work with the philosophy of Karen Barad, I map the membranous relationships that Bulut describes across discontinuous zones of space and time, examining how discrete agencies at great spatiotemporal removes coalesce in sound through the embodied activity of collective voicing (Toksöz Fairbairn 2022). I position the chimeracord as an agent of what Sara Ahmed describes as "'becoming oblique' of the world" (Ahmed 2006: 162), exploring how its discordant hybridity invites us, as listeners, to engage in constructive, collective, and intransitive complicities. Whereas previous chapters revolve around media of material agency, this conclusion follows that material fugitivity into the *borderland* (Diouf 2014), reorienting our attention towards the human capacity for responding to this material agency and collaborating in its communal creativity. This reorientation situates materials at the center of their own story, inviting our complicity while still voicing their own narrative self-(re)generation. It closes by turning back to the chimeracords themselves as they diffract the bodies and spaces they encounter into innumerable strands of joyfully hybrid reverberation.

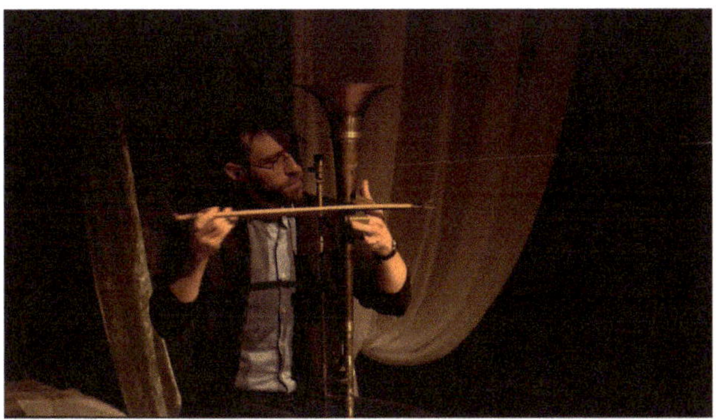

Fig. 6 Attending to the instrument. Photo by Davids Danoss (2025).

Situating the Work

While this text circles the idea of the workshop and the plot, probing for metallic agencies and the human senses that might perceive them, it remains tethered to the particularity of the workshop where I have personally trained, as well as to the land on which that workshop lies. Although ensuing chapters will draw the reader's attention to increasingly global histories of mining and material marronage, this story nonetheless remains rooted in the small, unassuming workshop where George first taught me how to attend to brass.

I started my apprenticeship while still in school, and so, in order to get to George's workshop from my childhood home, I had to drive about half an hour up the Virginia Peninsula, named—like the state around it—after Elizabeth I, the 'Virgin Queen' of England (by way of the Virginia Company, the English trading company that lay claim to thousands of kilometers of Atlantic coastline along the present-day Eastern Seaboard). My home itself lay even closer to the pulse of this colonial history, situated in a suburban neighbourhood just a few kilometers upriver from the first permanent English settlement in the so-called New World: Jamestown (named after Elizabeth's cousin and successor). Lying on Powhatan land, Jamestown survives in history as a unique epicenter and metonymy of colonialism, the site not only of England's first permanent incursion onto Indigenous land but also of the sale of the first slaves in North America in 1619.

This is the land on which I was born, though centuries ago the settlement of Jamestown was already subsumed within the colonial trading town of Williamsburg, named after the Dutch William III, who married into English monarchy. This union remains preserved in the still active College of William & Mary, where my parents and much of my immediate and extended family received their university degrees. Although within the anglophone world this William is known as William of Orange, in his native Holland that moniker is reserved for his grandfather, William I, who established the university that funded the research and writing of this book. These entangled and ongoing histories of colonialism suffuse all of my research and artistic practice, from my early training in Virginia to my position now as I write these lines. My relationship to these lands and occupations are stitched into work that—despite spanning many years, continents, and disciplines—remains firmly rooted in the land where I first learned my craft and the external forces that shaped it. Even as my apprenticeship with George would ultimately teach me how to listen to brass, to its metallic ontogeny, and to its material fugitivity, the craft tradition that brought me into contact with these materials-in-flight are indelibly, inextricably threaded through with the same histories of extraction, genocide, and exploitation that suffused the soil beneath his workshop, itself now dismantled and dispersed.

This is the workshop where I learned to attend to brass. It is the space in which I learned first to subdue it, and then later to coax and cajole it, before eventually learning also to listen to and learn from it. These various dispositions—from control to curiosity—are completely incompatible while also somehow coextensive. Like all craft knowledge, working with metal requires a constant interplay between expectation and reaction. The apprentice quickly gets a sense for how metal responds, and over countless repetitions, this sensitivity is further honed, until their body builds a catalog of metallic subjects that it can factor together. Such craft knowledge often revolves around embodied affinities for material trends, probabilities, averages, and predictions. But unsurprisingly, like so many other things in life, these expectations derive from the accumulated traces of irregularities. There is always some minor perturbation, some little wrinkle or inconsistency that requires a minor adjustment. These minor discrepancies will all get smoothed out and assimilated into muscle memory, but the craftsperson's expertise will ultimately stem from their ability to navigate these endless deviations rather than from any comprehensive understanding about general metal behavior. In the workshop, every preparation is also in implicit reaction. All foresight is already folded into the inevitable variability it will encounter.

And no matter how long one trains, no matter how many iterations are subsumed into one's embodied knowledge, each new workpiece will still require the same attentiveness. There is never a stage where these deviations can be predicted and ironed out in advance. The craft itself will still revolve around one's ability to address a singular, unique piece of metal in a particular point in time. In the workshop itself, all of these countless minor deviations will pass through our hands. They will each be held and attended to, a physical weight in our hands, forming sweat on our brows. Our bodies slowly attune to their patterns of resilience, absorbing and diffusing each fleeting aberration and irregularity that emerge within their roiling currents of implacable instability. Materials drift and buck, a turbulent tangle of wayward agencies. Learning the trade means learning how to smooth out these ripples, developing the skills to mediate between material friction and a smooth workflow. Craft, then, is a study in particularity.

Each piece of metal requires a careful calibration, soliciting the craftsperson's body to react and transpose. All general knowledge is diffracted through its situated application, one piece at a time, responding to the specific touch of each individual hand, tool, or treatment. The perfect piece of metal will never appear, pure and pliant, bending effortlessly to the craftsperson's will. Working metal is a sleight of hand, crafting the illusion of perfection out of endlessly imperfect material. Inconsistencies are smoothed out and variations kneaded into regularity. But in learning to craft this mirage of material consistency out of maddeningly temperamental, fluctuating metals, the craftsperson is paradoxically entraining an affinity for precisely those volatilities. A trained metalworker can identify tiny faults almost instinctively, discerning nearly imperceptible variations in the material or its responsivity. In learning to make metal obey, the craftsperson's body is actually gaining fluency in material vocabularies of insubordination, disobedience, and defiance.

The chimeracord reimagines craft, then, as an expertise of exception. It celebrates the peripheral, the surprising, and the aberrant. It asks how an instrument might sound if it embraced the oblique, following the grain of the material as it reimagines its own constitution. The chimeracord articulates questions that I first learned to imagine while working unruly pieces of metal in George's workshop over two decades ago. What stories might this metal tell if we followed its inclination?

What instruments do they imagine when they wriggle free from our forms? Can we map the infinite lexica of their acoustic interpolations? And could we access those voices in an instrument—could the metal in a chimeracord itself germinate these speculative sonic hybridities?

As this book progresses, it follows two paths: one backwards through the chimeracord's material history, tracing its gestation in workshops, mines, and mountains; and the other forwards through its performance, presentation, and interaction with listeners in the world. But even as these investigations expand outwards, incorporating broader histories of exploitation or wider audiences, they are still rooted in the particularity of these instruments, the fugitive materials that they contain, and my own personal practices as craftsperson, artist, and researcher. This book and the instruments that it presents attempt to mediate these disparate scales of inquiry, bridging the situated experience of my particular workshop to more general cultural, social, and political concerns that affect us all. But within this discussion, I entreat the reader to consider this material not as subject but as interlocutor. As I argue that material voices both exist and are audible, I am also trying to reorient the reader as listener, attending to these materials themselves, to the provocations they offer, and to the histories, epistemologies, and imaginaries that they voice. The recordings that accompany this text are not supplementary but rather fundamental. They are the skeleton of the work and the lifeblood that circulates through it. They root my speculation in the particular, directing the reader not to a general materialism but to the chimeracord's specific perspectives on material marronage and the collective cultural imaginaries that it affords.

The recording that accompanies this chapter reflects this aspiration. It documents a very typical performance with the chimeracord, a performance that invites the visitor to relearn how to listen. Although I will often (but not always) join the chimeracord onstage at some point in a performance, I often reserve time at the beginning to allow it to sound alone, in its own time and space. Although the audience might reasonably expect me to immediately perform on the instrument myself, putting it through its paces and showcasing its hybrid complexity, they are confronted instead with two, five, sometimes even ten or fifteen minutes of unaccompanied chimeracord. The droning harmonic tapestries that emanate from its metallic cords, chambers, and dispersions shift and evolve, languidly but perceptibly, gradually attuning the audience's perception to its evocative vocabularies of obliquity and fugitivity. The chimeracord here offers an invitation to listen otherwise, to voice complicity.

1. Monochord

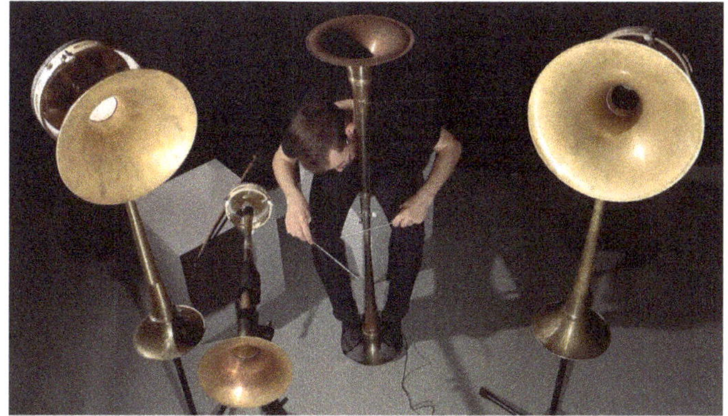

Fig. 7 Solo performance with chimeracord: *Verdigris.* Photo by author (2024).

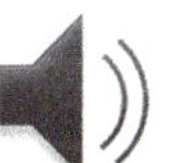

Audio Recording 3 *Verdigris*. Recording by author (2024),
http://hdl.handle.net/20.500.12434/47aac5b5

Video Recording 3 *Verdigris*. Recording by author (2024),
http://hdl.handle.net/20.500.12434/862b78b8

The chimeracord is a monochord of sorts, with a single cord of steel wire strung from end to end of its long hourglass body. This string runs directly through two small holes drilled in the tubular brass body

 https://doi.org/10.11647/OBP.0476.01

itself, with a small bit of copper winding placed at each point to help thread it into the sound chamber and, on one end, back out the other side to a tuning peg. The term monochord refers to this single string, and like all monochords, the chimeracord is in some way defined by this single strand's tension, vibration, and amplification. But monochords have evolved in many different cultures around the world (such as the Vietnamese *đàn bầu*, the Chinese *duxianqin*, or the musical bows popular throughout Africa and the African diaspora, such as the Brazilian *berimbau*), and the history of such single-string instruments presents an abundance of technical, musical, and cultural variation. Some are plucked or struck while others are bowed. Some are melodic while others are rhythmic, though many blur these boundaries altogether. But perhaps the greatest variation is in the mode of amplification. Monochords around the world map an endless capacity for invention, using human bodies, gourds, tubes, boxes, and even the earth itself as resonators and sound boxes for amplifying a single string. Each of these monochords embodies a particular imaginary, an expression of the peoples and places and cultures that produced them, and the chimeracord is no exception. Although developed only recently—and quite literally millennia after many of its monochord cousins—the chimeracord reflects not only the histories of the metals in its body or the workshops in which it is crafted, but also the cultural context in which those metals and workshops are embedded. It emerges in dialogue with traditions of Western music and harmony that interweave with the histories of material extraction and capitalist production that accompany its genesis.

Within this tradition of Western culture and music, the monochord occupies an exaggerated position. As a foundational character in the origin story of Western thought, this instrument has acquired totemic significance, compounding and growing with every passing century. Nonetheless, as in every other culture, before it was a symbol, it was simply an instrument. In fact, according to the standard mythologies passed down in music history textbooks to this day, the history of the monochord in Western music can be traced back to a single, particular instrument crafted two and a half millennia ago, and just as in any other culture where monochords emerged, it reflected the particular materials, sounds, and stories that surrounded it. But in this case, its story accrued a different kind of interest over time, as the unassuming monochord purportedly crafted by Pythagoras in Samos evolved gradually into metonymy, becoming not only *the* monochord in Western imagination, but also the embodiment of an entire system of harmony and, indeed, even of philosophy. Before that, though, like any other instrument, this Pythagorean monochord was just an object with its own unique story: a single string strung taught across a box—a commingling of catgut and wood—whose physical resonance burst and decayed in real time and space before being swallowed up by its unique history and interpretation.

This monochord occupies a special place in the mythology of Pythagoras, emerging as a kind of material muse, both loud enough to grab Pythagoras's attention but also somehow voiceless—more a tool of scientific measurement than a musical instrument. With the benefit of this hindsight, it is perhaps unsurprising that this monochord's story begins from Pythagoras's dissatisfaction—one might even say contempt—for the materials used to build musical instruments in his day. As we are told in numerous accounts, Pythagoras had exhaustively examined materials like gutstrings and wood, ultimately deeming them too erratic to rely on in his search for the immutable laws of harmony. With strings, for example, Pythagoras had found that "more humid air may deaden the pulsation, or drier air may excite it, or the thickness of a string may render a sound lower, or thinness may make it higher, or, by some other means, [alter] a state of previous stability" (Boethius 1989: 18). And he had encountered this problem not only with strings, but with other instrumental consorts as well, "[a]ssessing all these instruments as unreliable and granting them a minimum of trust" (Boethius 1989: 18). But the story continues, for, having seemingly exhausted these resources and therefore abandoning any hope of progress, Pythagoras then stumbled upon a breakthrough far removed from the spaces of musical performance or philosophical speculation. As the legend goes, when walking by a forge where a number of smiths were at work, Pythagoras was struck by the remarkable consonance sounded by the clamor of their hammer blows. With his curiosity sufficiently piqued, he rushed inside to discover the source of this remarkable concord. He first considered the materials being hammered, but they turned out not to be relevant. He then considered the muscles of the men doing the hammering, but again, these variations proved to be a dead end. Eventually, he turned to the hammers themselves, whereupon he discovered that each of the four hammers he examined produced a different tone as they were used, and that, moreover, their different masses mapped a series of proportions whose ratios would famously spark Pythagoras's incalculably influential investigations into harmony, rationality, and purity.

There are a number of notable details about this story—not least among them an illusory additional hammer, immortalized with the single phrase: "The fifth hammer, which was discordant with all, was discarded" (Boethius 1989: 18). We might ask ourselves, what else has been discarded along the way? As this monochord slowly transcended the physical boundaries of its single string's finite resonance, breaching the realms of philosophical speculation, which strands of materiality, culture, and history were uprooted? As the actual sounds and music that Pythagoras heard have receded, how has this story been reshaped and repurposed? Because Pythagoras was, by all accounts, an avid listener. Indeed, as the histories we have inherited acknowledge, he had already inquired exhaustively of other instruments before the hammers and the forge triggered his experiments with the monochord. This is, after all, the same Pythagoras who, according to legend, mollified a belligerent drunk by instructing the nearby aulete to change his harmonic mode, demonstrating his intimate fluency with musical harmony, instruments, and their affective capacities:

> Who does not know that Pythagoras, by performing a spondee, restored a drunk adolescent of Taormina incited by the sound of the Phrygian mode to a calmer and more composed state? One night, when a whore was closeted in the house of a rival, this frenzied youth wanted to set fire to the house. Pythagoras, being a night owl, was contemplating the courses of the heavens (as was his custom) when he learned that this youth, incited by the sound of the Phrygian mode, would not desist from his action in response to the many warnings of his friends; he ordered that the mode be changed, thereby tempering the disposition of the frenzied youth to a state of absolute calm. (Boethius 1989: 5)

While posterity has not recorded more of this encounter, it was an oft-cited proof of music's intimate connection to the soul and, indeed, even to the more fundamental composition of the human body and its humours (cf. Quintilian *Institutio oratoria* 1.10.32, Sextus Empiricus

Adversus musicos 6.8, Elias, *Prolegomena philosophiae* 2, Ammonius *In Porphyrii isagogen sive v voces*, Augustine Contra *Julianum* 5.5.23). This singular soothing intervention managed to provide the anecdotal basis for generations of philosophical speculation about how "the whole structure of our soul and body has been joined by means of musical coalescence" (Boethius 1989: 7). But it also indicates Pythagoras had far more than a passing acquaintanceship with the musical modes and practices of his day, which in turn casts doubt on his supposed dissatisfaction with the strings of the *kithara* and the reeds of the *aulos* before his fortuitous encounter with the forge.

Was Pythagoras truly so exasperated by the fickleness of these instruments? While it is surely true that the response and intonation of strings would vary with fluctuations in humidity, temperature, or tension (as his experiments with the monochord would later confirm), these issues are really only problematic when making comparisons over longer durations or with more dissimilar instruments. The strings available to Pythagoras would certainly have provided enough stability for a comparison between pitches within controlled conditions (as, once again, his own experiments with the monochord would later demonstrate). And as for the reeds and tubes of the *aulos*, how are we to reconcile the conflicting propositions that they were an untrustworthy basis for investigating the mathematical rules of harmony while simultaneously a stable base to understanding the harmonic foundation beneath complex human emotions and dispositions? The *aulos* is, of course, an instrument uniquely capable of foregrounding harmonic relationships; it was precisely this compelling interplay between melodic and drone pipes that allowed Pythagoras to exploit the affective power of musical modes to calm the storms of drunken rage.

It is quite unlikely that the strings, reeds, and pipes of his day were indeed completely unsuitable to the needs of his scientific inquiry—especially considering that it was those same catgut strings that were later stretched across his famous monochord. Despite what were certainly appreciable fluctuations with humidity or construction, it is unreasonable to entertain the idea that the same *kitharas* and *auloi* whose modal legibility could excite and soothe human temperament were incapable of rendering the relationships of harmonic proportion equally legible. On the contrary, it is perhaps safe to suggest that rather than turning to the serendipitous intervention of the forge after exhausting the limits of the musical instruments around him, Pythagoras had in fact *not* been on the search for the truth of harmonic consonance *until* that moment when it was literally hammered into his skull by the smiths he was lucky enough to overhear. It was the materials themselves—and their utility—that impelled this act of discovery. The hammers voiced their consonance, revealing a tactile foundation beneath the harmonic series and its cascade of rational overtones. They generated both the means and the medium for this initial breakthrough, for as Pythagoras asked the smiths to attempt different configurations of hammers, hands, anvils, and other tools, he came to realize that the harmonic phenomena that had drawn him in derived not from the strength or speed of the strike, or from the hands that bore them, but from the very masses of the materials and their proportion to one another. The four hammers were not only different sizes, but their masses were directly proportional to one another, providing Pythagoras a key to unlocking a fundamental relationship between harmony and proportion. These ratios would construct the scaffolding that supported an entire philosophy of universal harmonic laws: Pythagoreanism.

But just as this lucky discovery lay rooted in Pythagoras's purportedly contemptuous disregard of the instrumental materials already available to him, so did these first steps towards his comprehensive elucidation of harmonic ratios also bear a subtle, disdainful betrayal of their debt to the hammers' material stimulus. This tension between the materiality of the forge and its immaterial, philosophical legacy is only one of many tensions dispersed beneath the surface of Pythagoreanism. Pythagoras's story includes an unrecorded but influential adjustment, a minor restructuring of material reality that allowed Pythagoreanism to leverage the resonance of the hammers into an intelligible, reproducible epistemological paradigm, thereby establishing a foundation for its vaunted philosophical vision of the world as an elegant, harmonic symphony. The monochord—in both its material and speculative forms—helps reveal this dissonance between Pythagorean idealism and the material reality that belies it.

By examining the hammers, Pythagoras was able to ascertain a link between their consonances and their materiality. He could move beyond simply identifying harmonic relationships—which had been known and cataloged well before—to ascertaining the underlying physical characteristics that engendered them. What the brute mass of the hammers showed Pythagoras was the "ratio [by which the] concord of sounds was joined together" (Boethius 1989: 18). Pythagoras had found that

> those which sounded together the consonance of the diapason were found to be double in weight. Pythagoras determined further that the same one, the one that was the double of the second, was the sesquitertian of another, with which it sounded a diatessaron. Then he found that this same one, the duple of the above pair, formed the sesquialter ratio of still another, and that it joined with it in the consonance of the diapente. These two, to which the first double proved to be sesquitertian and sesquialter, were discovered in turn to hold the sesquioctave ratio between themselves. (Boethius 1989: 18)

This complex set of four-way relationships could be simplified, though, allowing the relative simplicity of their whole number ratios to become more evident.

> So that what has been said might be clearer, for sake of illustration, let the weights of the four hammers be contained in the numbers written below.
>
> 12: 9: 8: 6.
>
> Thus the hammers which bring together 12 with 6 pounds sounded the consonance of the diapason in duple ratio. The hammer of 12 pounds with that of 9 (and the hammer of 8 with that of 6) joined in the consonance of the diatessaron according to the epitrita ratio. The one of 9 pounds with that of 6 (as well as those of 12 and 8) commingled the consonance of the diapente. The one of 9 with that of 8 sounded the tone according to the sesquioctave ratio. (Boethius 1989: 19)

At this point, deigning to sully his hands with the inconstant and unreliable resources of musical instruments, Pythagoras set out to mirror the ratios of the hammers in other media. The specific ratios that he derived from the hammers—and which he apparently translated successfully to strings, percussion, and reed consorts—became famous in their own right. These four numbers garnered a unique valence, representing not only Pythagoras's initial burst of genius, but also its extrapolation to other applications, as shown in this famous illustration of his varied experiments in Franchinus Gaffurius's *Theorica musicae* from 1492:

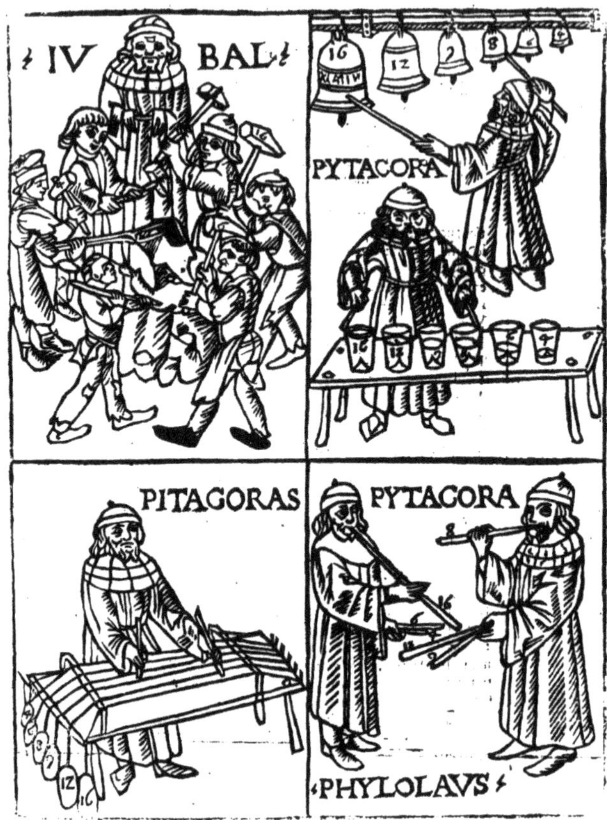

Fig. 8 Illustration of Pythagoras's experiments in Gaffurius's *Theorica musicae* (1492). Wikimedia Commons, public domain, https://commons.wikimedia.org/wiki/File:Gaffurio_Pythagoras.png#/media/File:Gaffurio_Pythagoras.png

Pythagoras's initial attempts to translate the hammers' proportional consonances into other media maintained a fairly analog correspondence. Mimicking the four hammers with masses of 12, 9, 8, and 6, he experimented by testing each of these proportional units in collections of similar objects: a bell, a glass partially filled with liquid, a tube, or a string with a weight attached to one end (to apply proportionally variable tension):

> Upon returning home, Pythagoras weighed carefully by means of different observations whether the complete theory of consonances might consist of these ratios. First, he attached corresponding weights to strings and discerned by ear their consonances; then, he applied the

> double and mean and fitted other ratios to lengths of pipes. He came to enjoy a most complete assurance through the various experiments. By way of measurement, he poured ladles of corresponding weights into glasses, and he struck these glasses—set in order according to various weights—with a rod of copper or iron, and he was glad to have found nothing at variance. (Boethius 1989: 19)

However, at some point he realized that these ratios and their harmonic ratios could be more elegantly demonstrated by a monochord. Consisting of a single catgut string stretched across a sounding board, one could divide that string with a finger (or centuries later, a moveable bridge) in order to generate the ratios previously expressed by these other experimental or musical apparatuses. By using a single string to compare different harmonic proportions, Pythagoras could demonstrate not only simple consonances, as with the hammers, but far higher orders of proportional harmonic phenomena, as well. And because these ratios could be quickly generated and compared on the same string, they were less subject to any vagaries of imprecision introduced by multiple strings, instruments, or other instrumental technologies. Fittingly, as the apotheotic tool for demonstrating these ratios, the monochord would come to be known as the *regula* or *canon*.

Although, as previously noted, monochord instruments are well-known and well-loved melodic instruments in many cultures, it never became a popular instrument in Pythagoras's time, nor in the ensuing centuries of Western fixation with Pythagoreanism. It was primarily seen as a tool, as an authoritative reference rather than as an expressive medium in itself. Only many centuries later did this gradually change, when Guido of Arezzo's introduction of the moveable bridge breathed new momentum into its evolution. "Shortly after the year 1000 A.D., [clavis (keys)] were applied to the monochord, which then was built with more than one string [...] As soon as the clavis was pressed down, [its] tangent would prick the string on the proper division of the scale and thus assure the sounding of the correct tone required for the guidance of the singers. The use of the clavis soon led to an increase in the number of strings [...] These experiments led finally to the invention of the 'clavicytherium'" (Dolge 1911: 28-29), which was, in turn, a forerunner of the clavichord, the harpsichord, and eventually the modern piano. It is curious to compare this history with instruments such as the *đàn bầu* (a single string zither that utilizes natural harmonics and a flexible rod to modulate string tension) or the *berimbau* (a musical bow with a resonator that can be manipulated and struck to produce overlapping layers of tones and rhythms), which are characterized by an array of inventive playing techniques that plumb their single string for hugely varied modes of melodic, harmonic, and expressive potential. In contrast, the evolution of the monochord followed a different path, essentially accumulating banks of strings each tasked with their own fundamental pitch. Rather than plumbing the depths of each string for its harmonic or expressive potential, these new instruments housed dozens of monochords in soundboxes that insulated them from contact, limiting their potential to the single plectra or hammers that would elicit each string's one, predetermined tone. Though these organological evolutions unfolded over centuries, and far removed from Pythagoras's Samos, it is difficult not to trace the threads that connect these developments back to the philosophical principles of Pythagoreanism. Through its adherence to principles of harmony and, by extension, purity, Pythagoreanism became equally inextricably linked to justifications for limitation and control, influencing not only localized, quotidian musical practices but also broader social and cultural evolutions.

At the heart of Pythagoreanism is an idealistic universality: an appeal for a rational, cosmic truth stitched through the heart of matter, from our quotidian world up to and through the celestial bodies themselves. One of the most alluring components of Pythagoras's initial discovery was the simplicity of the ratios that seemed to govern harmonic consonance. The original sets of proportions that the hammers represented generated whole number ratios, such as 2:1 for the octave, 3:2 for the fifth, and 4:3 for the fourth. The difference between the fifth and the fourth—what would come to be known as a single tone—could be demonstrated by a similar ratio further in this series, 9:8. These ratios are all similar in that they are formed by two successive whole numbers in relation to one another, which the Greeks called "superparticular," possessing "the mathematical shape of $n+1:n$. Each of the three intervals that Pythagoras identified in the mythic forge shares this arithmetical nature" (Heller-Roazen 2005: 34) That is to say, this arithmetic rule can define and generate each of the musical elements originally voiced by the hammers: the octave, the fifth, the fourth, and the single tone between the latter two.

But despite their compelling arithmetical elegance, these ratios didn't account for all of the musical intervals that characterized the musical modes of the day—those same musical modes that Pythagoras knew so intimately. In fact, even the most basic consonances produce strange misalignments when these simple ratios are rigorously applied. One of the most well-known is the progression of fifths. If one tunes a fifth in perfect harmony on the monochord, at the ratio of 3:2, and then proceeds to tune the next fifth at 3:2 of the former, after twelve iterations of this tuning exercise, the original fundamental pitch is once more generated. The only problem is that, if one actually does this, the fundamental that is reached by this cycle of fifths is not, in fact, identical to the original fundamental, but is instead a notably higher pitch—a pitch notably discordant with its original counterpart. How could it be that these immutable consonances could result in such literal discord? And there were further problems, as well, some even more troubling for musicians of Pythagoras's day. Despite their pride of place as the most pure consonances, music did not consist of only fourths and fifths, and the definition of smaller intervals triggered heated debates lasting generations. "According to Aristoxenus, the fourth-century thinker whose *Elements of Harmony* contains the most detailed surviving account of the subject, the music of the ancient Greeks was conceived in an intervallic expanse of two octaves. Each octave was composed of two fourths, or tetrachords, joined by the one tone. Within the fourth, two outer positions were fixed, while two inner ones varied" (Heller-Roazen 2005: 31). This tetrachord was clearly too large to contain two single tones, and yet far too small to contain three.

Aristoxenus himself proposed that this intervening harmonic interval could be construed as half a step, meaning that the tetrachord would comprise two whole tones and one half tone.

"Aristoxenus's argument about the fourth implied one major proposition that, to the ancients, was anything but self-evident. His claim clearly suggested that to define the extension proper to the fourth, one must imagine parts of the single tone, admitting, simply, that this basic interval may be halved" (Heller-Roazen 2005: 32). Halving the tone in this manner, though, was a mathematical operation totally incompatible with the Pythagorean logic of ratios and proportion. For the ancient Greeks, there were two, fundamentally discrete modes of mathematical operation: arithmetical operation, such as ratios, in which new terms are generated by multiplication of whole numbers (with, as in the case of ratios, the reduction to simpler whole number terms when possible, such as representing the ratio 8:4 as 2:1); and geometrical operation, such as the mathematics of the circle, in which continual subdivisions of the whole could be represented by precise divisions. For the Pythagoreans, then, having established harmonic consonance as a phenomenon of arithmetic ratios, the geometrical halving of the single tone was a distinctly irrational procedure. Halving a tone implied applying a geometrical operation to an arithmetical ratio—an irresolvable insolubility. "The Pythagoreans pronounced that solution untrue, as well as mathematically incoherent. Yet they thereby obligated themselves to find another answer to offer in its place." (Heller-Roazen 2005: 35). On its surface, this was not the most difficult task, for surely there would be some ratio that could generate this interval. After all, the succession of superparticular ratios that defined the octave, the fifth, and the fourth produced ever-diminishing intervals as the series progressed, such as the single tone itself. But the rational identity of the mysterious musical interval left over by the two whole tones in the tetrachord proved distinctly elusive.

> To find the exact quantities of tones that compose the fourth, it sufficed for them to "withdraw" from the fourth two tones. Originally, that operation may have been difficult to perform, but by the fifth century, if not sooner, it had been done. Then, it could be shown that, after the "subtraction" of two tones from the tetrachord, an interval remained that was less than half a tone. This was an inequality that could be defined by a complex arithmetical ratio: two hundred and fifty-six with respect to two hundred and forty-three (256:243). That seemingly arcane relation was to be found not only in the works on harmonics. Plato's famous investigation into cosmology, the *Timaeus*, contained it too. Explaining the secrets of the world soul, Timaeus recounts that in his act of making, the demiurge chose to "fill up" the interval of the fourth (4:3) with the intervals of the tone (9:8). An "interval," he explains, then "remained," and it was equal to two hundred and fifty-six to two hundred and forty-three (256:243). In deference to that passage, thinkers after Plato called this subtle ratio *leimma*, or "remainder." (Heller-Roazen 2005: 35-36)

Although not superparticular and well beyond the capacity of normal human beings to conceive of on the soundboard of a traditional monochord, this ratio at least provided some rational foundation to the claim that there could be no such thing as half of a single tone. It allowed Pythagoreans to persist in asserting that, by the rational extension of the series of harmonic proportions, the mysteries within the melodic tetrachord could be explained by the arithmetic (not geometric!) laws of the universe. Unfortunately, though, just as with the imperfections generated by the cycle of fifths, this explanation only led to further conundrums. Because of their superparticular construction, according to the rules of arithmetic, "neither one mean number nor several mean numbers will fit in proportionally" (Boethius 1989: 118). In simpler terms, this means that by finding the ratio to explain the "remainder," the interval of 256:243 effectively divided the single tone slightly lopsidedly, just as it had with the tetrachord: this alternative to the half tone was slightly larger than half of a whole tone, raising the question of how to define that altogether new leftover interval. And so, once again, the discrepancy between this new interval and the rational proportion that it related to had to be explained, leading to ever more extravagant ratios.

> The discrete quantity of the *leimma* could be compared with that of the tone; the difference between the two could consequently be measured in a ratio. They called this inequality the *apotomē*, literally, "what is cut off." At the limits of imaginable relations, this interval could be expressed by the ratio of exactly two hundred and seventy three and three eighths to two hundred and fifty-six ($273^{3/8}$:256, or 2187:2048). Venturing still further into the subtleties of logistics, the Pythagoreans also envisaged the difference between the *leimma* and the *apotomē*. They called this last remainder "the comma" [...], "what is struck out," defining its ratio as 531,441:524,288. (Heller-Roazen 2005: 36)

These irreducible remainders gnawed away at the heart of Pythagoreanism, a nagging irrationality in their arithmetical certainty. Maintaining the rational edifice of harmonic order demanded that these subtle incommensurabilities be erased, and yet as their arithmetical calculations to resolve these remainders grew ever more complex and arcane, the remainders themselves not only persisted but were themselves amplified by these operations. And yet rather than placing these mathematical conundrums in dialogue with the acoustic resonances that they sought to describe, Pythagoreans turned away from the sound of harmony altogether. When faced with practical questions about harmonic intervals and the inconceivably complex ratios that defined them, they abandoned the acoustic reality of strings, bells, and hammers, and dove headlong into theoretical abstraction. "Once his disciples committed themselves to the mathematical study of nature [...] they found that, at a certain point, the ways of conscious perception and arithmetical consideration must part. Then, to the perplexity of their contemporaries and later commentators, the disciples of Pythagoras resolved to follow an unexpected path: they renounced the evidence of their senses for the certainty of their arithmetic" (Heller-Roazen 2005: 37).

This resulted in a strange entrenchment, devoted simultaneously to two conflicting endeavors. On the one hand, Pythagoreanism reinforced the bulwarks against irrationality with continually evolving arithmetical proofs, seeking to establish beyond any shadow of a doubt the harmonic laws stitched into the cosmos at every level. On the other, they developed a conspiratorial intensity, insistent that these mathematical laws be shared only with the initiated and limiting awareness of these irreducible irrational remainders to the true believers of their mathematical truth.

> [N]umerous records [...] indicate that the Pythagoreans never intended to divulge their knowledge of such matters to those uninitiated into their teachings. It is said that a Pythagorean revealed to the ancient world the existence of mathematical "irrationalities," but it is also said that he was punished as a result [...] Iamblichus recounts that [...] "[n]ot only did they banish him from their community of study and their way of life. In addition, they built for him a tomb, as if the one who had once been their companion had truly departed from the life of men." Other reports suggest that as a consequence of his impious deeds, the Pythagorean suffered a far more violent fate: the gods drowned him at sea. (Heller-Roazen 2005: 41)

This story served primarily as a caution against the consequences of sharing such potent knowledge with the proverbial masses. Contemporary commentators considered it a "parable [about] the soul which by error or heedlessness discovers or reveals anything of this nature [who then] wanders thereafter hither and thither on the sea of non-identity [...] where there is no standard of measurement" (Pappus, trans. Thomson 1939: 164). As this mindset solidified, Pythagoreans "resolved not to name that immeasurable reality[, ...] develop[ing] means to moderate it as best they could, reducing asymmetries to the ordered inequalities of measured multitudes" (Heller-Roazen 2005:

29). Their commitment was an existential admission: the threat these remainders posed was not to something as simple as a mere mathematical tool for calculating consonance and harmony, but was rather a threat to the foundations of their entire metaphysical paradigm. Pythagoras had extrapolated from the rules of harmony in the hammers a complete system or order that stretched even into the celestial realm, declaring "a doctrine of the intelligibility of the natural world" (Heller-Roazen 2005: 9). His successors were therefore committed to obscuring any small discrepancies in this system that might suggest, however minutely, that there was some limit to its correspondence with reality.

In his far-reaching monograph on Pythagoreanism, linguist and critic Daniel Heller-Roazen identifies this lurking irreducible remainder with the character of the discarded fifth hammer, that long-forgotten character in the Pythagorean origin myth. In identifying this irresolvable incommensurability as a form of corrosion within the millennia-spanning Pythagorean project, he points out that by erasing the fifth hammer—"which was discordant with all" (Boethius 1989: 18)—from history, they revealed a much more subtle but damning limitation to the Pythagorean ideal: "What is this 'all,' if something—if even only one thing—sounds in utter dissonance with it?" (Heller-Roazen 2005: 16). In Heller-Roazen's astute examination of the Western world's long and intimate relationship to Pythagorean harmony and philosophy, this question continues to gnaw away in the background. Because no matter how florid or arcane their formulations, so long as they failed to resolve that irreducible remainder revealing Pythagoreanism's ultimate non-correspondence with the natural world, the universality they claimed to represent was held together by censorship rather than truth. They could only define the natural laws of the universe by carefully curating what counted as part of that universe to begin with.

Throughout the institutional progression of Western harmony, musical theorists devoted text after text to mathematical proofs defining the Pythagorean authenticity of the musical advances they gradually sanctioned. Propelled by a constant friction between practical innovation and the conservative idealism of Pythagoreanism, the harmonic and rhythmic palette of Western music grew increasingly more refined and complex. But even as this seemingly inevitable process ground slowly forward, Pythagoreanism persisted as a metric by which to judge or justify these innovations. Following Boethius's influential *De institutione musica* from the sixth century (largely just an extension of classical texts), centuries of Western music theory was framed by Pythagorean discourse and the language of ratios. Even though the practical application of thirds, sixths, and passing tones often preceded their theoretical explanation—just as the tetrachords and half tones of Aristoxenus reflected practical usage exceeding the Pythagorean imagination—these expansions of the melodic and harmonic palette were all eventually married to a Pythagorean rationalization (Burkholder, Grout, and Palisca 2014: 157). These evolving understandings of harmony were often linked to the similarly evolving discourse of tuning and temperament, which also often justified their specific intonational decisions in the language of Pythagorean ratios. And just as with the Pythagoreans before them, their appeal to the language of ratios proved equally exclusionary as inclusionary, as with the influential theorist Gioseffo Zarlino, whose elegant Pythagorean rationalization of thirds and sixths helped retrench the discordant designations of sevenths, elevenths, and other higher order whole number ratios (Partch 1949/1974: 378).

This appeal to mathematical purity was not limited to harmony, though, and as the rhythmic complexity of Western notation evolved, it fell into this same orbit, sucked in by the gravity of Pythagorean idealism. "Just as Boethius defined five types of ratio corresponding to five kinds of related multitudes, so in the fifteenth century Guilelmus Monachus, Gaffurius, and Johannes Tinctoris would admit in their doctrine five rhythmic 'proportions.' And just as, for the ancient thinker, multitudes were collections of ones, so for the medieval composers, such ratios of rhythm would be commensurable by nature" (Heller-Roazen 2005: 48). With their theoretical imaginations of not just harmony but also temperament, rhythm, notation, and other musical elements rooted firmly in Pythagorean arithmetical language, these Western appropriators of Pythagoreanism displayed the same preoccupations that the ancient Greek adherents had before them. Categorization was paramount: defining the limits of consonance mattered far more than exploring how or why other sounds might also be expressive or pleasing. These foundational and influential theoretical texts continued to value the circumscription of reality by ideal rationalization over the perception of their senses and the gradual but inexorable development of Western harmony. These attitudes can perhaps be summarized most pointedly by Boethius, a man more mathematician than musician, whose work's influence derived less from "what is written in it [than| by whom it is written, when it was written, and for how long its words were read by musicians" (Williams and Balensuela 2008: 24). Boethius was the primary intellectual link between Pythagoras's monochord and its later Western outgrowth, and he made clear that this instrument was more metrical than musical. In a play on words between the double meanings of the Latin word *regula* as both a metrical stick and a system of judgment, Boethius makes clear that, although he refers to the carefully demarcated sounding board of the monochord as a *regula*, the term derives not from its similarity to a ruler, but from its unique role as a vessel of the "rule" passed down from Pythagoras (Boethius 1989: 19). But rules only exist when there are elements that persist outside the boundaries they demarcate. In its stubborn drive to regulate both the awareness and the interpretation of the real-world remainders that bled at the edges of the monochord's rule, Pythagoreanism sought to define an idealized description of the universe that had, in fact, been flawed from the moment Pythagoras first examined the hammers.

While Heller-Roazen astutely asserts that the discarded fifth hammer helps symbolize a Pythagorean predilection for control, the decisive turning point in this choice between regulation and accommodation actually lies back in the story of the other four hammers. The myth surrounding Pythagoras was firmly rooted in his Promethean journey into the forge, where he wrested the laws of harmony directly from these four physical hammers before transcribing their ratios and revealing the immutable universal *regula*. Despite Pythagoreanism's glorification of reason over sensation, its claim to authenticity had always been reliant on an appeal to the material authenticity of Pythagoras's discovery. But that material foundation was flawed from the beginning, for even that initial set of simple ratios—the immortalized '12: 9: 8: 6' that triggered the ensuing tangle of remainders, apotomēs, and commas—were already based on an unrecorded discrepancy. As composer, theorist, and lutenist Vincenzo Galilei noted in 1589 (after approximately two millennia of Pythagorean influence on philosophy, culture, and music), the initial ratios that Pythagoras recorded were inaccurate or, one might even say, dishonest. Whereas Pythagoras claims that the simple ratios such as 2:1, 3:2, and 4:3 translated into consonances in each of the variety of masses, strings, weights, and tubes that he tested (as shown, for example, in Gaffurius's illustration), these different media do not in fact produce these identical harmonic relationships at corresponding proportional relationships.

By reconstructing these experiments, Galilei discovered that the ratios were in fact more varied, and that, for example, in masses such as the original hammers, the ratio required to produce a fifth was not 3:2, but 9:4, and that this adjustment carried over into all of the other consonances, as well. In short, unlike the simple multiplicative proportions that applied to string length, the proportions describing the consonances in mass—which, Galilei found, also applied to tension (such as the experiments with weights on strings)—must be squared rather than simply multiplied. Moreover, when calculating the same consonances with volume (such as in a tube), these proportions must be cubed! Put simply, the historically received record of Pythagoras's initial experiments was a flagrant misrepresentation of material reality. Rather than revealing a simple analog correspondence between these different media, his experiments would have shown a much greater divergence of proportional relationships. What is most striking about this lacuna in Pythagorean lore is that, despite these complexities, each of these proportional relationships are still so clearly related to one another (by square, by cube, etc.), and that when placed alongside each other, they describe a straightforwardly scalar spectrum of proportional harmonic rules; it would not have been difficult, one thinks, to present these exponential divergences as even stronger proof that the foundational ratios of this spectrum described a powerfully intrinsic relationship between proportion and harmony. But even at this very first hurdle, when translating the proportions of the hammers into strings and tubes and other media, Pythagoras and Pythagoreans preferred to obscure divergence and complexity behind a thin facade of elegant simplicity. It was as though the rule was more important than the physical resonances it described, and ultimately the hammers had to be "discarded in order to save the model (tonality) from its materiality (sound)" (Dyson 2014: 21).

Once Galilei had shown that the most basic tenet of Pythagoreanism—that is, that "[w]hatever the work, whatever the instrument, whatever its matter, certain arithmetical regularities were bound by nature to produce certain consonances" (Heller-Roazen 2005: 65)—was based on unstable, shifting ground, other recreations of Pythagoras's physical experiments were also found to generate as much doubt as explanation. In his own reconstruction of the monochord and Pythagoras's experiments, the seventeenth-century polymath Marin Mersenne found further elisions. Mersenne, who was inspired by Galilei's work and maintained regular correspondence with his son, Galileo Galilei (who had assisted his father's acoustic experiments), "discovered the overtone series [and] observed that these produced the 'major' chord but that the series did not stop there, and [...] [s]eeing the series go beyond the 'major' triad, he proposed the inclusion of [seven] as an integral musical resource" (Partch 1949/1974: 382). Somewhat surprisingly, in the centuries since, the idea of Pythagorean intonation has come to be associated with precisely these extensions of the overtone series, far removed from the ascetic limitations of the hammers' initial four intervals. Despite their spurious Pythagorean attribution, these overtone-derived harmonies are largely antithetical to ancient Pythagorean ideals; whereas they derive from a sensorially tactile immersion in sympathetic resonance, the early Pythagoreans valued the arithmetical simplicity of the smaller ratios early in the overtone series and held little real interest for their practical acoustic qualities. But this gradual shift in interpreting the relationship between Pythagoreanism and extended proportional calculations was indicative of a broader trend. In fact, over time, much of the terminology associated with Pythagorean harmony underwent a strange inversion: "We are now confronted with [a] complete change in terminology, from ancient to modern: the Harmonical Proportion is now the overtone series (Mersenne); the Arithmetical Proportion is now a limited 'minor' tonality (Zarlino); Aristoxenean approximations are now any of various temperaments [...], and Pythagoreanism is now more often one of the 'cycles of perfect fifths'" (Partch 1949/1974: 382).

As strange as these inversions may sound when viewed in hindsight, they may also be traced back to that fundamental paradigm of Pythagorean thought: that the rule transcends the resonance, and that the discourse surrounding harmony was more valuable than the sensorial experience of those harmonies. Just as they discarded the hammers from the forge, they ignored the monochord's *regula* just as soon as it actually began to sound. The monochord became an instrument, to be sure, but not an audible, musical one; rather, it became a metonymy, an instrumental assertion of a philosophical law. It was not valued for its musical utility but for its embodiment of an entirely immaterial rational idealism whose true cultural influence lay far outside the concert hall. As Heller-Roazen notes, Pythagoreanism's defining characteristic was this drive to contain all irreducible exceptions at the liminal outskirts of the rule, rendering them unpronounceable. Scholar of cinema and technocultural studies Frances Dyson builds on Heller-Roazen's observations in her own extensive reckoning with the legacy of Pythagoras and his monochord, *The Tone of Our Times*. She notes that this Pythagorean compulsion to silence or obscure its most fundamental irrationalities triggered "a logical glitch at the very beginnings of Western thought" (Dyson 2014: 4), allowing certain paradoxes to not only survive but thrive. As Pythagorean harmony subsumed these glitches and remainders into a comprehensive cosmology, this capacity for paradox seeped into every pillar of society, "enabl[ing] the progression through the centuries of something like a metaphysical wormhole into which the materiality of power, the force of legislation, the division of populations and their enslavement" disappeared (Dyson 2014: 4). Instead of resolving these remainders, Pythagoreanism simply banished them from view, insulating them from resolution in order to protect the fundamental tenets of their harmonic cosmology. This ultimately invested these glitches with a transformative capacity to absorb and neutralize the most irrational paradoxes, sowing a tolerance for imbalance and inequality directly into the fabric of Western thought and society. Dyson argues that this "accommodation of irrationality and incommensurability at the highest level of imagination (God, the infinite, cosmic time, and space) produces a form of 'cognitive dissonance[,' enabling] governance as an institution and governments in democratic nations to sustain massive contradictions without falling, like a house of cards" (Dyson 2014: 4).

Dyson posits the Pythagorean remainder as a seed of what would become a defining trait of Western thought, that the model could be more perfect—and therefore more true—than the world it represents. As a suspended state of the "unresolvable incommensurable," this remainder's erasure from Western cosmology embodied a rot at the core of the model—the secret "that the world can only be mathematical by plugging your ears" (Dyson 2014: 23). This wilful dismissal—rooted in an infatuation with the intellectual purity of the model at the expense of the world it sought to explain—allowed the simple harmonic rules derived from the monochord to undergird a massive intellectual evolution in Western culture:

> The cosmology that Pythagoras developed launched the monochord into the heavens, leading scholars to argue that the planets, given their geometrical rotations and relations, must, as moving magnitudes, also be sonorous since movement produces sound. For whom would they sound though? As the planets required an ear to hear them, a mind to perceive them, and a reason for their co-relation, they affirmed the existence of a divine being, an infinite universe. (Dyson 2014: 27)

Pythagoreanism blossomed from the strings of the monochord into a model of cosmological universalism, but "these neat correlations instituted one of the major flaws of unitary thinking: the impossibility of change" (Dyson 2014: 27), with the "necessary consequence" of also discarding "the excess baggage of social injustice, inequity, and the always questionable rationality of ethics, within what was supposed to be a perfectly harmonized cosmos" (Dyson 2014: 21). The Western world would resolve these problems in the same way that the Pythagoreans before them had dealt with the remainder, the apotomē, and the comma: by constructing a deliberate aporia at the heart of the system, neither resolving nor denying but merely preserving these incompatibilities in a state of eternal disregard.

Dyson's work shifts elegantly from register to register, revealing how the harmonic consonances endorsed by Pythagoreanism scale seamlessly upwards into the right to have a voice in society. She shows how the musical evolution of the monochord's tonal system morphs into the discursive control of contemporary capitalism, dictating what can and cannot be said, and in many ways even what can and cannot be thought. In sketching the trajectory of these transformations over the last two millennia, Dyson identifies the role of the church and the liturgy as an important fulcrum leveraging the philosophical scaffolding of Pythagorean harmony as a platform for the institutional exercise of discursive (and in many cases also material) power. Following Giorgio Agamben, she bases this analysis in the concept of acclamation, like the "amen," an "incantation [...] that is always in response to something said and always in agreement [...] a form of echo" (Dyson 2014: 36). But in the static harmonic perfection of a Pythagorean cosmos, this echo never dies; this acclamation is rooted not in the ebb and flow of quotidian life but in the eternal choir of celestial harmony, an "eternal repetition [that] confirms God but also obliterates the possibility for a silence that might make room for a different voice" (Voegelin 2019: 20). Dyson relates how this deployment of acclamation as a means to curate unitary discourse modulates over time from the church to the state and eventually to the more amorphous power of capital. But Dyson also notes that these operations replicate the stubborn Pythagorean compulsion to organize the world around an ideal model overlaid on the palimpsest of an effaced but persistent material reality. Even today, contemporary intellectuals appropriate "Pythagorean accounts of [...] social and cosmic harmony [to] adopt acoustic resonance as an analogy for the math neoliberalism and biopolitics use to create social inequalities" (James 2019: 22). And just as with the irreducible remainder lurking behind the mathematical logic of consonance, the discursive control that these regimes exert rely on a disavowal of material reality and the bodies and voices that compose it. "[U]niversal concepts and projections into the infinite seem to flow as if part of a logical formula. Yet the actual trajectory of this formula passes everywhere but through the physical reality [... T]hese are all strategies of dematerialization [...] of escape from the sweat of industry and animals" (Dyson 2014: 36).

With this in mind, Dyson sounds a call for resistance that she roots in corporeal potency. This "resistive echo-ing, or echopraxia" (Dyson 2014: 152) counters the ontological flattening of the eternal, ceaseless acclamation by asserting the agencies contained in the "the materiality of bodies—the sounds that they make, the atmosphere they breathe, the ground on which they walk, the space they occupy, and the interactions that occur between them" (Dyson 2014: 146). As she notes, the static continuity of this acclamation leaves no space for breath, eliminating the pause and silence of the "comma" (Dyson 2014: 23), and thereby eliminating any opportunity for meaningful response, misdirection, or dialogue. In opposition to the immaterial permanence of the acclamatory echo, she proposes a more worldly echo—rooted in the "eco" (Dyson 2014: 1-2, 17)—and formed from the rhythms of breath and voice within communal interaction. She proposes the concept of the "people's microphone," popularized by the Occupy Wall Street protests, as an example of how this echopraxia might emerge within the convergence of sounding bodies in social space:

> When related to the so-called Arab Spring, occupations in Spain, Syntagma Square in Greece, and riots in London that occurred in 2011, many commentators have noted the importance of corporeal occupation and a horizontal system of organization—such that there is no identifiable leader and everyone has a chance to speak. "The people's microphone" acts as a poignant enactment of these features: it enables multiple voices to be heard, its echoes incorporate its participants—indeed the participants are the echoes, materially and consensually—and it presupposes the occupation of a common space where the entirety of the sensible and sensory environment is shared. (Dyson 2014: 150)

For Dyson, the people's microphone is an "articulation" of the "physical act of occupying and reclaiming the common," imbuing corporeal rhythm to an "echoing [that] punctures, or inserts a comma, a pause, in the covering up of power" (Dyson 2014: 17). In her thoughtful and incisive reflections on "the political possibility of sound" (Voegelin 2019), philosopher and artist Salome Voegelin embraces Dyson's "echography of material practice[, which] does not produce a visible geography, an organization of the invisible on a map, but explores the unseen reverb of reflection where plural causes become visible and their consequences thinkable, and where other voices can make themselves heard rather than theorized" (Voegelin 2019: 21). Nevertheless, "while agreeing with the affirmative of her echo practice," Voegelin critiques its binary relationship to the power structures it resists, noting that "her resistive echo-ing implies a politics of the antis, the anti-stance of the 'people's microphone' and the centrifugality of its dissonance as a counter-politics remains trapped in the circularity of harmony and discord, violence and anti-violence, as the anti-nomic logic of power" (Voegelin 2019: 21). Voegelin suggests an echopraxia that is perhaps more alternative than resistive, imagining "a more agonistic and playful dispersion,"

> a sonic practice whose voice does not rise against harmonic tonality, the dominant self, but sounds itself, and whose clamour therefore, cannot be silenced in its opposition, but whose possibilities are inexhaustible: generative of an unfamiliar world that sounds actuality's hidden pluralities. (Voegelin 2019: 21)

Whereas Voegelin turns to the eco-corporeality of breath to articulate a less binary practice of resistive echoing, researcher and artist Annie Goh opens the concept up to a wider "echo-logical" perspective in which, as "material-semiotic actors, echoes are to be considered as neither purely acoustic, material and 'real' nor entirely symbolic, metaphorical and figurative[; ...] they are entangled in nature *and* culture as *natureculture*" (Goh 2019: 258). In attending to these material-semiotic valences, Goh situates echo alongside Donna Haraway's cyborg. Goh's echo expands on Haraway's influential figure, though, leveraging the porous boundaries between vibration and signification to embody a "*sounding* feminist figuration" (Goh 2019: 27). She probes the act of acoustic reflection that *produces* echo, problematizing concepts of originality and difference to help undermine a binary understanding of sound and its perception. Instead, she asks how we might embrace the speculative agency of echo, unlocking resonance as a form of "border thinking" (Anzaldua 1987) that unlocks the collective agency of human and more-than-human bodies that meet and merge in its diffractive mediation. In noting that "situatedness does not necessarily arise out of embodiedness" (Goh 2019: 141), Goh reaches beyond the envelope of a single sounding moment. Instead of regarding echo as a purely physical phenomenon, she proposes that echo can also "mediate between sound and the production of knowledges[, ...] a boundary figure, alerting us to the contingencies of subject-object relations and other pervasive dualisms" (Goh 2019: 27). In postulating an epistemological dimension, Goh's echoes reach towards the philosophical-political imaginaries of an 'elsewhere' and 'elsewhen' (Goh 2019: 276-277). Goh further invokes the mythological character of Echo to embody this disruptive, cyborgian intervention in sonic knowledge production; this Echo is not interested in "the 'truth' of the echo, but its truth-effects[, ...] less interested in what an echo *is* and more interested in what an echo *does*" (Goh 2019: 28). In this context, situatedness remains rooted in physical, haptic proximity, but also reaches out to suture disparate modalities of agency across time and space. Goh's Echo is not a tool for scientific positivism but a facilitator for collective imaginaries and world-building, a figure capable of "foreground[ing] human-nonhuman relationality in its multi-faceted richness" (Goh 2019: 276). Goh uses this conception of Echo to ground her theory of "sounding situated knowledges" (Goh

2019: 14), in which sound is more than just a physical phenomenon but also a powerful mediator of potential material and immaterial creativity. Sounding situated knowledges embrace Echo as an agent capable of supplanting the scientific positivity of a dying vibration into a form of "persistent questioning" (Goh 2019: 267) that binds the momentary transparency of sympathetic resonance to the multivalent "opacity" of our environment (Glissant in Goh 2019: 268).

With the assistance of Echo, Goh helps indicate how sounding situated knowledges carry the imprinted traces of the myriad agencies and spaces that converge in their coming-into-being, opening up Dyson's and Voegelin's resistive practices to additional, unexpected orientations towards plurality. Goh's Echo sounds a call for situated awareness that both affirms and extends the ecological embeddedness of Dyson's and Voegelin's political echopraxia, reminding us that resistance is an ongoing form of collective creativity that emerges from the human and more-than-human relationships that are cultivated over time and in space. Together, these three evocations of echo articulate a call to resist linear, teleological temporalities. They point us towards sound's powerful mediating potential, capable of calling our attention and orienting our imaginations, encouraging us to seek landscapes and communities that embody the responsivity that is Echo's indelible imprint. Positioned in opposition to the dematerialized essentialization of Pythagorean echoes (embodied in the ideological reverberation of the monochord), the shifting confluences of Dyson's, Voegelin's, and Goh's echoes celebrate our material entanglement in the world as opportunity for call-and-response, sounding out not-yet-imagined possibilities for collective human and more-than-human futures.

This more-than-human call-and-response disrupts the linear, hierarchical reductionism of Pythagorean space by scaling up its singular teleological gaze to a pluralistic multi-dimensional field of awareness. Echo's capacity to respond introduces a sonic contingency, an embedded awareness of the other as a physical interlocutor; rather than an abstract ethical consideration, the other within the echo demands an immersion in time and space in order to be heard, experienced, and engaged with. Echo-praxia confronts the ideological constraints of Pythagoreanism, reclaiming the commons—as Dyson suggests—and planting the seeds for alternative, multi-dimensional political imaginations—as Voegelin proposes. Goh's echo takes one further step, though, by attuning to echoes bridging more complex spatiotemporal and cultural divides. One encounters this echo in the spaces where she resides, in the edifices of ancient civilizations but also in the landscapes and environments that they found refuge in, inhabited, and became a part of. Again following Haraway, Goh proposes "[c]onceiving of echo as a companion species," enabling "us to purposefully blur the boundaries" and "foreground human-nonhuman relationality in its multi-faceted richness" (Goh 2019: 276). For Haraway, "'[c]ompanion species' thinking inquires into the projects that construct us as a species, philosophical or otherwise. 'Species' is about category work. The term is simultaneously about several strands of meaning—logical type, taxa characterized through evolutionary biology, and the relentless specificity of meanings" (Haraway and Gane 2006: 140). In appropriating the language of biological taxonomy, Haraway moves beyond a posthuman conception of the cyborg to explore similarly hybrid tendencies at larger scales, inviting a sweeping "interrogation of relationalities" (Haraway and Gane 2006: 140) across spectra of community, species, or even animacy.

In this guise as companion species, echoes pool in the collective awareness and agency of the bodies, buildings, and landscapes that imbue its diffractive call-and-response with murmuring vitality. Just as with the people's microphone that Dyson describes, this echo-praxia is not yet truly formed when sound radiates from a central source, but rather when that agency slowly distributes in a wider arena of actors and affordances. Goh's formulation of echo as companion species undermines Pythagoreanism on a far more fundamental level than the pluralistic reclaiming of the commons that Dyson describes. If an echo is simply reflecting and returning, defined by its relation to—or perception by—its acoustic source, then it simply delays and complicates that sound's eventual absorption into the linear course of history. By embracing material and more-than-human capacities in echo as companion species, Goh turns our attention to a much more complex interdependence, in which the situated sounding body is as much an echo chamber itself as it is a sounding source. In examining multiple genres of echo as modes of attentiveness and epistemology (see Chapter 6 for further discussion), Goh reveals the agencies latent in the land that echoes and in the bodies, materials, and accumulated stories that produce their own echoes therein.

From my own positionality as a performer, scholar, and luthier in Western traditions, I have sought to embrace these echo-praxias through engagement with materials, themselves. Mindful of Pythagoreanism's disregard for the physical resonance of hammers and strings, I propose here a response to Pythagoras that is articulated not by words but by physical (re)constructions, material interventions in the story of the monochord. Well before beginning this text, I turned my attention to the forge and the metals that are shaped there, embracing my expertise as a luthier and metalworker to revisit both the echoes of the workshop as well as the human and more-than-human bodies that produce them. The instruments that emerged from this endeavour, *chimeracords*, help turn our attention towards these material echoes and the agencies that pool in their acoustic activation. Through their collection, construction, performance, and reception, these chimeracords formulate questions about how collective human and material imaginaries might help generate forms of "resistive echoing" and thereby contribute to voicing the world's "inexhaustible [...] hidden pluralities." I envisioned a monochord free from the straitjacket of the *regula* and the *canon*, a monochord whose umbilical cord to the material phenomena that birthed it had not yet been severed. Rather than simply building an alternative monochord (there are plenty of such instruments that already exist), the chimeracord returned to the forge that Pythagoras stumbled upon, diffracting the sound of the hammer into alternative monochordal imaginations, thereby inviting material complicity into collective echo-praxias.

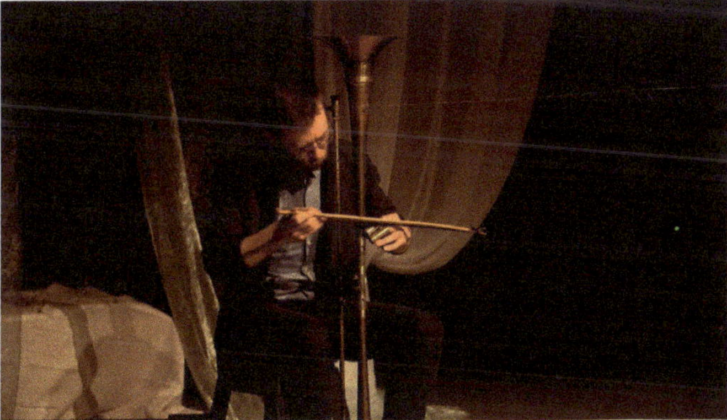

Fig. 9 Chimeracord in performance, bowing the string. Photo by Davids Danoss (2025).

Although the chimeracord has only a single string (like any proper monochord), that string passes across the entire body on one side, through the inside of the sound chamber, and then halfway back down the body. Through these three interlinked transversals, the unity of the "mono"-chord already starts to dissolve. As each of these three stretches of cord are played, they pull and stretch each other, their tensions intrinsically interlocked, perfectly mirroring each other's wavering vibrato, pitch, or timbre. Pulling or plucking any one leg of this string will also alter the others, enacting a sympathetic entanglement in which their harmonies and resonances merge, meld, and shimmer in tandem.

Monochords around the world utilize a huge variety of materials for their resonating chambers, from wooden boxes to gourds, from the human mouth to the earth itself. Because the chimeracord emerged as a response to the Pythagorean monochord—attempting to reimagine a relationship to the forge upstream from Pythagoras's mythical diversions—it has a sound chamber formed of metal that might have been found in that forge. In this case, it is brass that has been cast, drawn, tapered, and spun into a long chamber comprising two conical sections joined in the middle. This resonator creates several strange effects as its volume and distribution (long and thin rather than round or boxy) modulate the resonance and harmonic overtones of the vibrating string that stretches across and through it. However, this brass sound box also affords several other acoustic possibilities, and it is through this metallic resonating chamber that the chimeracord's hybridity is further refracted into a broader spectrum of organological superposition. This brass resonator invites a confluence of instrumental consorts, weaving together not only the string of the monochord but also the unique affordances of reed, percussion, and brass families, as well.

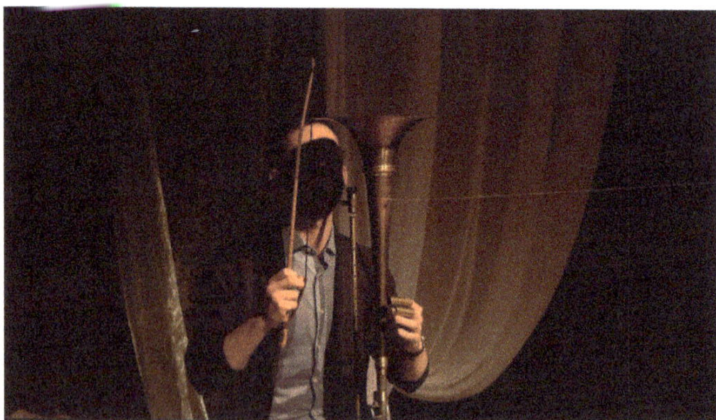

Fig. 10 Chimeracord in performance, bowing the bell. Photo by Davids Danoss (2025).

Like any soundbox, the chimeracord's resonator can be struck or scraped like a percussion instrument. From berimbaus to zithers, resonators have always afforded at least the capacity for percussive interpolations. But as the brass in the chimeracord resonator flares outwards at either end in its distinctive hourglass shape, it produces more varied and malleable acoustic vocabularies. Borrowing from the craft tradition of brass instruments like trumpets and horns, these brass flares are drawn and spun, stretched thin onto a steel mandrel, like a ball of dough kneaded into a thin sheet. But while a traditional brass bell would be reinforced around these sometimes paper-thin edges, the chimeracord's flares remain thin and fragile. In addition to the metallic frequencies of the soundbox's main body, these thin flares can be bowed or struck like a cymbal. These flares are much thinner than a traditional cymbal, though, voicing unique and highly reactive harmonic overtones and clusters when activated. Echoing then through the body of the resonator and back into the surrounding space, these flared apertures of the chimeracord's brass resonator produce unique and vibrant vocabularies that weave into the upper partials of the monochordal string resonance vibrating in the brass body.

The tubular construction of the resonator also opens up the possibility to be activated not only as a resonating chamber, but as a column of air, which in turn invites traditional wind instrumental practices—ranging from flute techniques to single or double reeds or even to lip buzzing, as with traditional brass instruments. The chimeracord has a small aperture at one end of the resonator that allows these different embouchures to activate its internal air column, projecting out the other end. This aperture can also be extended back up the instrument, effectively doubling the length of the activated column of air, thereby increasing the amplitude as well as lowering the frequency of the pitches it produces. These lower frequencies inhabit deep pitched registers that weave together with the low tones of the long monochord, while simultaneously the reeds and toneholes also access higher overtones and harmonic spectra within the resonating fabric of the composite instrument.

Given its inclination towards multiplicity and hybridity, the chimeracord has continued to grow and evolve beyond these basic sound-producing syntheses. Using repurposed steel string wire attached to the brass body and the monochord string, the chimeracord stretches outwards in space, building small networks of collective amplification and variation through a series of vibrating membranes mounted on smaller flared brass hourglasses. These additional resonators function as primitive analog amplifiers, absorbing and transmitting the sounds produced by the chimeracord, even as these additional cords, membranes, and flares introduce their own flickering variations of harmonic spectra and sympathetic frequencies to the composite voice of this ever-expanding instrumental collectivity.

As an experiment postulating how a monochord might develop if left to germinate in the forge rather than extracted and dissected in a Pythagorean laboratory, the chimeracord embodies a diffractive hybridity synthesizing discrete organological paradigms that congeal within the vibrating air column inside its strange brass body. It invites seemingly incompatible instrumental families into an entangled embrace, dissolving polyphony into a corporeal union—a chimerical fusion of reeds, strings, and metals. As they activate each other, vibrating in mutual tension and release, they declaim a provocatively polyvocal story of hybrid ontogenies and entangled collective futures.

Pythagoras's monochord epitomized a teleological mentality, its single string mirroring its single-minded purposefulness. It was first and foremost a tool and a metric, a means to measure the universe and tabulate its dimensions. And as attested to by the inaccurate or misattributed proportions in his early experiments, it was a masterpiece of preconception, an instrument designed to amplify its master's voice. Pythagoras's monochord was not an experimental device built to explore the harmonic phenomena of the world, but rather a valedictory monument, crafted to enshrine the foretold truth of a static, immutable law of consonance. Its single string, stretched taut across its wooden sound box, was never truly meant to sound, but to silence. It was not the opening of a mouth, but the foreclosure of a sentence already pronounced and complete.

The chimeracord attempts to articulate stories and histories that have been muffled by their absorption into the univocal acclamation of the monochord, to return to the constituent materials constrained and contained therein. These stories stretch into the soil beneath the forge itself, radiating out from the workshop into ecology and society alike. just as the gut strings and the wood that Pythagoras deployed, the materials in the hammers themselves were also extracted, refined, and repurposed. The metals from the forge have their own ontogenies, encompassing both the lands from which they were torn and the bodies that extracted them, arcing in long trajectories across space and time. Within the workshop, these metals still carry the accumulated scars of these journeys, and the metallic voices pealing under hammer blows in the forge are the ongoing echoes of those material memories.

In their material, and in the tools that work them, we are able to place an ear against the machinery by which ecology is subsumed into economy. As both raw materials of modern industrial production and cultural megaphones for creative expression, these pieces of brass help to problematize some of the ways in which "the connection between space, sense, and eco (meaning the management of a home and 'ecology') has been smothered under centuries of de-coupling, abstracting, separating what are essential relations between the extensiveness of space, the perceiving, understanding and experiencing of sense, the resonance of echo, and the flows, currents, and currencies of cents" (Dyson 2014: 1). Like Pythagoras's monochord, whose *regula* sucks the air out of its voice, deadening its corporeal vibration within a vacuum of philosophical idealism, this brass is beaten into predetermined forms and smothered in a blanket of enamel to ensure its sheen never dulls, an interchangeable mouthpiece voicing a cultural ideal in which plurality is silenced by "the absence of the environment in which echo can occur" (Dyson 2014: 151). But as they are nurtured into the evolving bodies of chimeracords, they are able to shed these forms of acclamation. In its place, these materials reach back through the violent echoes of their own extractive manufacture, recuperating what traces of their ecological ontogeny still persist as their organological hybridity helps give voice to the ores and flames, the chemicals and hammers, that are smelted together in the molecular lattice of their alloy.

In these new guises, they embrace an inquisitive pluralism, generating new forms of autopoietic material agency through the sounding materialism that reverberates within their chimeric brass bodies, spilling out into their environment as inquiry, as invention, and as invitation.

2. Place-Thought

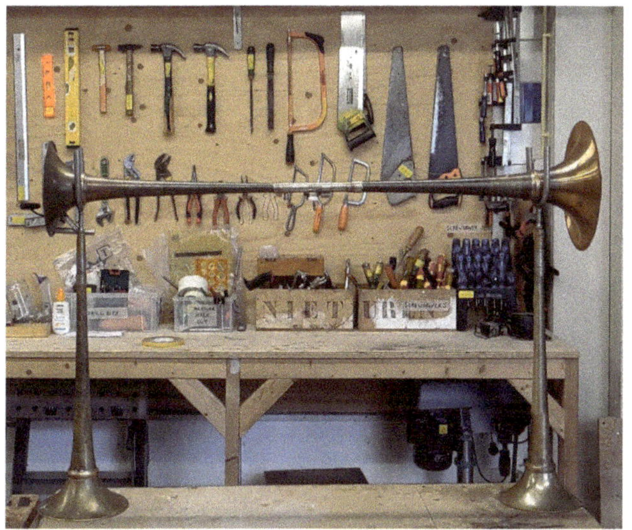

Fig. 11 Chimeracord under construction in the workshop. Photo by author (2024).

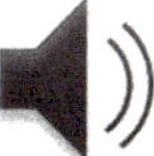 

Audio Recording 4 *Attending*. Recording by author (2024), http://hdl.handle.net/20.500.12434/6ef31249

Video Recording 4 *Attending*. Recording by author (2024), http://hdl.handle.net/20.500.12434/f57bd789

 https://doi.org/10.11647/OBP.0476.02

The chimeracord grew out of slow, careful, intermittent, and at times even aimless experimentation with salvaged brass—blowing, tapping, bowing, rubbing, scraping, and endless hours of careful, patient listening. These instruments are in many ways not just experiments, they are themselves agents and observers; which is to say, they are themselves experimenting. If I provoke the brass with a new string or a strange reed, it is the brass that absorbs and records that event. It is the brass's molecular lattice and internal volume that resonate and react, alternately muffling or amplifying these interjections, suppositions, and queries. In the workshop, brass can access a deep and fundamental responsivity. By the time brass gets to the workshop, it is already cast into sheets or tubes. The raw minerals that have been refined and alloyed in its body have already been distilled into these forms, but they have not yet been molded and soldered into the new, organological forms that will reinforce and restrict them to their utilitarian purpose. In these states when they are simultaneously processed and in-process, they are highly reactive, sensitive to vibration, and ripe with their own murmuring resonances.

Although I have the expertise as a craftsperson to hijack this organological trajectory—bending and soldering tubes into imaginative new configurations or elaborate networks—I prefer to be a listener, to approach these materials inquisitively and to wait until they reveal their own acoustic predilections or proclivities. As a component or collaborator in these experimental processes, I am not here just to recreate my own fantasies or imaginations, nor am I simply effacing myself or my agency in this process (and surely no one reading or listening to these instruments would ignore my own exaggerated influence on proceedings and results). Attending to material in these states requires equal parts intervention and reservation, a choreography of patient probing, meandering, and listening. In developing my practice of speculative craft and performance, such superficially trivial differences—between guiding material towards a preconceived design and attending to its own murmuring momentum—produce radically different results. In other domains of my practice, outside the purview of this study, I have built instruments determined by my own fantasy rather than any predisposition latent within the material itself. I have designed other hybrid instruments, even, including kaleidoscopic reimaginations of trumpets or zurnas or bagpipes, which feed into collaborative music and noise projects with other (human) performers. And I have designed innovative new models of traditional instruments, including multiple new models of valves for brass instruments, which remain firmly ensconced in fields of conventional music performance and trade production. But the construction of these chimeracords (as well as some of their other brethren in my wider instrumental family) departed purposefully and proactively from these working methods, embracing instead experimental orientations rooted as firmly as possible in practices of listening, attending, and responding.

The craft that flows into these chimeracords reflects my desire to amplify the sounds or agencies that I encounter here, rather than to shape or transform them. And because these practices entail long hours of careful attending, they merge and meld with their surroundings, with the tools and spaces of the workshop, with the years of apprenticeship that bring all these materials and tools into each other's orbit, and even with the centuries of accumulated expertise that provided the platform for that transformative apprenticeship. In these moments, the workshop is not a tool itself, to be deployed by the craftsperson, in service to some higher intellectual design. It embodies instead a confluence of bodies, materials, and trade practices that settle in the soil of each other's unfolding presence, germinating in the fertile ground of their situated entanglement. Only with time and care can these seeds begin to sprout their own acoustic imaginations, and conventional workshop spaces are—unfortunately but very deliberately—designed to foreclose these forms of multivalent agential seepage. With enough patience, though, the workshop can still foster a vibrant fecundity, a communion of agencies and expertises and material affordances that collectively formulate their own genre of thinking, acting, and sounding.

But this conception of the workshop—as a site for listening, for interaction, for collaboration—must be cultivated, for the workshop is fundamentally a site of utility rather than care. While this type of awareness to material is in some ways natural to the workshop—where craftspeople spend large amounts of time in close proximity to material, building acquaintanceships sometimes far deeper than those to their human colleagues—it is not inevitable, and in many cases the workshop's teleological momentum towards productivity limits or precludes such awareness. Despite the workshop's capacity for connection and collectivity, not every such space remains enmeshed in the material and social fabrics that surround it. Utility abstracts intimacy, diverting the craftsperson's heightened attunement to material towards specific, entrained practices of disciplining and shaping it. Material becomes merely workpiece; it becomes a prototype of its finished product rather than a particular object, each embodying its own unique response to the workshop's intervention. Although in constant states of negotiation, as its unruly rawness is carefully honed into obedient utility, the material is abstracted into a state of quasi-stasis: matter awaiting form, a mass untamed and yet defined by its eventual domestication. It can only ever be a single, teleological product, and its slow assumption of that form is simply a process of gradually coming into focus. In these spaces, the workshop is not a site of listening, but a site of command.

Both because of and in spite of the fog of mythology surrounding Pythagoras's trip to the forge, that site provides an interesting window into the plasticity of the workshop space. As Pythagoreanism divests itself of its material tethers in order to hone its philosophical understanding of the cosmos, it renders clearly how a workshop can become abstracted and dematerialized. Pythagoras never truly entered the forge, even though his body may (or may not) have encountered its literal space. He remained oblivious to both the forge and the bodies that animated it—to the skills developed and the tasks undertaken—even though he observed them in search of some fundamental law of harmony. He approached it with a clear goal—to observe and identify a particular sonic phenomenon—and his entire interaction retained this single-minded purpose. His investigations of the hammers never engaged with the reasons why each hammer might have required a different mass in the first place, nor with how the interaction of these different tools related to the hands of the smiths who wielded them, nor with the relations between the objects struck and the hammer blows that resounded. He remained oblivious to the carefully articulated choreography of heat and metal incrementally shaping resistant material into the deliberate forms of tools and utensils. He treated the creative locus of the forge as though it were outside time and space, a neutral entity producing tools and utensils whose very purpose is in fact not their own form, but rather their capacity to foment and realize other forms, a pure utility serving purposes beyond its own scope. The forge gives shape to the tools that will allow certain ideas or desires to become reality while foreclosing others. If, as the famous phrase goes, everything looks like a nail when one is holding a hammer, then it is the forge—which forms that metal into a hammer instead of a plow—that is responsible for the limits of perception and imagination, cultivating which realities become possible and which do not. As Pythagoras approached this cradle of material transmutation, he ignored the forces actually shaping that reality, reducing his observation to a predetermined focal point of perception: the consonance of four hammers and the mathematical rules that they—however illusorily—intimated.

Despite his close observation of the hammers and their chordal architecture, he only registered this sonic phenomenon, maintaining a stubborn remove from the spaces and bodies (and their intertwined agencies) that produced it. As Frances Dyson notes, Pythagoras's journey to the forge encapsulates "a scenario replete with all the elements that operate today in sonic capitalism: a thinker, a member of the privileged class, visits (as in 'goes down' to) the forge, where he notices not the men, but the instruments, and not the purpose of the instruments, but rather the sounds they make" (Dyson 2014: 20-21). And just as any good capitalist might do today, Pythagoras plucked what he desired while passing through, without ever noting the ground from which it was uprooted. He descended to the forge and mined it for "the mathematical formula [that provided] a model for the numerical quantification, transcription, and notation of nature" and thereby underlying Western (and eventually also capitalist) "musical, scientific, philosophical, and religious doctrine" (Dyson 2014: 20). In this guise as Promethean proto-capitalist, Pythagoras embodied the ethos of extraction, regarding the forge purely as an expedient opportunity, an exotic source from which he could extricate what truths he desired with no need to consider the context in which they emerged.

This teleological extractivism stems from a worldview rooted in linearity, in which the forge is merely a temporary stop along Pythagoras's wayfaring journey. It sees objects in a landscape as inherently separable, as fruits that can be disentangled from their context and withdrawn. They are absorbed into a telos, and through their consumption they further its progression and purpose rather than their own. Whatever remains of them after serving this purpose may be discarded along the way, their seeds never returned to the ground in which they sprouted. In this linear perspective of utilitarian teleology, as a single strand stretches from one point to another, the line constitutes an ideal in and of itself—an ideal external to the spaces it traverses or the points from which it departs. With his canonical monochord, Pythagoras helped to entrench this cosmological template in Western consciousness, and indeed, the seeds of this Western compulsion for so-called progress and development can be identified already in Pythagoras's descent to the forge and his approach to the hammers he found there.

This previous chapter detailed the misrepresentations and inaccuracies in the actual proportions and ratios that Pythagoras purportedly discovered in the forge. And although these discrepancies are jarring in hindsight, they are not indications of any malicious intent or deliberate obfuscation. Rather, they reveal a startlingly efficient aspect of the perspective that produced—and over centuries continually reproduced—them. In distilling the actual proportions of hammers and strings down to simplified formulas, including those made famous by the monochord, Pythagoreanism demonstrates both how effectively a hermeneutic grating can curate perceptions of reality as well as how powerfully that perception can shape how people go on to engage with that reality. In the story told by Pythagoreanism, the specific qualities and vessels of our knowledge about reality are easily overlooked, because in this telling, our gaze remains trained firmly on the inquisitive sage as he traverses the city, discovers the forge, investigates the hammers, and whirls away to his complex experiments with strings, weights, tubes, and glasses. The hammers feature only as a spark to light the philosophical insight of our hero, and they recede into the background as soon as they've helped to train his attention towards the vision that awaits at the end of his journey: the universal harmonic proportions that infuse the entire fabric of reality. With this backdrop, it is easy to forget that the hammers are not just musical instruments, that they sounded and reverberated in relation to a trade, to its materials, and to the humans who wielded them. It is easy to overlook the entirely non-coincidental utilitarian concerns that placed those particular hammers in sonorous relationship to one another as Pythagoras walked by. The line passes through the forge, and although the hammers are absorbed into his trajectory, they are again discarded further down the line, all nonessential characteristics boiled away in the crucible that refined Pythagoreanism.

This story encapsulates a teleological linearity that distinguishes the Western canon into which it was later subsumed. As a specimen of the origin myth genre, it demonstrates a pattern within Western culture that Indigenous philosopher Vine Deloria Jr. describes as a conception of "creation as the beginning event of a linear time sequence in which a divine plan is worked out" (Deloria Jr. 1973/2003: 77). This worldview inheres in the particularity of the points along this linear time sequence, from its instigation in an act of "creation as a specific event" (Deloria Jr. 1973/2003: 77) through to the interpolations of specific historical events. This structure is perhaps best exemplified by the evocation of messianic intervention, whether that be the historical birth and death of Jesus of Nazareth or his recapitulatory return as an agent of redemption, resolving the long teleological arc of history. In Western culture, specific actors and actions define the course of history, charting its linear course by grasping the agency necessary to plant its defining moments along a trajectory that they set. These interventions ascribe meaning to long arcs of seemingly less eventful coexistence, inscribing purpose by organizing vast swathes of activity around decisive focal points. Actors like Pythagoras invest history with its direction, puncturing the unfolding thread of history and segmenting it into sharply defined vectors of historical progress. Like the gutstring of the monochord he built, this history is formed from countless threads of living, breathing corporeality, all of which are painstakingly extracted, woven into a single braided strand, and stretched taut with its ends severed—firmly notched into a retroactively particularized, self-contained, and teleological cosmology.

In this conception of time and progress, Pythagoras's descent into the forge functions as a limit point, fixing the origin of Pythagoreanism firmly in a single historical time and place. All of the discrepancies that were noted in the previous chapter between the actual material reality of the forge and Pythagoreanism's appropriation of it are rendered quite literally immaterial, for its historical function is dictated not by Pythagoras's role in the unfolding story that surrounds him but rather by the particular meaning invested in it by the unfolding purposefulness of Pythagorean rationalism. In this worldview, paradoxically, the

Pythagorean presumption of a universal law of harmony does not in fact clash with the material facts of the forge that fail to conform to it because, in extracting the seeds of rational proportionality and spinning them into a cohesive systematic understanding of the world's harmonic fabric, Pythagoreanism retroactively refines and defines the material reality of the forge. The success and intelligibility of the Pythagorean system renders the forge's irrecuperable material discrepancies invisible and inaudible. In walking out of the forge and continuing on his journey—having plucked what value he could from the hammers and discarded the rest—Pythagoras silenced the forge and its reality as it receded from the onward march of his story and, indeed, from the entire arena of history's forward progress.

As strange as it seems when told like this, this hermeneutic recalibration of material reality is neither unique nor remarkable. Because this linear purposefulness inheres in particular interventions by discrete actors, it elides the particularity of all other points along the line, especially those points that might drift away from the trend that it charts. Precisely because this conception of history is embodied in the heavily distilled particularity of defining events, it also obscures (or outright erases) the particularity of the times and spaces that surround those events, radiating outwards in their own tapestries of complicated interrelation and superposition. The forge becomes a brief tableaux in Pythagoras's journey, disentangled from the contexts in which it emerged and remained enmeshed. It makes one wonder what truths might emerge from the forge if its own discrete spatial particularity were enabled to unfold over time, divested of its Pythagorean purpose. What forms of agency and relationship might emerge if we returned to the forge, if we stayed there and listened to the hammers within their metalworking web of materials and agencies, and if we allowed them to voice their own stories of proportion, harmony, or consonance?

Just as the metalworking forge continued to resound in his absence, stubbornly pronouncing ratios irrecuperable to Pythagorean truth, other potential forms of historical consciousness provide alternatives to this linear interpretation of history. Even as Western culture traversed the world, its single-minded progress scything through innumerable other cultures along its imperturbable path, those other traditions persisted in their own understandings of time and space, cultivating forms of history and storytelling attuned to alternative consonances, discords, and realities. In contrasting the linear temporal cosmology of the West with Indigenous North American perspectives, Deloria notes the fundamental incommensurability between the evental particularity of Western creation myths and an Indigenous conception of "creation as an ecosystem present in a definable place" (Deloria Jr. 1973/2003: 77). While the former operates with an unarticulated assumption that both creation and our experience of its aftermath are driven by causal relationships, the latter asserts that creation is inseparable from the web of agencies that inhabit its echoes. In the context of creation as an ecosystemic process, time is not a linear force but a spatial relationship. "Space [...] is determinative of the way that we experience things [...] because to have time, there must be a measurable distance to travel during which time can pass" (Deloria Jr. 1973/2003: xvii). And furthermore, if, as Deloria suggests, "space generates time" (Deloria Jr. 1973/2003: 70), then "[t]ime is merely a measure of motion" (Cordova 2007: 227) and temporal relationships are not causal but rather spatially entangled. All other aspects of an individual or communal cosmology may be diffracted through this awareness of situated spatial emergence. In contrast to Western teleological linearity, in which divine redemption can intervene at a particular future point to alter the fundamental meaning of all existence, these Indigenous traditions embrace "revelation [...] as a continuous process of adjustment to the natural surroundings and not as a specific message valid for all times and places" (Deloria Jr. 1973/2003: 66). This revelation is entangled with very real, specific locations, and it inheres not in the punctuated intervention of messianic actors, but in the "complexes of attitudes, beliefs, and practices fine-tuned to harmonize with the lands on which the people live" (Deloria Jr. 1973/2003: 69). "Sacred places thus inform us of the particularity of revelation" (Deloria Jr. 1973/2003: 67), and in so doing invest that particularity not into specific human actors or dramatic historical moments, but into the land, its context, and our unfolding entanglements therewith.

A Standing Rock Lakota citizen, Deloria recognized the many differences between Native traditions and philosophies in North America, but citing also certain notable shared features, he nonetheless sought to write from a broader Native perspective, as have other

Indigenous thinkers, such as Jicarilla Apache philosopher Viola F. Cordova, who remarks:

> One of the objections to studying 'Native American philosophy' is that the groups called 'Native American' represent too diverse a group to subsume under one label. The ideas of each group, it is argued, might be so different as to require an exploration of each group. In other words, one cannot generalize about the Native American peoples. [...] Nevertheless, there are [...] spread throughout the Americas, some similar concepts that allow one to speak of Native American thought in general. (Cordova 2007: 33)

With this in mind, I will seek to navigate through conceptions of place, sound, and duration from a collection of loosely related Indigenous traditions in North America, outlining a system of thinking with and through place that will inform new insights into the forge in this study, proposing an ecosystemic approach to regarding the materials and metals it houses, as well as the instrumental voices that such an approach might generate. In later chapters, this discussion will also leave the forge, though not as Pythagoras did—by departing through the front door—but rather by following the grain of the metal itself, tracing its course through the landscapes from which it was mined as well as through the contemporary industrial landscapes in which it persists.

As political scientists Gina Starblanket (Cree/Saulteaux) and Heidi Kiiwetinepinesiik Stark (Turtle Mountain Ojibwe) remind us, "Indigenous knowledge and traditions exist in relation to specific contexts" and are "neither [...] fixed [n]or fundamental" (Starblanket and Stark 2018: 175). Through their connection to place, they can be both as mutable or immutable as the land, itself both "context and process" (Simpson 2014: 7). Knowledge and tradition are rooted in the land in an organic sense. Santa Clara Pueblo author, artist, and architect Rina Swentzell underlines the fact that "*community* and *watershed* are synonymous," and that this coextensivity incorporates the individual human body into a network of nested, interscalar "organic systems where connections and communication between parts and other wholes can happen. Any watershed and any human body are both a whole and a part of another whole at the same time [...] Both are home, each is where we live" (Swentzell 2012: 29). As Michi Saagiig Nishnaabeg author and musician Leanne Simpson describes, these senses of place "include[ ] all aspects of creation: land forms, elements, plants, animals, spirits, sounds, thoughts, feelings, energies and all of the emergent systems, ecologies and networks that connect these elements" (Simpson 2014: 15), and to learn from the situated knowledges that emerge through this experience of space requires a participatory, collaborative immersion. Anthropologist Keith Basso calls this process "place-making," describing the durational, multi-species, communal gestation through which particular "place-worlds" emerge, "constructing history itself, [...] inventing it" (Basso 1996: 6).

Place-making, though, no matter how immersive or emergent it might seem, remains intensely particular. After all, the iterative "reconnection of people with one another, and of individuals and the land isn't necessarily transformative in and of itself" (Starblanket and Stark 2018: 177). Not all relationships to place are the same, and certainly not all relationships to place can facilitate coherent cosmologies. Indigenous practices of place-making emerge from specific ecosystemic relationships that enable that knowledge to evolve and flourish through a long-standing entanglement with the particular material realities of the place-worlds which they inhabit. These are not romanticized caricatures of man's communion with nature; they are material relationships developed over countless generations of communal coexistence rooted in everyday sustenance, survival, and flourishing. As Deloria asserts, Indigenous traditions in the Americas do not speak of "nature as some kind of concept or something 'out there.' They talk about the immediate environment in which they live. They do not embrace all trees or love all rivers and mountains. What is important is the relationship [they] have with a particular tree or a particular mountain" (DeLoria Jr. 1999: 23). As referenced previously in the diversity of these traditions, there are distinct and fundamental divergences between the knowledges that emerge within each landscape and ecosystem. "The key to knowing is not to determine universals and derive particulars, but to know the particulars" (Rosiek, Snyder, and Pratt 2019: 7).

Cordova stresses the importance of this particularity, noting that this "sense of place [is also] a sense of *bounded space*" (Cordova 2007: 333; emphasis in original). These Indigenous traditions embrace the centrality of their situatedness within a particular land, building their cosmology around particular features that actively participate in their life. These traditions nearly all have "a sacred center at a particular place, be it a river, a mountain, a plateau, valley, or other natural feature" (Deloria Jr. 1973/2003: 66). These sites are sacred because of their rich entanglement in the lives and well-beings of the whole ecosystem, such as those in the dry, arid landscapes of the Pueblo people, where "water and place are [...] inseparable. Where water emerges from the ground is of great significance. Shrine places are often located there. They are symbolic openings for the emergence of all life" (Swentzell 2012: 30). What makes these spaces sacred is precisely what makes them bounded: their intimate complicity in the development and continuation of the ecosystems with which they are consubstantial. Their sacredness "is taken directly from the world around them, from their relationships with other forms of life. ... Thousands of years of occupancy on their lands taught tribal peoples the sacred landscapes for which they were responsible and gradually the structure of ceremonial reality became clear" (Deloria Jr. 1973/2003: 66). The sacred and ceremonial capacities of this landscape are indistinguishable from the material constraints for life within its reality. In their entanglement they constitute the particularity of the discrete ongoing, evolving ecosystem in which they are embedded. Anishinaabe legal scholar John Borrows describes these relations as "place-based cycles of life" (Borrows 2018: 52) and emphasizes how "[t]hey must be continuously reproduced for Indigenous peoples to live harmoniously with the earth" (Borrows 2018: 50). This continual reproduction of ongoing relations is also a highly particularized activity—it is not an abstract awareness of the land but a literal and ceaseless interaction with it, as for the Pueblo, whose relations of care to the water sources that sustain their bounded space require a constant peregrination through the foothills and valleys around them, "[s]ince all waterways are connected to lakes, hills, and mountains." The iterative and processual enactment of these life-sustaining relationships "on an almost daily basis [make] the entire region intimate[,] familiar[, and] intensely known" (Swentzell 2012: 33).

Because these features within the landscape are so intimately implicated in the most minute as well as the most monumental occurrences within their ecosystem, they also delimit its natural sustainable limits. By referring to this sense of place as *bounded*, Cordova maps the networks of complicity that stitch together their ecosystem.

Cordova describes how even the cardinal directions are not infinite horizons but palpable boundaries and reference points for the ongoing collective activity of existing in a particular shared space (Cordova 2007: 332-344). Deloria echoes this, noting that the sense of gravitational emplacement in their landscape's spatial "center enables the people to look out along the four dimensions and locate their lands, to relate all historical events within the confines of this particular land, and to accept responsibility for it" (Deloria Jr. 1973/2003: 66). By evoking a sense of responsibility, Deloria places human inhabitants in relationship to their human and nonhuman—and even organic and inorganic—cohabitants. Cordova reinforces this idea that "being a part of a bounded space is [...] to adapt to the place that they see as, not only a home, but an extension of themselves as people" (Cordova 2007: 337). This bounded space suggests a kind of homeostasis, in which the maintenance of equilibrium is a dynamic, ceaseless collaboration between a collective of mutually implicated bodies, materials, and landscapes. "[I]t is not simply 'the environment' that they accidentally 'occupy'—they are the children of that place. There is no such artificial distinction between themselves and some alien 'other' that is termed 'nature'" (Cordova 2007: 354).

Despite the intensely material particularity of this coextensivity, it is not a purely physical relation. Anishinaabe and Haudenosaunee sociologist Vanessa Watts relates how thought and philosophy are also produced through this intimate connection to the land's bounded space. In acknowledging that "we (humans) are made from the land; our flesh is literally an extension of soil" (Watts 2013: 27), Watts disputes outdated and racist conceptions of Indigenous thought as simple or "mythic" by emphasizing that "[i]t is not that Indigenous peoples do not theorize, but that these complex theories are not distinct from place." (Watts 2013: 22). The particularity of the land and its ecosystem engender the particularity of Indigenous philosophies, and the theorization of these relationships unfolds not only in words but also in deeds—in the particularized deliberateness with which Indigenous traditions engage their environment in the unfolding space and time of their everyday lives. "Human thought and action are [...] derived from a literal expression of particular places" (Watts 2013: 23). The material conditions for thought and philosophy are also produced by the homeostatic dynamism that characterizes Indigenous conceptions of their physical relationship to the environment. As these traditions of thought and philosophy are then naturally enfolded into material activity and interaction within the world, they are also invested with the concentrated particularity of the bounded space in which they emerge. Watts terms this multimodal materialization of particularity "*Place-Thought*" and describes it as "a theoretical understanding of the world via a physical embodiment [...] Place-Thought is the non-distinctive space where place and thought were never separated because they never could or can be separated" (Watts 2013: 21).

Just as with other relations to the land and the ecosystem, place-thought is a non-linear, non-singular action. Its particularity is braided together from the multiplicity of bodies and agencies that flow into it and it is contingent on the continuous, reiterative enactment of multi-species relations within space. Place-Thought is a vital activity, and while it accommodates metaphysical abstraction, these theoretical strands are still continuous with the material, bounded space in which they are embodied. Place-Thought, therefore, helps to conceptualize how human thought and agency are enacted through dynamic ecosystemic relations, and if these relations form the particularized conditions for human thought, then it follows naturally that the agency of place-thought is also shared with other nonhuman and inorganic entities. "Place-Thought is based upon the premise that land is alive and thinking and that humans and non-humans derive agency through the extensions of these thoughts" (Watts 2013: 21). As an energetic force flowing from the land through its embedded interrelation, place-thought is not unique to humans—nor are, by extension, other forms of thought, philosophy, or agency. Just as the human capacity for place thought hinges on the complicity of other species within their shared network of bounded space, this web of complicity also animates other nonhuman and inorganic species. The presence and, indeed, antecedence of this agential ecosystem is a central concept within many Indigenous traditions, whose "origin stories [maintain] the idea that humans were the last species to arrive on earth" (Watts 2013: 25). This detail is critical not for its chronological importance, but because it situates human activity within a functional and pre-existing ecosystem. "[H]umans arrived in a state of dependence on an already-functioning society [...] The inclusion of humans into this society meant that certain agreements, arrangements, etc., had to be made with the animal world, plant world, sky world, mineral world, and other non-human species" (Watts 2013: 25). Human assimilation into this society entails a certain humility, a willingness to learn from the land and negotiate with its other inhabitants, who are drawing on networks of communication and interaction that outstrip human perception and memory. Humans persist in a novitiate state, apprenticed to the wider context in which we are embedded. If we hope to partake of the fruits of that environment, then we must enter into these relations with the awareness that our participation is contingent on our ability to mediate with other, more experienced non-human species. As Deloria reminds us, "Unquestionably, we have a human-plant relationship but one in which the human is the less sensitive participant. The human [has] to be particularly aware of the bush and pay unusual respect to it in order to use its fruit" (Deloria Jr. 1999: 35).

Cordova traces this idea of nonhuman agency to a fundamental conception of the universe as a dynamic system:

> If something exists
> it is in motion
> and if there is motion
> there is life.
> Everything that exists
> is in motion
> Therefore, everything that exists,
> is alive. (Cordova 2007: 183)

For the Indigenous traditions that Cordova describes, this dynamism underlies a multiscalar spectrum of agency and animacy, a vast homeostatic network of "Stable shifting / Shifting stability" (Cordova 2007: 184). Because motion instigates a form of interactivity between forces or bodies, by existing, we become "*participants* in a process of motion and change" (Cordova 2007: 229)—complicit in the ongoing maintenance of the equilibrium that this unceasing motion solicits. However, humans are neither alone nor even exceptional in that compact. Through the reiterative dynamic process of existing, humans are densely entangled with all other bodies and scales within their bounded space, no more or less agential than "[a] blade of grass [...], a mountain, or a molecule of oxygen" (Cordova 2007: 265). But far from flattening ontological differences, this conception embraces the notion that, by virtue of being rooted in motion and change, these various agents (grass, mountains, molecules, humans) are neither meaningfully discrete nor interchangeable, but are entangled in a more profoundly dynamic vitality:

> Motion and existence are necessarily interrelated [...] What exists has motion; what has no motion does not continue to exist. The universe is one 'thing,' that is, energy, although, whether the quality of *thingness* is applicable in a Native American context is doubtful. This 'energy' seems to have a natural tendency to 'pool,' that is, to gather in various degrees of concentration. The 'pooling' causes the diverse 'things' in the universe. Thus, [...] there are not 'things' but rather the world consists of 'events': *being, peopleing, mountaining*, and so on. (Cordova 2007: 225)

For Cordova, each moment in time and each body in space bears attention as a congealing of vibrant energy, but they are, on a larger scale, incorporated into broader currents of "perpetual motion and change—*is-ing* occurs, *being* happens" (Cordova 2007: 316). Entities or events are instantiations of an existence that is defined by verbs rather than nouns, "manifesting [...] as something temporarily distinct from [their] surroundings" (Cordova 2007: 380), but nonetheless still implicated in the currents of energy that, though momentarily pooling, continue to circulate. The agency that we have as humans is neither unprecedented nor extraordinary. However, rather than viewing human existence as inconsequential, these Indigenous traditions acknowledge the exceptionality inherent in the animacy of all of these entities as they collect into eddies of motion and energy.

It is once again important to underline that, from an Indigenous perspective, these are not generalized, abstract notions but physical realities. Citing her own community's traditions, Watts pointedly asserts this: "A river may act (i.e. flow) but does it perceive or contemplate this? An Anishnaabe perspective would respond in the affirmative" (Watts 2013: 24). Deloria makes a similar assertion of how Native Americans "knew that stones were the perfect beings because they were self-contained entities that had resolved their social relationships and possessed great knowledge about how every other entity, and every species, should live. Stones had mobility but did not need to use it. Every other being had mobility and needed, in some specific manner, to use it in relationships" (Deloria Jr. 1999: 34). From these perspectives, water and stone retained certain wisdoms and capacities from their deep and longstanding relationships to the land and their cohabitants. Having collected wells of pooling energy for however many generations they have been part of their landscapes, they offer humans not only material resources but even more so materialized knowledge. "Each of these forces possesses powers of communication, which humans can discern if they pay attention to their larger natural environment and are immersed [...] for sufficient periods of time" (Borrows 2018: 52). Watts reminds us that much of the activity we are prone to consider agential is also fleeting, superficial, and that entities such as water or stone embody agencies no less potent for their immeasurable duration. In contrast to the teleological agency characterized by Pythagorean actors, these "non-human beings choose how they reside, interact and develop relationships with other non-humans. So, all elements of nature possess agency, and this agency is not limited to innate action or causal relationships" (Watts 2013: 23). Indigenous traditions understand this durational agency as a unique and special knowledge practice and seek to learn from it, as noted by renowned Anishinaabe elder, storyteller, and scholar Basil Johnston as he describes this emergent material wisdom as a "methodology [...] embedded in the earth [...] which we should strive to emulate" (Borrows 2019: 4-5).

Cordova grounds an Indigenous sense of ethics in our ability to contextualize our relationships in these diverse modes of place-thought and embodied knowledge, incorporating human agency into various scales of individual, communal, and ecosystemic consciousness. Although this ethics may be expressed on an individual basis, it is contextualized by the group and its bounded space. "The existential and geographical circumstances of the group will provide the basis for [their] ethical considerations" (Cordova 2007: 330). These ethical systems are forms of place-thought, emerging from nested scales of human and nonhuman agency and varying from group to group with their bounded space and ecosystem. Because these ethical relationships evolve as forms of ongoing place-thought, they are also not universal, and Cordova cites only two generalized principles, namely that "[h] umans are not alone [and that they] occupy a specific place" (Cordova 2007: 330). Once again, the particularity of place-thought supersedes the general. When describing how Indigenous peoples emerged in a situated place that anteceded their interpolation, Watts notes specifically that these networks of nonhuman agencies included ethical systems, constituting "an already-functioning society with particular values, ethics, etc." (Watts 2013: 25). Deloria cites this concept as well, broaching a wider discussion of ethical concerns with a discussion of the common Native colloquialism, "We are all relatives." Deloria asserts that, when taken as an ethical imperative, this phrase becomes a "methodological tool for obtaining knowledge [... from] the total set of relationships [that] mak[e] up the natural world as we experience it" (Deloria Jr. 1999: 34).

Within even this short exposition, what becomes clear is that place-thought is a collaborative activity by which nested multiscalar communities of agency co-constitute their material, theoretical, metaphysical, and even ethical conditions for existence. When contrasted with the Pythagorean tradition, place-thought articulates an alternative to the Western "epistemological-ontological divide [that] contribute[s] to colonial interpretations of nature/creation that act to centre the human and peripherate nature into an exclusionary relationship" (Watts 2013: 26). Human participation is not devalued, but it is deprivileged and decentered, ensconced within a wider ecosystem of land and materiality. This allows human agency to unfold as a processual interaction with its context, both aided by and answerable to the network of other agencies in which it is enfolded. When actions and decisions are expressions of place-thought, they transpire as the temporary eddying of mutual energy that Cordova describes, temporarily accumulating agency from a range of human and nonhuman sources before that energy is absorbed back into other forces and movements within the universe. Decisiveness becomes a communal momentum rather than an individual interjection. In the Western paradigm that developed through and around Pythagoreanism, action is pointillistic, interpolated into the linear flow of history. By reserving agency for human intervention, this theoretical paradigm extracts agency from the land, which "becomes scaled and modified in terms of progress and advancement" (Watts 2013: 26). The land becomes material, and material becomes stock: literally, an accumulated mass of resources segmented into consumable fragments.

The conception and construction of his famous monochord illustrates this dematerialization of the land and its resources. The forge that Pythagoras visited housed craftspeople, themselves working with extracted materials—metals smelted from ore. The following chapter will consider this ore and its origins in more detail, but in focusing specifically on the forge that Pythagoras visited, we encounter a collection of tradespeople toiling with tools and metals with which they have a tremendously intimate knowledge. Not only do these particular human bodies display a complex prosthetic relationship to the hammers, tongs, and flames of the forge, they are also embedded in a trade that evolved over centuries, themselves shaped by the gradual evolution of their predecessors in the forge. Their expertise flows from generations of bodies working closely with metal, learning and navigating the seams of metallic plasticity that can conform to the persuasion of the forge, its tools, and the hands that wield them. While the forge—taken as a localized site where multi-generational craft knowledge is threaded through material particularity—is a faint shadow of the landscapes and ecosystems that produce genuine Indigenous place-thought, it still bears the seeds of a complex material agency with serious theoretical and ethical implications (for both human and nonhuman bodies).

Let us consider the hammers; they were, after all, the reason that Pythagoras even entered the forge in the first place. Without these hammers, Pythagoras would have simply walked past the forge, blissfully ignorant. It was the hammers who called out, who accosted Pythagoras and demanded his attention. It was their collective voice that reached out and touched Pythagoras, their vibrations in his eardrums, enveloping his consciousness. And as intoxicating as the consonance of the four hammers' sympathetic vibrations may have been, there was a discordant fifth hammer in their choir, and it was the sound of all five that coalesced into the reverberating force that hailed Pythagoras and diverted his journey. But before these hammers were cataloged by Pythagoras—reduced from four to five and segmented into individual units for examination—their relationships were rooted in the bounded site of the forge. Their relative proportions were related not to musical consonance, but to the physical properties of their proportional mass. The five together formed a unit of varied potential, each hammer with its own mass tailored to specific purposes in the forge, calibrated to particular sizes and shapes of metal, and to varied levels of heat and malleability. Their proportions were related to the hands that wielded them and the range of skills that they had to apply: forceful or precise, pointed or distributed, rapid or attritional. The five different hammers that Pythagoras discovered were carefully attuned tools, complementing each other along the long arc of metalworking tasks that could take hours or even days to accomplish. Indeed, these five hammers would certainly have been just five out of many. The specific five that resounded together in that moment would have been determined by the nature of the work—not by the hammers, nor even by the craftspeople who wielded them (though their own tendrils of agency would have been braided into the moment). These five hammers would have been chosen in relation to the particular metal they struck, chosen by the metals' size or by their shape, by their resilience or by the nature of their work-hardened shape-shifting. The metal itself, in its elemental materiality, would have dictated precisely which hammers were entwined in sound, reverberating in the streets and, in so doing, hammering their coextensive, interrelational proportionality deep into Pythagoras's skull.

The trade environment into which Pythagoras stepped would have been a microcosmic bounded space. All of the tools had been painstakingly crafted through centuries of accrued knowledge, tailored to the specific demands for each and every shape of metal, degree of workability, or acumen of its wielder. The humans themselves would have been shaped by the forge, apprenticed to their predecessors and trained by the materials, their bodies molded to the constraints of their work: muscles strengthened, coordination honed, injuries sustained. There is nothing arbitrary in a workshop like the forge; from the tools to the people to its distribution in space, it resonates at every level to the efficiency and efficacy of the task and its execution. It is all the more remarkable, then, that Pythagoras could enter that space and see only isolated consonances. As recalled in the texts referenced in the previous chapter, he did not initially comprehend what variables produced the consonances he perceived. Already at this stage, Pythagoras had assessed the network of bodies, tools, and metals in their finely-tuned choreography and seen them not as a collective but as isolable, interchangeable components. He had already, at first glance, reduced the co-constitutive space of the forge to a finite set of discrete units, each equally as extractible or dispensable as the other. Within this set of variables, he sought first to cordon off human power, having the workers exchange hammers to see if their corporeal diversity could account for the harmonic intervals they produced. "But the property of sounds did not rest in the muscles of the men; rather, it followed the exchanged hammers" (Boethius 1989: 18). Once identified, the hammers could be extracted, compared, measured, preserved, or—in the case of the fifth hammer—discarded.

Having uprooted the hammers from their environment for closer scrutiny, Pythagoras then sought to mirror their effects in other media. From his perspective, the hammers were modular components of the universe, units of distinct study whose behavior could be replicated by other units irrespective of the complex entanglement of bodies and metals that had shaped them to their particular dimensions. How fascinating it is, then, to reconsider the swerve that Pythagoras performed at this stage. After ascertaining the role of proportion in the consonant frequencies sounded by the hammers, he was unable to replicate their effects with the exact same ratios in other media, and yet, rather than basing his study upon this diversity of proportional interrelation, he chose instead to privilege the most simple ratios (i.e. those of vibrating strings) over those deemed less suitable or more confusing (i.e. those of mass or volume). Despite having required the facilitation of the hammers' material and environmental agency to even notice such proportionality, Pythagoras immediately dissolves that agency into the service of an abstract ideal. Already extracted once physically, the hammers are thus subjected to a further extraction through this abstraction. They are effectively dematerialized—stripped of their true physical characteristics and replaced with an immaterial caricature. This caricature is then preserved for millennia in the triumphant tale of Pythagoras's descent into the forge, where he steals the harmonic secrets of the universe from the threshold of materiality before returning to consecrate those truths at the foundation of Western civilization. Despite its complete and utter alienation from material reality, it is this version of the hammers which survives well after the actual physical specimens and the space in which they were forged have crumbled to dust, their concatenated agencies subsumed back into the soil.

This caricature of the hammers was subsequently projected onto the monochord as a thin veneer of mythic origin ornamenting an otherwise simple—and by absolutely no means innovative—instrument. The monochord that Pythagoras built was a museum, in a way, only it did not preserve the tools by which he explored proportional relations in the world but rather the only surviving tools that conformed to the ideal proportions he chose to amplify. Having settled on strings as the ideal vehicle for this abstraction, he constructed (or had constructed for him) a simple instrument with a single long string stretched across a wooden frame or box. All of this technology predated Pythagoras, having been used for centuries in various traditional string instruments throughout his region, such as the popular *kithara*. In fact, the design of the monochord is less a creative process than an act of erasure, eliminating extra strings and ergonomic frames in order to pare the idea of an instrument down to its most minimalist form. Even in this act of construction, Pythagoras continues to eschew material agencies sedimented in cultural practice for generations, opting instead for material artifacts as detached as possible from their cultural or utilitarian context. Even the wood and strings themselves seem to personify this drive: in contrast to the metals of the forge (which are malleable when heated and coaxed into novel forms through manual persuasion), the wood and string of the monochord must be cut, treated, severed, and reassembled. The construction of the monochord—even compared to that of a *kithara*—typifies the logic of extraction, segmentation, and isolation that infect the entire grand project of Pythagoreanism. All of the innovations to this instrument (such as the moveable bridge introduced by Guido of Arezzo) followed many generations later. Pythagoras's monochord was a paragon of simplicity, an idealization of abstraction designed to efface even its own materialization.

But of course, that was very much the point. For Pythagoreanism, all of these materials—metal, wood, string—are simply tools. The monochord itself was seen more as a scientific tool than a musical instrument, concerned with precision measurement rather than artistic expression. The story of the Pythagorean monochord can be told in many ways, and in many versions, this abstraction is the symbol of victory, the crucible through which reality can be refined into theoretical truth and beauty. For the adherents who mastered this science of proportions and then promulgated the gospel of rationality, this distillation of the forge into, first, the monochord and then, ultimately, the universal philosophical system of Pythagoreanism was a resounding triumph. It evidenced both the solid foundation of their system as well as its capacity to transcend its humble, material origins and reshape society on a much broader scale. The critique that emerges from the version of this story I share here is not intended to diminish the success of that operation nor to distort the very real proportions and ratios that guided it. Rather, it hopes to reveal the insidious blindness that this system inculcated, an outright hostility towards not only materiality but any alternative hermeneutic that threatened the fragile scaffolding that upheld its vision of the universe and humanity's (privileged) place within it.

Because ultimately this attitude manifests as a form of intellectual object impermanence, in which physical objects in the world cease to hold their actual features, dimensions, and interactive capacity as soon as the observer's attention has shifted away—in this case, shifting away to the abstracted idealization of rationality. Far removed from the particularity of the forge and its agential coagulation of sweat, flame, and metal, Pythagoreanism imagined a world of pure ratios in simple, linear alignment. Their ability (or for that matter, desire) to suppress any irreducible remainders out of sight and out of mind follows naturally from Pythagoras's initial swerve away from the materiality of the hammers. The origin myth of this ideology is rooted not in space or place but in total abstraction. It embraced dematerialization in both theory and practice, carving out a world utterly divorced from the land and the bodies that comprise it. But the alacrity with which Pythagoras turned away from the forge—and away from the hammers altogether—also opens up a lacuna in which we can continue to write other stories and histories. The forge as a space remains and the hammers who generated those primal harmonies were never truly assimilated into the Pythagorean project. In part because of Pythagoras's bizarre success in erasing their materiality (and the inelegant proportions they embodied), the hammers' bounded metalworking space was never properly absorbed into the gravitational pull of the monochord.

If Pythagoras had remained in the forge, or if he had entered the space as a listener rather than as an observer, what might he have heard? If four hammers extracted and sanitized of their context could reveal a few lower order ratios, what might Pythagoras have encountered if he had remained to listen to the other sounds in that space—to the other hammers, the other anvils, the bodies around them, the metals they modulated or even the shifts in tone and timbre from those modulations themselves? These sounds don't reveal themselves so easily; they lack the revelatory directness of the open consonances those four hammers shared. These other sounds require more patience to uncover, listening not only to the space itself but to the ebb and flow of its swirling, eddying energies. The workshop soundscape flows from these energies on many different scales. There are, of course, the daily rhythms of workflow that shift like tides. There are also rhythms and patterns that emerge from the physical demands of the work, such as the metronomic regularity some smiths use to help absorb the hammerblows' recoil (limiting attritional fatigue and injury). All of these rhythms emerge from complex interplay between the organic bodies of the workers and the demands of the materials as they are slowly worked. They cannot be observed in a single moment nor contained in a single calculation because they are relational, emergent phenomena that reflect the congealed agency of the entire bounded workshop space. Nevertheless, as anyone who has spent time in a smith or a metalworking shop can attest, the experience of these sounds and energies over time accrues into an intricate sonic tapestry. As bodies and metals rebound against one another physically and acoustically, the acoustic envelope of the workshop begins to mold and transform like the metal being worked, glowing with molten energy in peaks of activity while simmering dully as that energy cools, ebbs, and pools back into the material density of the space itself. As an acoustic chamber, the workspace becomes a type of crucible, collecting and distilling the integrated energies of the bodies and materials implicated in its activity and distilling them into concentrated streams of collective agency, which dispels slowly, suffusing the temporal duration of the workflow with a saturated tactility.

The materials themselves provide a valuable entry point to this sensorial sonic space. While the tools and the human bodies that wield them wear and tear over long temporal arcs, the materials that they address together are transformed more quickly and, crucially, into a wider variety of forms. Within the overlapping arcs of their treatment, they are capable of embodying blocks, spheres, tubes, sheets, or any other evolution of these forms. Each of these forms is accompanied by a shift in the sonic signature of not only the material itself (resounding and ringing in response to its handling), but also in the tools and craftspeople. In a workspace dominated by loud noises, where human communication can often be limited to nonverbal signals, the acoustic experience of these shifting forms and workflows cannot be underestimated. And with that in mind, the materials themselves offer the only means of indexing these sonic strata as they swell and morph over time. A particular piece of metal's form—encompassing its shape, its density, its resilience, its responsiveness, etc.—provides a core sample of the bounded workshop space and its unfolding acoustic ecology. It bears testament to the hammers that resounded in its transformation, its very morphology cataloging its processual coming-into-being as well as the haptically sonic space that reverberated sympathetically with that emergent process. The metal becomes not only agent but also witness, each permutation in its materiality indexing a cross-section of the stream of energies that resound in its body, echoing the stories and histories woven together through the durational unfolding of its creation.

In contrast to Pythagoras's monochord, the chimeracord draws from the material of the workspace in its capacity as acoustic agent and sonic witness. The pieces of metal that comprise this instrument provide a tangible archive of the durational tactility of the workshop and the fluid intermingling of energies that permeate it. The monochord is rooted in a teleological origin myth and its gradual dissolution into the overarching intellectual project it metonymized provides a template for the historical paradigm it embodied: that creation be conceived as a singular impulse instigating a linear trajectory. The chimeracord, in contrast, rejects the entire notion of an origin myth and situates creation within an ecosystemic bounded space—in this case the workshop and the generation-spanning collectives of materials and bodies that are bound together within its horizon. The components of the chimeracord derive—due to their irrecuperable decay—from vastly varied and essentially arbitrary stages of the workflow. As such, their individual and composite bodies co-constitute a material archive of the agencies that pooled in their creation, core samples of the echoing vitality of hammers and human bodies. They catalog the many sounds and substances of the creational ecosphere, threading these vibrations through the unfinished, evolving materiality of the metal tubes, sheets, and bars that cohere in the chimeracord. The instrument tells a story through the durational acoustic materiality of the bounded workshop space itself. It does not describe this emergence, but rather physically, haptically narrates it.

Duration and narration are keystones in the scaffolding of place-thought. Just as with concepts such as multi-species communication or material agency (or animacy), the emergent qualities of place-thought are entirely non-metaphorical, which is to say, they are based in ongoing practices of world-making. In the case of place-thought, one primary element of its embodied practice is its durationality. Place-Thought is not a marker of a particular concept or disposition, performing an agential intervention in the linear progression of everyday life. On the contrary, place-thought is an iterative re-constitution of inter-agential relationships with, through, and within the land. The interscalar relationships that comprise the ecosystems and bounded spaces of our environments engage in ongoing acts of place-thinking that require space and time to unfold. Deloria refers to time as a relational traversal of space; place-thought requires that bodies and energies negotiate their coexistence in physical space, generating time through the literal mingling of bodies with all of the compromises, conflicts, and symbioses that that entails. Through the process of negotiating the evolving form that this catalysis takes, the parties to place-thought generate the densely frictive temporality of their own world-making practice.

In these Indigenous traditions, sound plays a critical role in place-thought's durational tactility. In addition to the fact that these interscalar interactions are conceived communicatively, their negotiation is also enacted very literally through storytelling. In these situations, the act of storytelling is not a simple narrative act but rather a modality of interacting with the world. It is not only woven directly into social, cultural, and everyday practices, but also generates those practices through an ongoing, participatory, and durational iterativity. Although Western interlocutors have tended to ascribe to Indigenous storytelling primarily narrative and historical—and thereby *repetitive*—functions, Indigenous scholars have detailed the far more complex functions that storytelling enacts. In addition to simply recording events, storytelling iteratively reinforces, reinvents, and reinterprets the world, grounding these activities in stories' ability to generate knowledge or shape society through unfolding activity rather than descriptive prescriptions. "[A] symmetrical power relationships have enabled conventional Western knowledge to produce hierarchies of knowledge that too often mute modes of understanding the world as deeply relational and interconnected" (Starblanket and Stark 2018: 181). Storytelling embeds meaning in relation, and grounds that relation in the particularity of the context in which it is embedded, rather than in the totalizing logic of Western paradigms.

These relations are dynamic, as is the bounded space they relate to. These oralities are not passed down so much as they are reenacted and reinvigorated. They are preserved not through their periodic repetition, but through the networks of community that make their reiteration possible. In emphasizing the dynamism at play in these oral modes of knowledge production, Starblanket and Stark note how a greater "understanding of how our mobility is generative can also enable us to see how discourses that fix us spatially (as well as temporally) are reductive" (Starblanket and Stark 2018: 191), helping to underline the literality of the story's dynamic reenactment (as opposed to the figurative symbolism of its repeated preservation). With respect to the Western compulsion to reduce these multifaceted capacities of the story to a simpler, monolithic function as history (or even more disparagingly, as mythology), Simpson asserts that "[i]t is critical to avoid the assumption that this story takes place in pre-colonial times because Nishnaabeg conceptualizations of time and space present an on-going intervention to linear thinking—this story happens in various incarnations all over our territory every year" (Simpson 2014: 8). As Deloria phrases it, "the story itself is important, not its precise chronological location" (Deloria Jr. 1973/2003: 97). As with place-thought, this intervention into Western conceptualizations of space and time derives from the particularity of relations that converge in the story; within the bounded space of these stories, connectivity is defined not as linear causal singularities but rather as networks of community.

As alluded to by Starblanket and Stark, this communality is crucial to any understanding of the generative dynamism of storytelling. Laguna Pueblo author Leslie Marmon Silko relates how "[e]verything became a story[, of which] the remembering and retelling were a communal process" (Silko 1986/2002: 1008). What many Western interpreters have failed to understand is that stories are not containers of some truth to be unpacked or interpreted. Their conceptual power lies not in the meanings they store but in the agencies for meaning-making that they enable through their retelling. "'Theory' is generated and regenerated continually through embodied practice and within each family, community and generation of people. 'Theory' isn't just an intellectual pursuit—it is woven within kinetics, spiritual presence and emotion, it is contextual and relational" (Simpson 2014: 7). And these agencies are necessarily multiple and diverse. If there were only one way to tell a story or only one voice to tell it, then it would lose the generative dynamism that relates it to the ecosystemic collectivity of place-thought. Basil Johnston refers to this as "the invitational nature of [...] stories," suggesting their purpose is not to record precepts but to provide tools and contexts "for adding our own interpretations and enhancing our own growth" (Borrows 2019: 4). In citing this, Borrows asserts that no one person can be "the authority in these matters" of interpretation and that the potency of storytelling inheres in its "collective endeavor." The invitation to recipients "to activate their own agency" fosters a vibrant interpretive community for whom "[n]uance is often valued over highly specific delineations" (2019: 4) and the construction of truth is an "ongoing contested process" (Napoleon 2001: 318). Silko describes this "communal storytelling" as "a self-correcting process" (1986/2002: 1008) in which a diversity of accounts enables a collective capacity for faithful preservation to merge seamlessly with the ongoing, interactive processes of revision, interpretation, and application. The emergent nature of storytelling helps reinforce this double helix of memory and imagination, reinforcing the importance of "a communal truth, not an absolute ... [a] truth lived somewhere within the web of differing versions, disputes over minor points, outright contradictions tangling with old feuds and village rivalries" (Silko 1986/2002: 1008). Borrows is keen to point out that these practices are neither ancient nor restricted to an idealized natural world, but that they can persist anywhere these peoples continue to activate their collective, generative agencies (Borrows 2018: 49-51).

These stories are "polyfunctional: containing a plurality of factual insights and conveying a multiplicity of truths" (Borrows 2001: 35). This plurality of function means that each song or story (or the objects and places that inhabit them) perform multiple roles as their context shifts. They take many forms spanning a vast range of formalities and types of transmission, including "memorized speech, historical gossip, personal reminiscences, formalized group accounts, representations of origins and genesis, genealogies, epics, tales, proverbs, and sayings" (Borrows 2001: 8). This polyfunctionality is not an ancillary benefit of stories and songs, though; it arises largely because stories and songs unfold through sound, which enables them to embody this polyfunctionality. They cannot be casually abridged or summarized; rather, they require a certain amount of time and space to emerge, and therefore, the particular times and spaces in which they are performed become entangled in their evolving meanings and functions. "Oral tradition does not stand alone but is given meaning through the context of the larger cultural experiences that surround it" (Borrows 2001: 8). The places and manners in which they are enacted vary widely, from private to public, encompassing "pre-hearing preparations, mnemonic devices, ceremonial repetition, the appointment of witnesses, dances, feasts, songs, poems, the use of testing, and the use [...] of place and geographic space" (Borrows 2001: 8). These social contexts invest stories with meanings adaptable to the collective demands and needs of a community. As Simpson notes, "Continually generating meaning is often, but not exclusively, done in ceremony and involves ongoing ethical systems of accountability and responsibility [...] These meanings, in all of their diversity, then become the foundation of generated collective meanings and a plurality of truths" (Simpson 2014: 11).

As Watts remarks, these "histories can sometimes take days to describe" (Watts 2013: 21). Their duration (re)enacts the meanings of the stories they relate, while those meanings in turn transform and adapt to the contexts in which they are voiced, "blend[ing] interpretation and incident" (Borrows 2001: 5). Their shifting functionality allows these stories' application to shift registers and disciplines, "bound up with the configuration of language, political structures, economic systems, social relations, intellectual methodologies, morality, ideology, and the physical world" (Borrows 2001: 8). What differentiates this communal generation of meaning from a Western conceptualization of interpretivity (i.e., multiple interpretations of a foundational text or communal truth) is its embodied and durational enactment. Rather than the exegesis of a monolithic code, storytelling emerges through a dialogue of ongoing exegeses formulated (and reformulated) through the navigation of diverse bodies living and cohabiting a particular environment. This is why it is so notable that these stories are not simply referential but must be continuously reproduced. Through their ongoing entanglement with the land and the places that shape them, these stories act as the seams of place-thought, stitching together the interscalar agencies of land, materials, and peoples.

If Indigenous place-thought emerges—through community—from the land, then that collective meaning-making often transpires through sound. Xwélmexw (Stó:lō/Skwah) artist, curator, and author Dylan Robinson describes how "land-based knowledge [is] encoded within songs [and] the indigenous sovereignties of squálewel, of knowing-feeling place are reconstituted through the actions of singing and listening" (Robinson 2020: 54). In noting how "[o]ften the crucial element in a narrative is the terrain" (Silko 1986/2002: 1009), Silko emphasizes how "the continuity and accuracy of the oral narratives are reinforced by the landscape—and the Pueblo interpretation of that landscape is *maintained*" (Silko 1986/2002: 1010). These oralities—songs, stories, histories—leverage the experience of their duration into a spatiotemporal relationship to place, akin to the embodied knowledge derived from traversing the landscape. Through these durational narrations, storytelling can provoke its listeners to "confront and interact with a particular land along with its life forms [and] to relate the community of people to each and every facet of creation as they have experienced it" (Deloria Jr. 1973/2003: 84). Storytelling is woven from but also back into the bounded space to which it is connected. Its duration allows it to iteratively resituate its roots in a place, becoming not only a part of the terrain but also a part of the spatiotemporal experience of coexisting within that terrain. Storytelling does not convey the image or the symbol of a sacred place, but rather the experience of traversing the landscape around it, and of living within its shadow. These sensorial capacities emerge through the orality of song and storytelling, as their sonic materialization stitches their experience into the unfolding inhabitation of place-thought that they relate.

When describing the foundations of place-thought in multi-species negotiation, Watts states explicitly that "habitats and ecosystems are better understood as societies from an Indigenous point of view; meaning that they have ethical structures, inter-species treaties and agreements, and further their ability to interpret, understand and implement. Non-human beings are active members of society. Not only are they active, they also directly influence how humans organize themselves into that society" (Watts 2013: 23). As humans are invited to participate in these inter-species agreements, the social, legal, and ethical codes that they enact through story and song are enfolded into the ongoing durational sonicities of these multi-species agencies, themselves negotiating their own continual collective articulation of place-thought. Materiality, then, not only contributes to the sonic enactment of place-thought, but actually helps mediate the more expansive collective agency within a bounded space. The animacies that these Indigenous traditions attribute to nonhuman and material entities are instigated by these entities themselves, inscribed through the stories they tell through their own sonic entanglement with their ecosystem. The ceremonies that give voice to these agencies are not constrained to humans but rather welcome and indeed invoke other nonhuman agencies as well, using storytelling as a means to bridge human and nonhuman spiritual agencies. When relating a story in which a tree helps share a form of land-based embodied knowledge, Simpson refers to the need to use ceremony to approach and communicate with the tree, requesting its reciprocal attention by sharing one's own. The human is obligated to "set up a relationship with the maple tree that is based on mutual respect, reciprocity, and caring[, ...] speaking directly to the spirit of the maple tree, entering into a balanced relationship of mutuality" (Simpson 2014: 12). Ceremony, and by extension its articulation, help negotiate the interspecies communication at the foundation of embodied place-thought and the multi-species knowledge-making practices that enact its collectivity:

> [S]piritual knowledge is a tremendous, ubiquitous source of wisdom that is the core of every system in the physical world. The implicate order provides the stories that answer all of our questions. The way we are taught to access that knowledge is by being open to that kind of knowledge and by being engaged in a way of living that generates a close, personal relationship with our ancestors and relations in the spirit world through ceremony, dreams, visions and stories. (Simpson 2014: 12)

The material world is a support to human participation in multi-species society, and the stories that the material world share are an intrinsic and critical component of the environment humans inhabit and the place-thought in which they partake. As Simpson demonstrates, these material agencies mediate the emergent becoming of the world, inviting and eliciting human involvement as or if they choose to. In the case of Simpson's tree, which participates each year in an ongoing story of symbiotic cultivation, the material world recenters the human gaze according to the functions that allow it to embed within the community and bounded space in whose continuity and homeostasis it is complicit.

Watts cautions against the impulse to metaphorize these complicities, insisting that the material interactivity of place-thought and storytelling retain their urgency as interscalar activities of both everyday and multi-generational, multi-species survival. As she notes, "flesh becomes action not because it is material but because it must do so for ears to remain open and low to the ground" (Watts 2013: 33). Cultivating the capacity to respond to and facilitate these complicities is a material obligation that suffuses storytelling with an accountability missing from contemporary Western discourses that have developed or appropriated similar terminologies. In this chapter, I have opted to maintain a strict focus on the network of North American Indigenous cultures whose voices from the last century have shared the rough outlines of place-thought and sonic agency referenced heretofore. I have done so not only because they do not require the mediation of Western or contemporary interlocutors in order to articulate their complex and compelling philosophies of ontology and mutuality, but also because such mediation would dilute their potency. While storytelling has become an increasingly popular methodology in Western discourse, and although certain new materialist trends in particular have begun to use the durational or immersive qualities of sound to help conceptualize humanity's place within a wider, emergent ethico-onto-epistemological context, their interventions are neither necessary to understanding the traditions presented here nor, in truth, evolved enough to engage in dialogue on equal terms. I remain mindful, in Métis anthropologist and researcher-artist Zoe Todd's words, of:

> [...] how a Euro-Western audience consumes [...] the arguments of others writing and thinking about the climate, ontologies, our shared engagements with the world[ ]without being aware of competing or similar discourses happening outside of the rock-star arenas of Euro-Western thought. I do not think [they all intend] to elide decades of Indigenous articulations and intellectual labour to render the climate a matter of common concern. [...] But the structures that produce [these discourses] make it easy for those within the Euro-Western academy to advance and consume arguments that parallel discourses in Indigenous contexts without explicitly nodding to them, or by minimally nodding to Indigenous intellectual and political players. Because we still practice our disciplines in ways that erase Indigenous bodies within our lecture halls in Europe, we unconsciously avoid engaging with contemporary Indigenous scholars and thinkers while we engage instead with eighty year old ethnographic texts or two hundred year old philosophical tomes. [... W]e implicitly give credit to the person at the lectern, and that person is very rarely an Indigenous thinker. (Todd 2016: 8)

Referencing Watts in particular, Todd continues, noting that,

> [...] the appropriation of Indigenous thinking in European contexts without Indigenous interlocutors present to hold the use of Indigenous stories and laws to account flattens, distorts and erases the embodied, legal-governance and spiritual aspects of Indigenous thinking. So there is a very real risk to Indigenous thinking being used by non-Indigenous scholars [...] without contending with the embodied expressions of stories, laws, and songs as bound with Indigenous-Place Thought (Watts 2013: 31) or Indigenous self-determination. (Todd 2016: 9)

In her own words, Watts expresses concern about the generalization of place-thought by Western commentators, noting that as Indigenous conceptualizations of nonhuman agency "becom[e] not only accepted by Western frameworks of understanding, but sought after in terms of non-oppressive and provocative or interesting interfaces ... [Indigenous] stories are often distilled to simply that—words, principles, morals to imagine the world and imagine ourselves in the world" (Watts 2013: 26). The real risk in this is not simply the unhealthy appetite with which Western culture consumes and misappropriates other cultures—what Robinson aptly terms "hungry listening" (Robinson 2020)—but the way in which this "reductive approach essentializes critical listening positionality" (Robinson 2020: 51). Watts notes in particular how this essentializing gaze allows Western commentators to appropriate these traditions while bleaching out the aspects of place and material agency that lie at its heart, absorbing their superficial characteristics into the totalizing framework of the Western ontological-epistemological divide (what Robinson describes as their hunger "for the felt confirmations of square pegs in square pegs, for the satisfactory fit as sound knowledge slides into its appropriate place" [Robinson 2020: 51]). Watts notes that, although this Western gaze may not be "inherently colonial," it nonetheless "creates spaces for colonial practices to occur," for even as "Euro-Western thought is beginning to embrace the contributions of the non-human world[,] the controversial element of agency is often redesigned when applied to non-humans, thereby keeping this epistemological-ontological divide intact" (Watts 2013: 28). As Watts continues by discussing prominent Western commentators who have attempted in various ways to de-essentialize their conception of nature and its complicity in our own ontologies (Watts 2013: 28-30), she notes the points at which they consistently fail, persisting with systems of thought that privilege human agency:

> In [their] relationship with dirt, humans are responsible to land the way an owner might be responsible for a pet. This type of dirt is not First Woman; it is a plaything asking for attention. [...] These interpretations of agency place humans and nonhumans in an interconnected web of cause and effect, where the plane of action is equalized amongst all elements. Agency, however, acts outside, within, and in between this web through carefully re-designed definitions where humans possess something more or special. These levels of agency are a product of the epistemology-ontology paradigm. Imbedded within it, as demonstrated, is the idea of human ownership over non-human things, beings, etc. The inclusion of the non-human, in this case dirt/soil, has been causal or instinctual in nature. Meaning that, although the dirt/soil has been granted entrance into the human web of action, it is still relegated to a mere unwitting player in the game of human understandings. (Watts 2013: 29-30)

As Watts notes, the Western gaze—of which this text is very much a part—often fails through its implicit biases towards a desire for totalizing understanding. This is, in a sense, the idea of a monolithic universality in which the varying components of human and nonhuman ethico-onto-epistemologies may diverge in certain respects while continuing to be subsumed within the whole on a higher order of complexity. In many ways, the Western intellectual project is simply the pursuit of this higher order of complexity, of which Pythagoreanism offered one influential conception—one requiring the silencing, flattening, and essentializing of other frames of thought in order to survive. The monochord exemplifies this, both as an instrument and as a metonymy for the broader philosophical strategy of totalization. As a craftsperson (and person) embedded within my own bounded space, I have sought to engage with the metalworking shop in order to explore the expressions of place-thought and material agency by which the chimeracord can (re)imagine the history and future of the monochord as a philosophical interlocutor in the Western world. Within this bounded metalworking space, I have sought to engage with the material voices that indicate other avenues of perception and, along the unfolding grain of its sensation, also conceptualization. By remaining in the metalworking shop and listening to the hammers and to the metals themselves as they are cast, annealed, and molded, I have sought to divest the story of the monochord from the trappings of creation mythology that have shrouded it since Pythagoras first extracted it from the forge. Instead, turning to the continual (re)instantiation of this bounded metalworking space as a creative ecosphere, the chimeracord immerses itself in the resounding articulation of the material agencies that cohere within that space.

As a person, craftsperson, and artist, I seek to join the other material bodies in the workshop space in facilitating the genres of place-thought that might emerge from these agential confluences. And as noted in previous passages, this work has almost nothing to do with any form of theoretical speculation or philosophical inquiry; it inheres instead in the continuous cultivation of response-able interactions. It coalesces around practices of listening and attending that welcome the agencies of obliquity, experimentation, and fugitivity that lurk within these materials and their mutual diffraction in the unfolding sympoietic construction of this workshop space. Although more or less impossible to convey in an excerpted cross-section of this densely entangled process, it is still possible to listen into these situations from the outside, to share moments of interactive discovery, where the chimeracord begins to voice acoustic inclinations that reverberate within its own resonant chamber while eddying and flowing outwards into the workshop spaces and bodies that it draws into its sonorous embrace.

In the recording that accompanies this chapter, the chimeracord has been raised on improvised brass stands, allowing the string's resonance to seep in and out its internal chamber on both ends, where microphones have been placed to capture the strange harmonic world of these border spaces neither inside nor outside the instrument. But these open ends of the chimeracord also embody a deeper organological aspiration, as well, weaving strands of attentive place-thought within the workshop through their eventual encounter with the outside world, as these instruments, like myself, are subsumed into a wider world of globalized nomadism—of workshops and ateliers that dissolve or resituate; of performance practices tethered to touring and residencies; and of lives and livelihoods that unavoidably uproot and transplant all of these human bodies, material fugitives, and their evolving, entangled composites. The instrument itself becomes a bounded space, both metabolizing the world around it—myself included—while maintaining its homeostatic integrity. Its acoustic resonance sketches both this corporeal integrity as well as its entanglement in its environment. The voice of this bounded instrumental body offers a sense of scale, of nested spaces bound in mutual embrace. It articulates how the precise boundedness of a space can embody both insulation and amplification, bridging various orders of place-thought that drift from the instrument's body through the workshop space and outwards into the environments and societies complicit in both material extraction and musical or cultural community.

But even within these interscalar networks of displacement and peregrination, the chimeracord retains a capacity to attend to the spaces and agencies that surround it. Through the open ends of its bells—that can collect as well as amplify sound—it invites the environments that it encounters into new forms of acoustic interaction. And in particular, when placed in its more typical hourglass configuration, the lower bell of the chimeracord places its open ear to the ground, absorbing the sounds of the building or the stage or the ground that it meets. It transmits its own vibrations into the soil even as it collects and amplifies the deep rumbling traces of that world bubbling back up into its body. Rooted in the ground beneath, the migrating chimeracord is a kind of delta, flowing out to meet the world even as it absorbs and assimilates the environments that, in turn, respond to these invitations.

The following chapters will embark from the foundations of place-thought established herein, but in acknowledging this work's irreconcilable relation to those traditions, it will follow the stories told by the metals within the chimeracord back to the lands from which they come and through the contemporary industrial and cultural realms in which they persist. The continuing experiments and dialogues undertaken alongside the chimeracord in the ensuing pages will seek to privilege the human agency that has, thus far, contextualized this discussion, and will instead probe the ontogenic becomings of this metal in order to attune to the conceptions of place, thought, and community that these metals' material agency render imaginable.

3. Extrusion

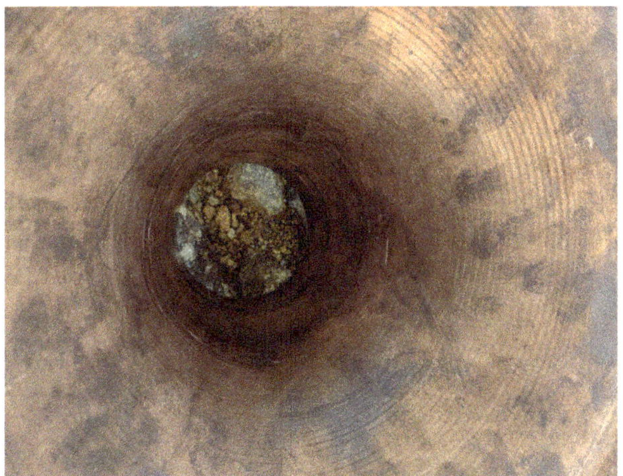

Fig. 12 Chimeracord bell with soil and stones at Balya copper mine. Photo by Işıl Toksöz (2024).

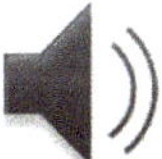 

Audio Recording 5 *Balya*. Recording by author (2024), http://hdl.handle.net/20.500.12434/b24b58d3

Video Recording 5 *Balya*. Recording by author (2024), http://hdl.handle.net/20.500.12434/c20be2d4

 https://doi.org/10.11647/OBP.0476.03

The chimeracord originally grew out of an attempt to return to the forge and the metal workshop while reimagining these sites through material capacities to react, resist, or even flee. From my own position as a metalworker, I sought to attend to rebellious brasses in precisely those states, facilitating their reorientation towards acoustic and organological imaginaries outside the rigid strictures of traditional craft or Pythagorean reduction. But this journey back towards the forge and its situated place-thought raised further questions about these materials' origins. The more time that I spent exploring alternative monochordal futures, the more driven I was to also attend to the histories behind these materials-in-flight. Metallic histories embody vast genres of motility. From the metallic core of the planet to meteorites crashing down from the heavens, metals congeal at every stratum and in every corner of our world. And whether buried in mountains, flowing through rivers, or burning in stars, they attest to an implacable inertia, an elemental momentum. Metals tear across the sky even as they slowly and inexorably extrude beneath the Earth's crust. Their stories help articulate the transformational capacity at the heart of any matter, each molecule dynamic within its own time and space, commingling in ceaseless collision.

But despite its elemental purity, precise definitions of metal are surprisingly elusive. On a quotidian level, metal tends to be defined by its luster and resilience. In scientific contexts, it is characterized rather by its ability to conduct electricity. But while conductivity may appear—superficially at least—more objective than shininess or hardness, upon closer scrutiny it is similarly inconsistent and imprecise. Many elements can take on metallic properties under certain conditions (for example, when subjected to variable states of pressure or extreme temperatures) and efforts to tighten this definition inevitably run into further ambiguity or outright subjectivity. But it does underline one fundamental trait of metal, namely, that its metallic nature derives not from a subjective assessment of its own properties, but from its relationship to other agencies or forces that it has the capacity to amplify. Although we often imagine metals to be quite hard materials, they are equally characterized by their plasticity under certain conditions; their luster is similarly remarkable in part because of its presence on a spectrum that includes dullness, tarnish, or even corrosion. Metals are distinguished by their ability to shift between these registers of physical properties, their metaphysical rigidity belied by a material plasticity. This metaphorical mutability is exemplified by their conductivity, through which metals act as medium, as facilitator, as bond, and as conduit. As inconclusive as a definition of metal may remain, it is inextricably linked to metals' relational entanglement with their environment—which is to say, metal is metallic only because these relations are possible and because metal facilitates their emergence.

Metal's interstitial relationality is typified by its geological emergence. In the previous chapter, I noted Vine Deloria Jr.'s assertion that "Stones had mobility but did not need to use it" (Deloria Jr. 1999: 34). But metals emerge when stones do use their motility, in their own space and time, and on scales far removed from our own perceptive capacity. Stones regularly traverse vast distances with the help of water, whether in the incremental drip of erosion, or in the currents of rivers, or absorbed into the inexorable momentum of glacial flow. But this transverse motility is far less potent than their gravitational motility, subsiding and sedimenting, absorbed beneath the amplified attraction of their accumulated mass in the Earth's core and crust, layer upon layer collapsing into each other in an ongoing, ceaseless geologic migration towards the Earth's core, itself an agglomeration of molten metals. These geological currents are not purely agglutinative, though, and the energy of their motility is not confined to simple compression. The various soils and stones that meet in this dance generate and share unfathomable energies, subjecting one another to chemical reactions and transformations as they slowly subside into a mutually cascading geological narrative. Metals not only form from and within these slow compressions, they also—and more commonly—merge and bond with other elements and other metals to form complex, but remarkably stable, molecular bonds. These mineral ores comprise elemental relationships between all manner of diverse metallic and non-metallic agencies, congealing across geological strata and suffusing the Earth's crust.

The stories that metals voice emerge from this relentless motility, a vast and volatile spectrum of murmuring energy. From the microscopic bubbling of chemical interactions to the brilliantly macroscopic inertia of geological compaction, metals embody an underlying current of mutability at the core of the Earth's illusory stasis. Just as metals themselves sketch the outlines of an energetic, electrical current coursing through the universe, metallic ores record ongoing histories of entanglement within the petrological coalescence of the Earth's very form. These ores run through the outer crust, narrating the diverse mineralogical interactions that characterize each evolving landscape that they stitch together. Metallic ores formed the seams of this planet long before humans walked on its surface, and for countless generations—indeed, for the overwhelming majority of human history—they remained invisible to human perception and curiosity. One wonders if they might have preferred to remain in that state, deeply embedded in their own stories of motility and interactivity, simultaneously illegible to human interpretation.

As it happens, though, their unique capacities gradually breached human consciousness, sparking the last several millennia of ever deeper interactions between metallic and human agencies. Indeed, metallic influence is so indelibly inscribed on human history that entire chapters of our cultural evolution are defined by it. Popular imagination (and no small number of textbooks) imagine humans' first encounters with metal as isolated flashes of illumination. As historian of metallurgy Paul Craddock notes: "Many histories of metallurgy commence with the scenario of the Paleolithic hunter picking up a gold nugget from a stream bed, attracted by its colour and sheen" (Craddock 1995: 93). But in contrast to this attractive fairy tale, the actual archaeological record suggests a surprising apathy in early humans towards the allure of gold and other shiny metals. On the contrary, "[i]f this eminently plausible event did take place then the interest must have waned pretty quickly, and the pebble discarded, for [such metal] has never been found on any Old World Paleolithic or even Mesolithic sites, even where decorative materials such as shells were in use as personal ornaments" (Craddock 1995: 93). A less common but similarly provocative myth attributes humanity's initial encounters with metal to meteorites. Rooted in an imaginative application of comparative linguistics to various Hittite, Egyptian, and Greek etymologies, this story suggests that iron meteorites falling from heaven first alerted humans to the presence of metal, sparking the knowledge that would eventually trigger the Chalcolithic, Bronze, and Iron Ages. Though its mythological (or even extraterrestrial) potency has allowed this story to survive a thorough debunking (see Bjorkmann 1973), it describes at most only a few isolated and rather unusual situations (such as the Innaanganeq meteorite and the Inuit people's knowledge and use of its iron) and almost certainly none from the linguistic regions supporting the hypothesis.

These narratives—each constructed in hindsight—ascribe metal's value to its reputation as a symbol of permanence, assuming that its luster and hardness reveal an inviolability that allows it to stand outside the fickle currents of human societies. But this reputation arose rather late within humanity's engagement with metals, and much to the contrary, early interactions with metal seem to have been driven not by its totemic power but rather by its quotidian utility. Metal's early interactions with humanity were dictated by its ability to effect change in its environment—by its capacity to write new stories into the dynamic unfolding of the world. As metal's overwhelming potency gradually inscribed these new stories ever more deeply into the fabric of human society, it became a symbol of irreversibility; but that air of permanence only coalesced incrementally, during broad epochal sweeps in which this potency came very slowly to bear—like a metallic ore extruding from the slow but implacable force of geological compression. Metal's stranglehold over human society (and its so-called progress) inhered in this incomparable range of utilitarian functionality, through which it became both a practical cultural symbol of change and transformation.

Although almost all metal in the landscape is woven into diverse mineralogical ores with other elements (most commonly oxygen and sulfur), occasionally the shifting geological and molecular tides will produce seams of pure elemental metals. Known as native metals, these mineralogical anomalies were the first metals to both attract and hold human attention. However, throughout the world, and in many disparate circumstances, the metal that elicited this interaction was not one of the so-called noble metals (which always occur as native metals, namely gold and the platinum group metals: ruthenium, rhodium, palladium, osmium, iridium, and platinum) nor even silver (which occurs occasionally but not always in its native form), but rather copper. Although copper forms primarily in ores, bound to other minerals, native copper nonetheless occurs on scales whole orders of magnitude greater than other native metals (Patterson 1971). And besides this relative abundance (in places), copper also proved unfathomably useful, providing a cutting edge for tools and weapons that would propel profound changes in human society.

A tool by itself is just another object, but through its application to other activities, it becomes something more; a tool amplifies both the energies of its wielder as well as the fruits of the work it addresses. An object becomes a tool through its mediation of the world, through its capacity to transform other objects. The act of chipping away a sliver of copper to form a point or a blade does not in and of itself produce anything of great value to human culture—which is to say, it does not generate short-term benefits like providing food, lighting fires, building shelter, etc. But once crafted, a copper-pointed chisel or a copper-bladed knife transforms the efficacy of many of those same activities. By radically altering the ease or efficiency of these tasks, copper's value within human society lay not in its physical properties as copper per se, but in the capacity for those physical properties to generate unparalleled utilitarian potential. In this way, metal transformed human society not through its luster or its (semi-)permanence, but through its mediative capacity. Once discovered and harnessed by human societies, copper leveraged its fundamental metallic agencies of entanglement, amplifying myriad forms of motility and transformation in human productivity and social development.

Copper's prolific utility derived not only from its sharpness or hardness, though. For among the many human societies who encountered native copper and developed means of chipping it away to form useful points, blades, and other simple forms, almost all of them would also soon discover its ductility. Like many metals, copper also inhabits a spectrum from malleability to resilience and it responds most notably to heat as a means to navigate between these extremes. When paired together, these two properties dramatically enhance copper's utility. Once humans were able to harness both copper's heat-induced malleability as well as its strength and incisiveness thereafter, its transformational effects on society exploded. If annealed (heated red-hot and then cooled), copper's molecular structure coalesces into larger, more symmetrical grains that render it appreciably more plastic. As it is then molded into new forms, these grains fracture into smaller, more asymmetrical clusters and the copper becomes once again harder and more resilient. The discovery of this specific property of copper would have an exponentially more profound effect on human history than any native metal alone could ever have done, demonstrating once more metal's unique agency as a facilitator of motility and transformation across widely varied scales of time and space.

In nearly every situation in which humans unlocked the transformative potential of annealing, they also discovered casting, smelting, and alloying in quick succession. Because while copper becomes drastically more ductile after annealing, additional heat will melt it entirely, allowing it to be cast into new—and potentially also entirely bespoke—forms. This led to two important changes in humanity's relationship to copper. First, casting allowed them to produce new objects designed specifically to purpose. This power would radically transform the effectiveness and inventiveness of metal tools, revolutionizing their everyday utility and availability. But the second effect of casting—despite a more limited effect on the everyday experience of copper tools—would alter the course of human societies even more dramatically. In addition to allowing far more invention in the design of copper tools, casting also invested small chips or less pure fragments of copper with sudden new value. Before casting, copper tools could only be made by finding (or breaking off) pieces of native copper both small enough to be portable and big enough to be useful, before chipping or hammering them into shape. However, with the development of casting, a far wider range of size or shape of native copper could be used. And crucially, as these smaller or more impure pieces were melted and cast, one could not help but discover two other crucial facets of metallurgy: that copper could be produced from melting less pure mineral deposits (i.e. mineral ores), and, even more amazingly, that in doing so, other forms of copper could sometimes be produced that were even stronger than pure copper. In the former case, humans discovered that native copper was not the only source of copper, and in due course would also discover that, in fact, native copper represented only a fraction of the copper available. And in the latter case, they discovered that other metallic minerals existed alongside copper in these ores and, moreover, that they could be alloyed crudely (or sometimes even entirely accidentally) by smelting.

These discoveries sparked humanity's deep obsession with both metallurgy and mining. Having discovered the relationship between heat and metal, the mineralogical landscape would gradually become more legible and thereby also exploitable. Suddenly the exotic power of native copper paled in comparison to the exponentially more vast reserves of less pure copper ore that could now be extracted and exploited at greater scale. Even with relatively primitive mining strategies—and while limited to mostly surface-level or -adjacent veins of ore—the stone itself provided far more useful material than isolated patches of native metal did.[1] And wherever humans discovered these new techniques, they began expanding their metallurgical agency, setting slow-burning fires along mineral-rich stone walls to soften the metallic deposits before hammering and chiseling away chunks of ore for smelting and casting. As they left behind their dependence on the native metals that were so much more easily identifiable than the mineral ores they now sought, the landscape itself would teach them how to read the metallic stories that had been inscribed in the terrain over countless eons.

Although initially ores would have been identified mainly through their proximity to native copper, other relationships within the environment would slowly become legible to human observation. Even where metallic ores were not directly visible (for example, from the green oxidation of exposed copper ores), various species of metal-tolerant plants that clustered and thrived in their terrain

1 Much has been written about the relative absence or late development of metallurgy in North and South America, which is generally attributed to the much greater abundance of native metals (most notably in the copper-rich Great Lakes region), which as a consequence generated a diminished necessity for experimentation with manipulation, annealing, etc.

would reveal their presence. Certain plants become well-known for their use in prospection, such as *Elsholtzia splendens* in China, *Sabulina verna* (sandwort) in Europe and parts of Asia and northern Africa, or *Polycarpaea spirostylis* in Australia. As would later happen with many other metals, minerals, and ores, copper's intensely intimate entanglement with its environment would eventually expose it to human scrutiny. After millennia spent intertwined with copper, the ecosystems into which it was braided would ultimately reveal its presence to human observation. And as human societies reoriented towards these new dimensions of exploration, these same ecosystems were subsequently exposed and subjected to increasingly intrusive extraction.

Even as other metals were discovered and tamed, copper continued to be one of the most important metals in human society. Although popular in part due to its prevalence, copper's unique physical properties were what truly made it so valuable. Highly ductile in its pure form, once other alloys were discovered, it became even more prized. The first alloy to be mastered by early metallurgists was bronze, in which copper is alloyed with tin. Bronze is even more resilient than copper and yet also more workable under certain conditions. By improving on copper's utility for tool-making and other practical purposes, bronze quickly drove further developments in mining and refining in the cultures that mastered its production. Brass soon followed, although as the next chapter will examine in more detail, the unique challenges that its alloy with zinc posed would remain problematic or even insuperable for many generations following the successful mastery of copper and bronze production. Nevertheless, copper in its various guises and alloys continued to provide the backbone for many of the critical components of society's rapid urbanization, reflected in a growing dependence on metal for tools, medicines, coinage, infrastructure, and all manner of other applications.

In describing this period of urban growth, philosopher Manuel DeLanda notes that "urban morphogenesis has depended, from its ancient beginnings in the Fertile Crescent, on intensification of the consumption of nonhuman energy," (DeLanda 2000: 28), such that "[c]ities appear as parasitic entities" (DeLanda 2000: 20). In order to sustain their growth and metabolism, they must become "veritable transformers of matter and energy: to sustain [their] expansion [...,] they extract from their surroundings sand, gravel, stone, and brick, as well as the fuel needed to convert these into buildings" (DeLanda 2000: 76). As European colonialism metastasized across all other continents, ever larger swathes of land succumbed to this "gradual conversion of the world into a supply region to fuel European urban growth" (DeLanda 2000: 106). This massive project of energy conversion swallowed up everything from material resources to the flesh and blood required to metabolize that material into usable fuel for expansion. The relationship between these two modes of extraction is both complementary and reverberatory. As more material became accessible (not only through the brute force of colonization but also through the evolution of better tools for identification and extraction), more biological power was required to accumulate and domesticate that material, and, consequently, even more biomass was required to sustain that manual labor as it continued to lubricate the ongoing, motoric reiteration of extraction.

These various chambers of material and biological fuel reverberate within each other's influence, amplifying both the power and the utility of their productive force while simultaneously stoking the appetites that require their continual expansion. In focusing on the stories of metal, we can note here that this is the stage in history where metal's value as symbolic power was finally minted, for currencies themselves arose in relation to urbanization. Because urban power relied on efficiency and fluid exchange in order to satisfy its material and biological hungers, metal coinage became essential as a means to lubricate this economic machine. And as some scholars have noted, the development of systematic currencies in these stages of urban development are also closely linked—if not directly caused by—the use of taxation to both subdue the surrounding reservoir of material, agricultural, and biological fuel as well as to fund the military forces that would enforce the stability of that arrangement. Although in one sense this marks the moment in which metals' resilience and luster (as opposed to its utility) take on valence, it also reveals how those qualities served primarily to codify and amplify human and material power relations. After the role that copper mines and copper-alloy tools played in revolutionizing human society and enabling early urbanization, those same alloys would go on to reify the state authority that both demanded and sustained their extraction.

But it would not be the divine right of kings or the accumulation of precious metals that ultimately powered the exponential expansion of mining and extraction worldwide, but rather the rapacious demands of modern capitalism. Because despite the technological innovations that propelled extractive mining—which was dependent on innovations in prospection, mine ventilation, transport, refining, etc.—the actual dents made in the landscape were surprisingly small compared to the massive footprints seen today. Even in the first few centuries of industrialization, up until the nineteenth century, the "environmental impact of [...] industrial developments [was] small by comparison with contemporary industry," even when accounting for the cascading effects of "toxic wastes discharged into streams or built up into unvegetated piles[, the expansion of] roads, canals and railways[, w]ater-courses already altered to provide power for the new machines [that] were further diverted, and [the] settlements [that] grew up to house the burgeoning workforces, replacing fields and other open ground" (Simmons 1989: 217). Several concurrent innovations began to accelerate the rate of expansion of both cities and their exploitation of surrounding resources, though, beginning with the introduction of new smelting furnaces. The long history of smelting charts a laborious, painstakingly gradual calibration of furnace technology to increase temperatures and reduce oxidation and loss of material through vaporization. These twin challenges saw a number of ingenious innovations in disparate cultures over several millennia, but the evolution of the reverberatory furnace in particular had a massive impact on the growth of urbanization and capitalist extraction. Although the technology of reverberatory furnaces had already existed for centuries, having been first used for casting bells in medieval Europe, their usefulness in smelting materials like lead, copper, and pig iron triggered an acceleration in their engineering in the eighteenth and nineteenth centuries, most notably the development of dramatically larger furnaces capable of processing and refining exponentially more metal than ever before:

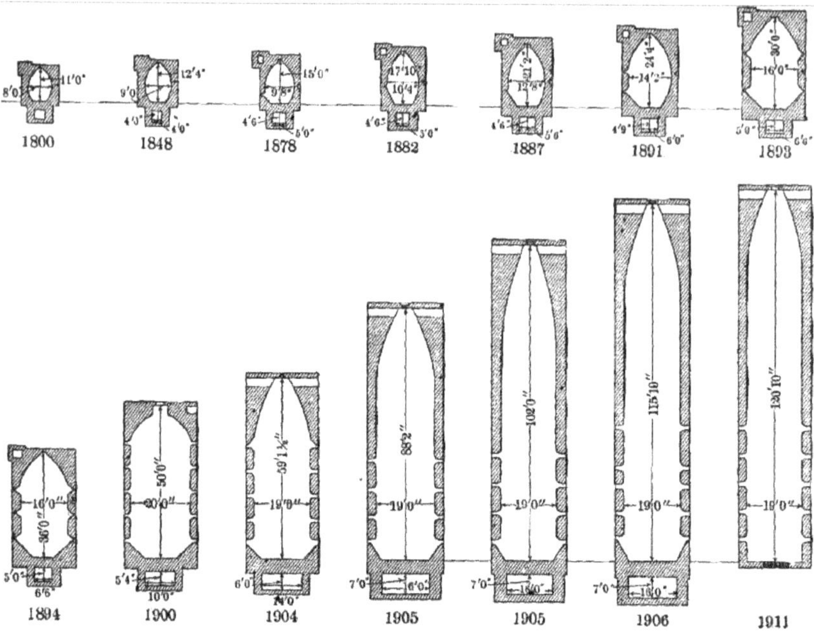

Fig. 13 Reverberatory furnace evolution. From Peters 1895: 444, public domain.

As can be seen in the evolution of reverberatory furnaces in this image, these expanded refining capacities were well underway by the end of the nineteenth century, but their development exploded even further when allied to an expansion in demand, for the copper that was processed in these furnaces was suddenly a key component in the explosion of electrical innovation. At the end of the nineteenth century, key developments in establishing larger and more efficient power grids sparked a massive expansion in the application of electricity throughout society and industry:

> Although the use of electricity as an energy source owed its origins to urban economies of agglomeration and the information they generate, once those meshworks had been internalized and routinized, electricity's future belonged to economies of scale. [...] The new intensification took place along several fronts. Size, temperature, and pressure were all intensified to generate economies of scale in the *production* process. Voltage, too, was greatly intensified, and positive feedback was created in the *transmission* process as well. Yet, as far as electricity's effect on society, the intensification that mattered most was that of *consumption*, which followed naturally from electricity's multitude of potential uses. (DeLanda 2000: 90-91)

Although similar expansions in the extraction and industrialization of other resources helped fuel this appetite (e.g. steel, oil, and plastics), the specific affordances of electrical infrastructure generated an outsized impact on urbanization in the ensuing decades precisely because electricity powered the explosions of scale in these industries as well as their accessibility and practical application in urban infrastructure and everyday life. As DeLanda notes, the skyscraper—that symbol *par excellence* of the contemporary cityscape—could never have existed without the electrical intervention of the elevator; and even the steel and glass that enabled these innovations were increasingly dependent on electrical infrastructure for their production (2000: 92). As evidenced in the evolution of smelting technology both before and after this electrical renaissance, the impact of electricity was not an isolated development but rather a node within a network of industrial innovations and expansions that amplified each other. Nonetheless, the specific role of electrical infrastructure (and of the outrageous amounts of conductive copper wire it required) can hardly be overstated.

The demand for the raw materials that fueled these interlocking industrial and urban expansions triggered an unprecedented expansion of mining. Open pit mining for resources like copper exploded and the already devastating impact of mining quickly reached levels previously unimaginable. The words 'open pit' are both horrifyingly apt and woefully inadequate to describe the scales of extraction that they perpetrate. Open pit mining describes a process in which mineral-rich land is incrementally dug up and broken down, digging a literal pit into the earth, creating city-sized holes stretching down hundreds of meters (over a kilometer, even, in the deepest open pit mine to date, Bingham Canyon) and often well below the water table. These mines have an extremely characteristic visual appearance, because the scale of their operation requires such heavy machinery that the edges of the pit are striated by the rings of shelves carved into its walls that render its entire surface area accessible to the vehicles that transport material, machines, and the labor power that maintains its operation. Like a perverse inversion of the organic histories recorded in tree rings, the stratified edges of these open pit mines document the incremental, decades-long extraction of entire landscapes. As they leave gaping holes festering in the surrounding land, these mines also expose and spread toxic chemicals and minerals that poison aquifers and ecosystems for generations if not indefinitely. Ironically, these toxic byproducts have generated yet another market for the industrial and electrical infrastructures they fueled: in order to prevent rising water levels in abandoned open pit mines from reaching the water table and poisoning the watersheds that surround them, these mines must be continually pumped—theoretically in perpetuity—thereby generating yet another unending demand for the very infrastructure whose appetite continues to carve out these pits. In many cases, the abandoned pits that require this attention are in close proximity to newer pits that are still expanding.

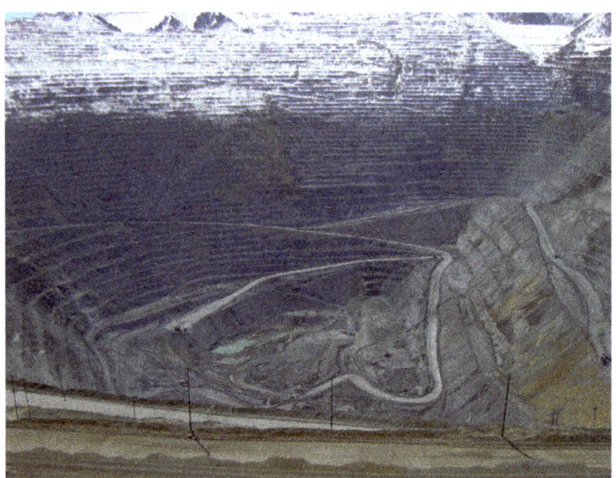

Fig. 14 Bingham Canyon. Note the depth of the pit, as well as the toxic pool collected at the bottom. Photo by Tim Jarrett (2005), Wikimedia Commons, CC BY-SA 3.0, https://commons.wikimedia.org/wiki/File:Bingham_Canyon_April_2005.jpg#/media/File:Bingham_Canyon_April_2005.jpg

In the process of building and researching the chimeracords in this book, I wanted to visit these mines, to experience for myself their perverse distortions of landscape and ecosystem. Although I originally intended to find the source of the brass in the chimeracords themselves, that ultimately proved impossible. Although these materials came from factories and workshops I knew, even with that information, their sources proved impossible to track down. The capitalist industries that consume these metals are perpetually seeking increased deregulation and cheap supply chains, and the brasses with which I was working were discarded by a company that sourced cheap and impure brass without proper documentation or certification. Unfortunately, their particular histories of mining and smelting remained frustratingly inaccessible, even after tracing their journey through various links in their supply chain. However, despite that disappointment, and with these materials' riposte to the Pythagorean tradition in mind, I turned instead to the sources of the metals that would have inhabited the forge that Pythagoras visited, which in the case of copper, could be found in mines dotting the low mountains ranging along the Aegean coast of Anatolia. Not only is this mineral-rich region directly adjacent to Pythagoras's birthplace on the island of Samos, but the first brasses produced here (the earliest brasses in the West, developed roughly one millennium after similar brasses were routinely smelted in Zawar, Rajasthan) were developed contemporaneously with Pythagoras's descent to the forge. In all likelihood, the metals that Pythagoras heard resounding beneath the mythical hammer blows he immortalized had been mined, smelted, and cast in these hills.

The first recorded instance of brass in this region comes from Balya (Craddock 1998), a small village about fifty kilometers inland from the Aegean Sea in the foothills of Balıkesir.[2] The rich veins of mineral ore in these foothills have been mined for thousands of years, and nowadays, a village still sits in the same spot, nestled between an active open pit mine and the older, inactive shafts that were first mined millennia ago. This village itself articulates a history of countless generations of mining, bearing traces from disparate eras and technologies of extraction, all of which are currently dwarfed by the growing pit that continues to strip and displace entire surrounding mountainsides.

When you approach Balya today, you encounter this mine long before you reach the village itself. Within these mineral-rich mountains, which have been feeding forges and workshops for centuries and centuries, contemporary mines can emerge unexpectedly around bends, appearing as great scars rent in the landscape, disrupting the rolling hills that surround them.

2 I was rather surprised to find this in my research as Balıkesir is also my father-in-law's birthplace. This surprising coincidence only further fuelled my desire to visit this particular mine at the root of Western copper production.

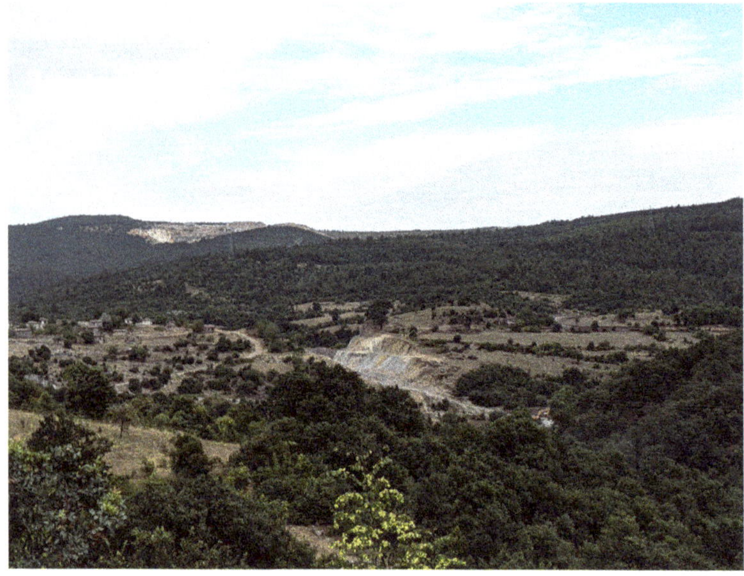

Fig. 15 Balya copper mine at a distance. Photo by author (2024).

These scars soon open up into the mines themselves, which can stretch for kilometers.

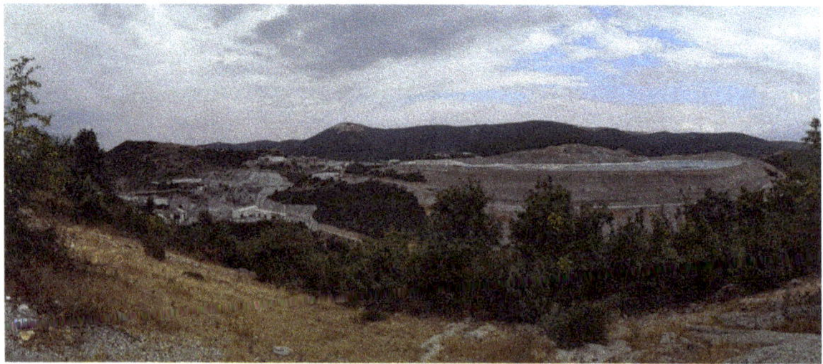

Fig. 16 Panorama of Balya copper mine. Photo by author (2024).

Today, these mines are still accompanied by the unique vegetation that first signaled their presence to ancient prospectors millennia ago. These ecosystems thrive around the mineral-rich soils, their prosperity paradoxically alerting invading industries to the veins of copper that saturate the earth beneath.

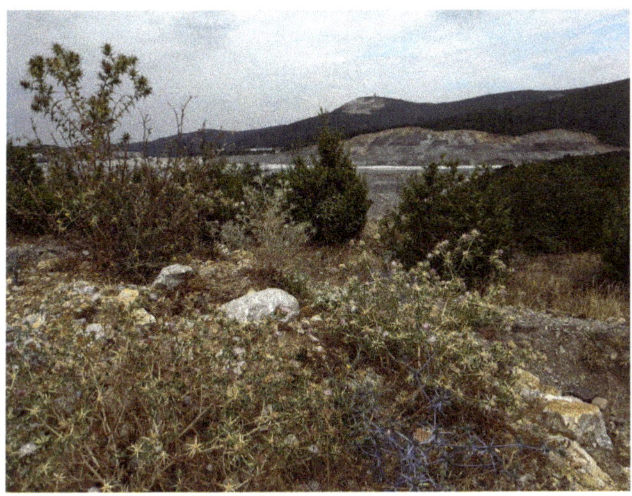

Fig. 17 Vegetation at Balya copper mine. Photo by author (2024).

Eventually one comes to the village itself, Balya, surviving both in spite of and because of the surrounding mines. This history is still palpably present, as traces of mines from many ages can still be found within the village and throughout the surrounding hills. Ranging from decommissioned, sealed pits to crumbling infrastructures, these remnants of bygone mining enterprises abut the active mines, whose bustling activities echo within their ruins.

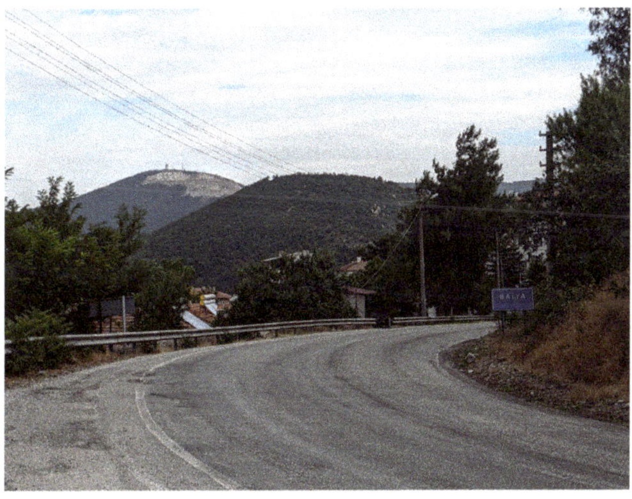

Fig. 18 Approaching Balya with Balya copper mine in the distance. Photo by author (2024).

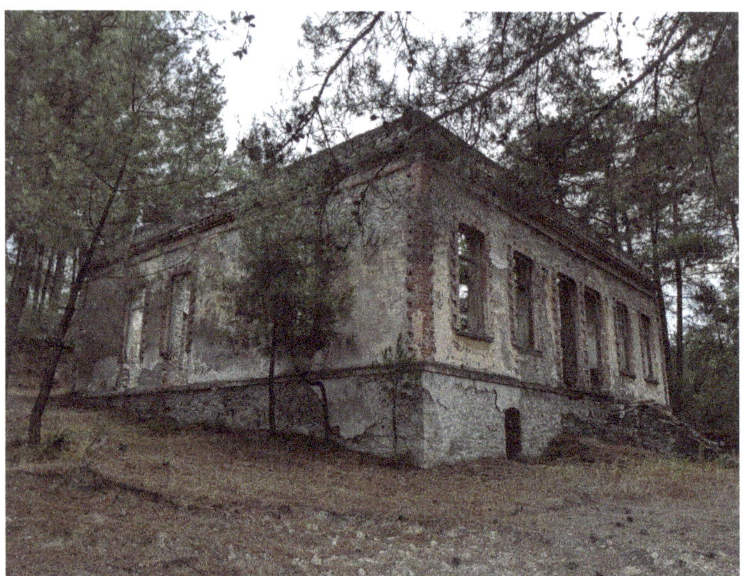

Fig. 19 Ruins of old mining infrastructure at Balya copper mine. Photo by author (2024).

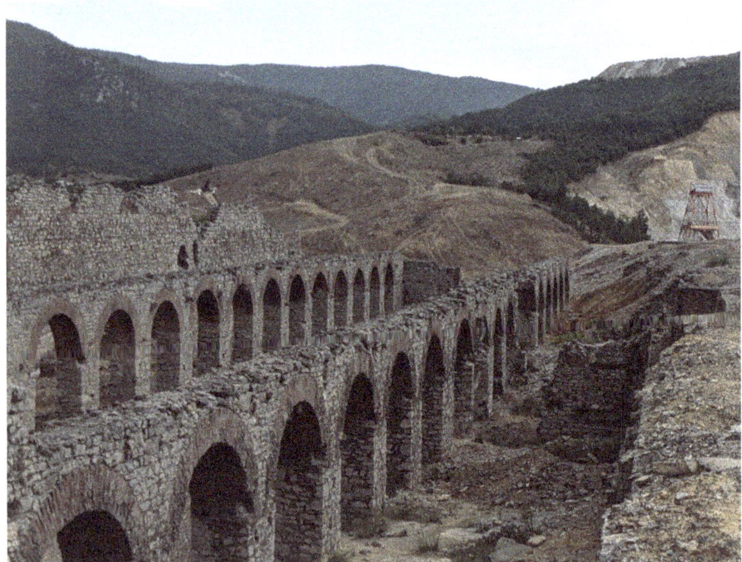

Fig. 20 Ruins of old mining infrastructure at Balya copper mine with active mine in the distance. Photo by author (2024).

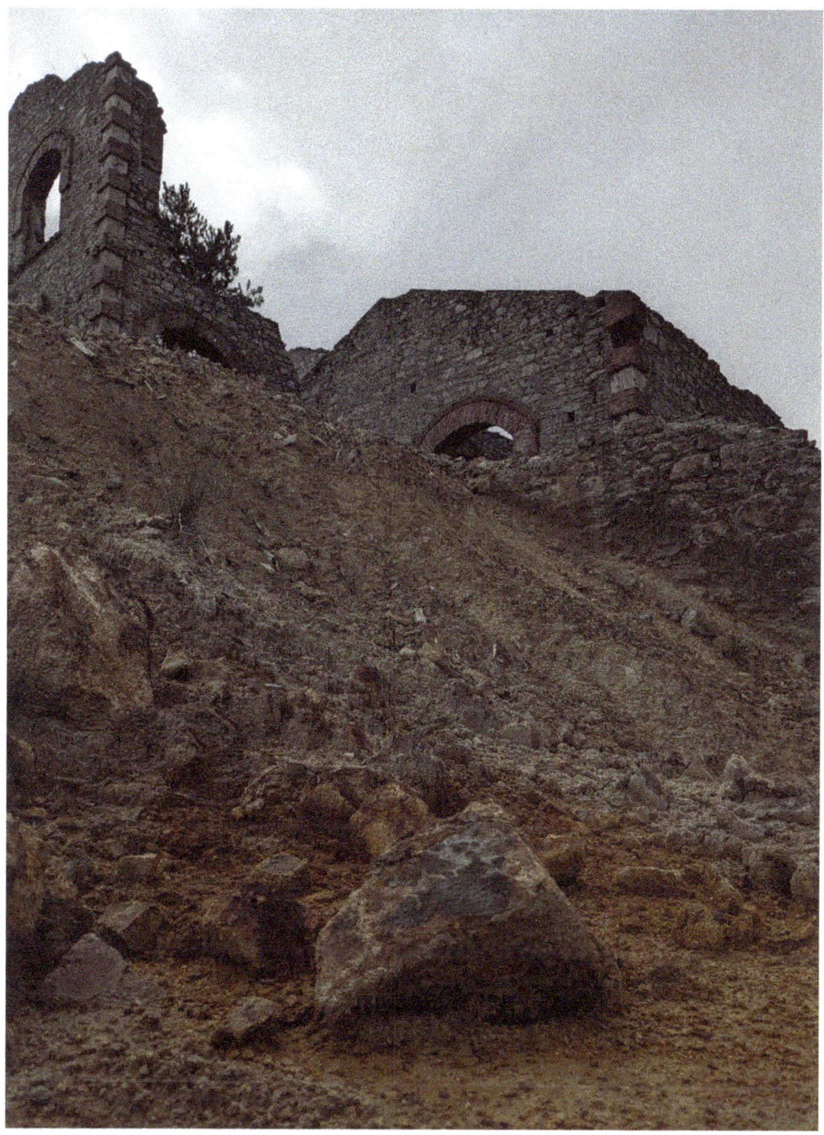

Fig. 21 Ruins of old mining infrastructure at Balya copper mine with copper-rich soil in foreground. Photo by author (2024).

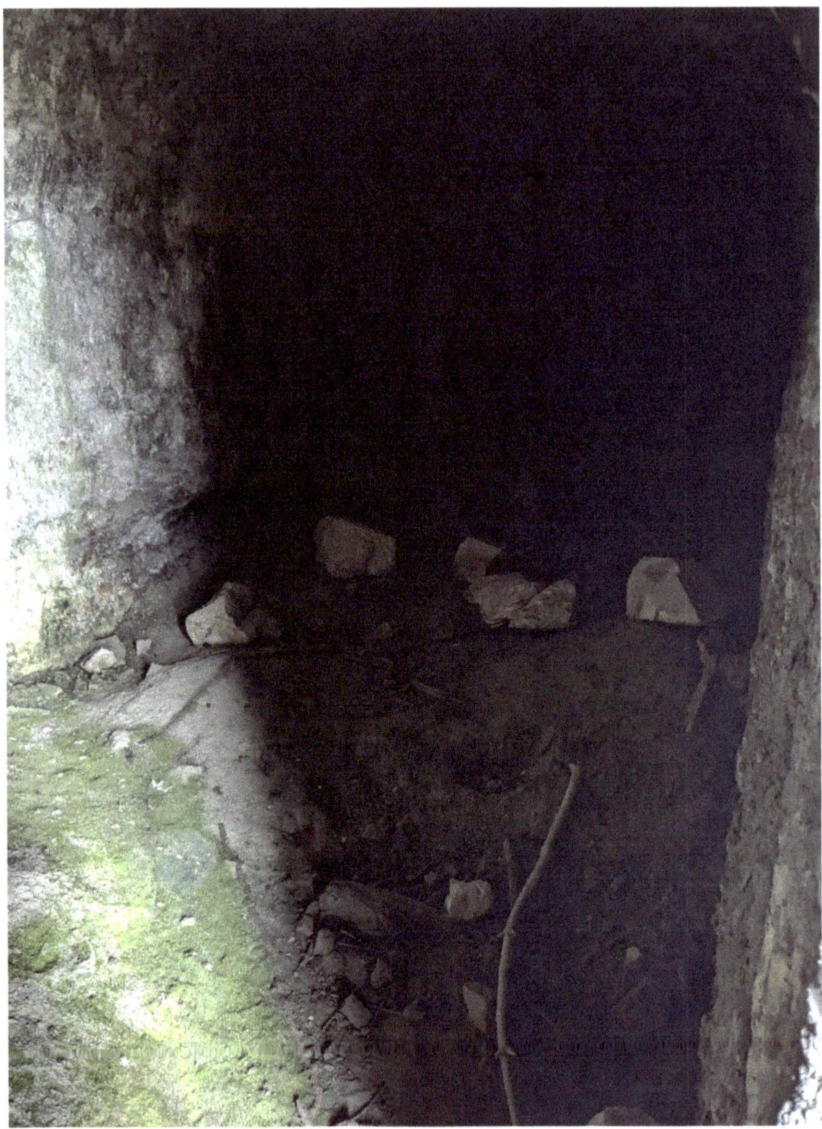

Fig. 22 Ruins of old mining infrastructure at Balya copper mine. Photo by author (2024).

Even as they wither and erode, these abandoned shafts and structures attest to this landscape's unbroken genealogy of extraction and exploitation. From the smelted copper of Pythagoras's forge to the unfathomably intricate webs of copper wire connecting every corner of the globe today, Balya reveals a deep and unrelenting addiction to these resources and their industrial affordances. But copper is not the only metal mined in these hills. In fact, this mountain range has supplied a vast range of metals and minerals over the intervening centuries, its resource abundance supporting countless cultures and governments. Just as the chimeracord seeks to bridge the workshop and the mine, mapping seams of agency that bind them together, the copper mines in Balya reach beneath the surface of the soil to other seams that stitch these histories into wider tapestries of extraction. Copper has always been an amplifier, increasing the potency and utility of countless other materials, especially—as previously noted—since the advent of electricity and its vast copper infrastructure. And because of this amplifying effect, copper mining has always been mirrored and amplified by the extraction and production of other key resources, as well, just as in the landscape surrounding Balya.

In fact, despite the astronomical amounts of copper required in order to service the maintenance and expansion of electrical infrastructures, copper is not even among the resources most devoured by early industrialization or contemporary urbanization. As architectural historian Mark Jarzombek remarks, these undertakings are and have always been "addicted to four basic products: steel, concrete, glass, and plastic," which together constitute what he calls "the Quadrivium Industrial Complex" (2019: n.p.). These materials have accompanied and amplified each others' impacts on modern life, enabling radical transformations and expansions of urbanization and the capitalist infrastructures that support and thrive alongside it. Just as the rapid growth of electrical infrastructure was dependent on the availability of copper, the materials of the quadrivium provided the scaffolding for the infrastructures supporting modern capitalism. As Jarzombek asserts, without the quadrivium's mutually reinforcing influence, "[n] ation states as we know them would be different. Steel alone lies at the political foundation of Europe and the United States. Thank god for the great Quadrivium! Skyscrapers in the desert? No problem" (2019: n.p.). But the accumulation of these materials entails a vast and overwhelming appropriation of countless landscapes, resources, and labor pools:

> Steel comes, of course, from ore and an array of toxic chemicals, extracted from mines in dozens of places around the globe. Concrete, glass, and

> rubber are no less complex in their constitution and fabrication, each compressing within its materiality a vast array of chemicals. Should we map even a single building backward, against the grain of its production—back to its molecular origins—we would find a dizzying global operation. (Jarzombek 2019: n.p.)

In analyzing the complex webs of control and appropriation that animate urbanization, DeLanda notes that "living creatures and their inorganic counterparts share a crucial dependence on intense flows of energy and materials" (2000: 104). While this interdependence coalesces into ecosystems when undisturbed, those same flows of energy can be hijacked and repurposed by the "parasitic relationship" through which cities transform other lands into "resource depots" (DeLanda 2000: 106). In part because "the circulation is what matters, not the particular forms that it causes to emerge" (DeLanda 2000: 104), cities are able to circumvent and redirect these relationships to serve their own parasitic interests. DeLanda devotes much attention to the way in which colonialist exploitation controls organic and, by extension, genetic materials, "appear[ing ...] not only as a means to redirect food toward the motherland, but also as the means by which the genes of many nonhuman species have invaded and conquered alien ecosystems" (DeLanda 2000: 20). Extractive colonial and capitalist policies dictate the reproduction or extinction of genetic material in every corner of the globe, from the plants that are cultivated for food or eliminated to make space for agriculture; to the control of local and Indigenous populations through aggression, introduction of disease, and labor; to the proliferation of weeds and microorganisms that invade the spaces left behind by the extinctions perpetrated at other scales. By controlling the flow of biomass necessary to secure their survival and continued expansion, cities also create the conditions by which the rest of the ecosystems and landscapes that surround those resources live or die, not just in isolation but across generations, centuries, and millennia.

The capitalist appetite thrives on simplifying the world it encounters: diverse Indigenous populations are decimated or assimilated; diverse ecosystems are razed to make way for monocrop cultivation; and diverse mineral landscapes are literally melted and vaporized to generate a reservoir of the few most desirable resources. Although it has now infected every corner of the globe and destroyed countless peoples and ecosystems, this genocidal mechanism is encapsulated particularly dramatically in the extractive machinery that erases landscapes—quite literally uprooting mountains and transforming them into the building blocks of urban sprawl. The land that is erased in these operations had formed the skeletons of the ecosystems they housed, as well as of the place-thought that those entangled webs of organic and inorganic agencies collaboratively enacted. This land embodied not just the mineral deposits packed beneath its surface, but also the watersheds and soils and all of the vast ecological polyphonies that intertwine within the bounded spaces they collaboratively bore. In order to siphon out the vast quantities of raw materials necessary to satisfy the contemporary thirst for copper, steel, glass, concrete, and petroleum products, this land must be not merely raided but literally disappeared. Melted and refined, these materials are transplanted into concrete cityscapes, leaving behind a vast, hollow emptiness comprising the erasure of entire bounded spaces and the ecosystems that inhered in their millennia-spanning coalescence, survival, and thriving.

What remains after this operation are the simplified realities capitalism thrives on: subdued labor pools, genetically uniform monocrops, and refined materials. In the case of these materials, such as the four components of the quadrivium, the industrial innovations that exploded in the nineteenth century have refined their production to such an extreme that it is now cheaper and more efficient to extract and refine new materials than it is to recycle or reuse what has already been produced. Not only do the quadrivium comprise the vast majority of material flowing into modern urban expansion, they are replacing discarded remnants of their own material:

> Tons of the great Quadrivium wind up in landfills. Building material accounts for half of the solid waste generated every year worldwide and the volume is expected to increase to 2.2 billion tons every year by 2025—more buildings [built] means more buildings to throw away. (Jarzombek 2019: n.p.).

Having now spanned several generations of urban inhabitation and gravitation, this proliferation of such a small subset of materials has infected whole cultural imaginations and interpretations of the world. Jarzombek diagnoses this in the way that these highly processed materials come to be identified as "raw" or "natural" in some way, as though steel grows on trees or glass flows in rivers. Citing the famous quote by architect Louis Kahn in which he asks, "What do you want [to be], brick?" (Kahn 2003; cited Jarzombek 2019: n.p.), Jarzombek underlines the way in which these materials have become so essentialized as to have lost all trace of the vast network of agencies that flowed into their creation—landscapes, minerals, organic and inorganic ecosystems, labor power, and even the capitalist infrastructures that generate and transplant them. In addressing the brick as such, Kahn betrays the complete erasure of the landscapes that bore its material and the hands that crafted it. In essentializing the brick, Kahn's address parodies the attentive relations of Indigenous peoples who originally cohabited with the clay and other materials extracted in the manufacture of that brick and its brethren.

In an attempt to recuperate some attentiveness to the agencies of the materials subsumed into these bricks and other building materials, Jarzombek reformulates Kahn's question to reflect the problematic complexity of these materials' generation, suggesting that the "question should have been 'What does a brick have to say?' [Or p]erhaps more relevant to today's architecture: 'What does a steel beam have to say?'" (2019: n.p.). Kahn's initial question—asking what a brick wants to be—remains aphoristically rhetorical, leaving no real space for the brick to respond, but rather disingenuously laundering the architect's fantasy into the essentialized ventriloquy of their brick puppet. In contrast, Jarzombek's reformulation of the question—asking what a steel beam might actually have to *say*—is stubbornly and insistently non-rhetorical, as evidenced by Jarzombek's brief speculation about a steel beam's hypothetical response:

> Would it tell us of the mines that sent contamination down into the streams below? Would it tell us of the lung cancer that the miners contracted breathing in cadmium fumes? Would it tell us of the corruption that was needed to quicken its unloading at the dock? Would it tell us of welders who sweated over their beads? Would it tell us the jokes of workers who sat on its beam a thousand feet in the air? Would it tell us the magic of the great chemical bonds that define its molecular existence? Would it tell us the governing logic of its alloy? Would it tell us of the great heat of the forges, or the cool spray of the presses? Would it tell us of its fear of water and fire? (Jarzombek 2019: n.p.)

Jarzombek insistently reminds us of "the speech-carrying capacity of materials," but these materials' voices are not, as he describes, "denie[d by ...] architectures of silence" (2019: n.p.). On the contrary, not only are they not silenced, they are in many ways amplified, for their material bodies constitute almost all of the acoustic media of contemporary urban soundscapes and the acoustic ecologies pulsing through the continuously evolving metabolisms of urbanization, industrialization, and extraction. Those of us who live within the bubbles of modern cities or the vast infrastructures that support them hear little else *but* the voices of these materials. The quadrivium's concrete, glass, steel, and plastics—and their accompanying hum of electrical transformers and copper wires—animate the acoustic soundscapes that dominate contemporary cities. They amplify or drown out every other voice in those spaces, simultaneously reinforcing the infrastructures of discursive control that saturate these urban spaces. They might once have had voices within the landscapes they were formed in, but those landscapes have been replaced by potent absence. Even the very echoes of the voices that once populated those spaces have been extracted, resounding and reverberating in the transplanted materials that now form the halls and walls of the cities whose existences document their extinction. The key issue with the extraction of these voices is not their silencing, though, but their censorship. Their voices persist, but only within the strict constraints within which they've been placed. Like Kahn's brick, their voices have been cast into the molds dictated by the colonialist regimes that appropriate them, reduced to simulating the articulations of the forces that puppeteer them.

Within the buildings and streets of our cities, we are listening to the displaced acoustic agency of entire landscapes—and, by extension and association, of the ecosystems and place-thoughts that they once housed. Acknowledging this relationship between the soundscape of the city and the distant landscapes it has subsumed complicates the problematic dichotomy of natural and urban soundscapes that has long troubled the fields of acoustic ecology and sound studies. This dichotomy reflects a common notion that "authentic nature appears only where humans do not" (Malm 2018: 4), and many conventional approaches to acoustic ecology consider "[m]arkers of healthy soundscapes [to] include the density and diversity of 'biophonic' and 'geophonic' sounds, which respectively refer to sounds produced by biological organisms and geological processes; the ability to hear distant sounds; and what [R. Murray] Schafer famously characterized as a 'hi-fi' soundscape" (Ouzonian 2017: 8). Many critics of this legacy, though, have noted, as geographer and sound artist AM Kanngieser does here, that a troubling "logic of purity [...] emerges from this complex antinomy of occupation and absence: who and what is considered the right kind of nature" (Kanngieser 2023: 695), which is in turn situated within an "enduring sonic inheritance [and] assumption consolidated over centuries that the white ear that listens is benign and objective;" this "dangerous and under-acknowledged construct [...] defines sonic colonialities, in which structural whiteness masquerades as 'lack of bias'" (Kanngieser 2023: 693). The more recent ontological turn in discourses of speculative realism, new materialism, and object-oriented ontology have influenced reactions within the fields of acoustic ecology and sound studies, as a new generation of theorists have attempted to rectify these troubled essentializations of nature and sound by "posit[ing] an internally coherent essence to sound in part to renounce anthropocentrism and attain a universal listening position" (Kanngieser 2023: 693). But in many instances these approaches have merely repositioned the presumption to 'lack of bias' in alternative but no less essentialized perspectives. As researcher and philosopher Marie Thompson has remarked, these developments in sound art and sound studies constitute a "white aurality" (2017: 1) that "names a racialized perceptual schema that is at once situated and 'modest' insofar as its own, active presence is obscured" (2017: 11). As Thompson writes:

> white aurality can be understood as not just relying upon but actively producing a series of bifurcations in its 'hearing-with': it amplifies the materiality of 'sound itself' while muffling its sociality; amplifies Eurological sound art and, in the process, muffles other sonic practices; amplifies dualisms of nature/culture, matter/meaning, real/representation[,] sound art/music and muffles boundary work; all the while invizibilizing its own constitutive presence in hearing the ontological conditions of sound-itself. (Thompson 2017: 7)

Far from being confined to theoretical or philosophical speculation, both of these conflicting approaches to sound have been consistently and extensively reproduced in sound itself. Since the inception of recording technology, the concept of field recording has influenced disciplines as wide-ranging as music, anthropology, urban studies, and even mining prospection (Banerjee et al. 2013). But from its first applications in anthropology, field recording has always gravitated towards "ambivalent relations to history" (Sterne 2003: 27). Housed within this emerging domain of anthropology, early field recording constructed fictional tableaux conflating the sublime and the wild with their cultural analogues: the primitive and the savage. But while this narrative proved highly influential, it masked the colonial relations that carved these imaginary states of nature out of the intertwined cultures and landscapes captured in early field recordings. As sound artist, researcher, and writer Mark Peter Wright describes:

> The field is built upon asymmetrical encounters underscored by the hegemony of Western anthropology. It is not natural or neutral as a consequence. It is not simply an outdoor location removed from borders or issues of power and agency. It is not necessarily a green or rural space. The field is very much entwined with the city, cage, and camp. Media devices such as the wax cylinder and gramophone allowed for the claim of objective measurement in the field, a means to assert scientific truth while establishing divisions of nature and culture, observer and subject. Field recordings were therefore intrinsic to the colonizer's toolkit. (Wright 2022: 16)

This toolkit encompasses far more than just the documentation or cataloguing of extracted sound. As with Kahn's brick and Jarzombek's steel beam, the voices captured in early field recordings were absorbed into, refined by, and preserved within the larger narrative infrastructure of colonial systems that molded them to specific purposes. As Wright notes, duplicity and secrecy were a necessary and powerful tool of early anthropologists, who often sought to hide from subjects that they were being recorded, and who thereby also robbed those subjects of any opportunity to exercise curatorial discretion over how or what they shared, and for what purposes. Often still preserved and studied in institutions directly continuous with their colonial extraction, these voices and stories remain shrouded in a "specter of appropriation" (Wright 2022: 17) that both obscures their own history while holding a mirror up to the history of the cultures and institutions that house them, demonstrating how "[s]onic media was part of the same colonial project that produced the physical exploitation of materials, places, and people" (Wright 2022: 13). And as with those other forms of exploitation, these sonic media were reproduced to serve very specific ideological purposes:

> Phonography's much-touted power to capture the voices of the dead was thus metonymically connected to the drive to dehistoricize and preserve cultures that the U.S. government had actively sought to destroy only a generation earlier. Permanence in sound recording was much more than a mechanical fact; it was a thoroughly cultural and political program. To a great degree, inventing reproducibility was about reconstructing sound and hearing and developing technologies to fit and promote these new constructs. (Sterne 2003: 27)

As Kanngieser notes, "[i]t is only through dehistoricisation that a wilderness recording can invoke the sublime without revealing the violence of its conquest," and in many ways "the foundational function of anthropological phonography was to preserve what had been destroyed without the context of history" (2023: 695). As such, the practice of field recording helps demarcate "the delineation of what a natural sound is—including selected sounds of Black, Indigenous, and First Nations cultures—and the claim to authenticity this serves" (Kanngieser 2023: 695). Kanngieser calls this process a "fabrication [of] environments" (2023: 695), reflecting the applied methods by which the material documentation practices of field recordings (re)iteratively construct these fictions. While many of these practical strategies have now sedimented into accepted—or even expected—practice, they are never accidental and require continuous reapplication and recalibration.

As human geographer Michael Gallagher underlines, "[f]ield recording [...] includes practices of listening, reviewing and editing recordings, composition and mixing, playback and audition[, which processes are] are arguably more geographically salient than the process of recording itself, since a single recording, if presented in different ways, can produce different spaces" (2015: 10). These refining techniques filter the spaces they record from the instant that their state of observation commences up to and beyond the contexts that surround their editing, documentation, publication, or presentation. The spaces of field recording are constituted less by the "field" per se than by "the material and technological spaces of microphones, loudspeaker arrays and headphones, or the architectural spaces of editing studios, art galleries and public installations" (Gallagher 2015: 29). And even as these painstakingly refined (re)presentations characterize practices of field recording from the academy to the gallery, in many disparate disciplines and discourses, the technological practices that produce them are elided, hidden behind the twin illusions of artistic purity or scientific objectivity. Historian, theorist, and sound artist Gascia Ouzounian outlines how these techniques function as rhetorical agencies:

> In acoustic ecology, field recordings (recordings of soundscape) are almost inevitably treated as evidentiary documents, as containers of acoustic 'facts': accurate or near-accurate representations of an acoustic environment at a given moment in time. The presence of the sound recordist is thereby typically diminished or effectively erased in these recordings [...] The use of spectrograms, 'soundtopes,' and other computational tools for quantifying, measuring, visualizing, and analyzing data pertaining to soundscape recordings has further helped to establish a scientific basis for acoustic ecology. Conversely, soundscape artists are typically understood as producing sonic 'fictions' by creatively altering, processing, editing, mixing, and re-situating environmental sounds in the form of compositions, performances, installations, and myriad artistic interventions. (Ouzounian 2017: 11-12)

All of this labor—comprising everything from "[t]he labour of the field recordist [to t]he labour that produced the equipment used [to t]he labour of distribution and infrastructure" (Gallagher 2015: 38-39)—aligns to produce carefully curated constructions of nature. "Most, if not all, nature sound recordings foster the illusion of healthy ecosystems; many times even the location being recorded is severely degraded, and only a combination of boundless patience in the field, careful editing out of human noise, or overdubbing of field recordings can recreate the primal fullness" (Cummings in Kanngieser 2023: 696). In part because of the deliberation inherent in the practical post-production this requires, these careful manipulations and curations "are always ideological-spatial formations" (Kanngieser 2023: 696):

> It is not only in the recording but also in the editing and post production of these recordings that such aesthetics come to bear. The application of audio filters and noise reduction to eliminate 'unwanted' voices and sounds further demonstrates the deliberate evaluation of who and what belongs in an audible natural environment. (Kanngieser 2023: 696)

The various social, technological, and institutional agencies that superpose in the creation and curation of field recording form an infrastructure that filters and edits reality much as a mixing board adjusts the specific equalization of a sound recording. Within these networks of technocultural manipulation, the physical audio documentation of "[f]ield recordings produce small spaces nested inside these larger networks, small vibrations riding on the back of longer, slower, waves," and as such "emerge not as neutral aesthetic objects, but as participants in the production of a global space of consumer electronics, international travel, digital media infrastructure, arts institutions, and engineering and design companies" (Gallagher 2015: 41). As composer, sound engineer, and historian of music technology Tara Rodgers reminds us, "Histories of sound and audio technologies are inextricably entwined with histories of the body" (2011: 516). In this case, it is the body of the land itself that is slowly unraveled and woven into new patterns and tropes by the technological intervention of recording technologies and infrastructures of dissemination. These practices are inextricable from and coextensive with colonialist conceptions of ownership and territory, as well as with the implicit right to extraction that those notions assume. "This aesthetic approach to making nature is important to situate within a wider framing of how land became differentially designated through colonial European practices as property, an extractible resource, a site of conservation, an inhospitable wilderness to be mastered, and a place of respite" (Kanngieser 2023: 694). Echoing the language of mastery, audio post-production reiteratively constructs an "environment [...] codified and represented through the European imagination in the service of scientific rationalism and the accrual of capital," contributing to the ongoing "categorisation and ordering of nature [...] underpinned by a calculus of expropriation and nation-building" (Kanngieser 2023: 695).

This relation between audio production and colonialist extractivism lends new valence to composer and sound artist R. Murray Schafer's famous formulation of rural and urban soundscapes as respectively "hi-fi" and "lo-fi" (Schafer 1977/1994: 43). For Schafer, these terms map straightforwardly onto a spectrum of "signal-to-noise ratio" (1977/1994: 272). He describes their differences by suggesting that a "hi-fi system is one possessing a favorable signal-to-noise ratio. The hi-fi soundscape is one in which discrete sounds can be heard clearly because of the low ambient noise level [...] In a lo-fi soundscape individual acoustic signals are obscured in an overdense population of sounds," and goes on to assert that "[t]he country is generally more hi-fi than the city; night more than day; ancient times more than modem" (1977/1994: 43). Schafer does acknowledge that this terminology of hi- and lo-fi derives from electroacoustics (1993: 272), but obscures the fact that these definitions of high and low relate specifically to the concept of fidelity, which is to say, to representation rather than to the one-to-one experience of real-time immersion. Originally referring to the ability to "reproduc[e] the full dynamic range, frequency range, and timbral nuances of live music" (Ouzounian 2021: 159), the concept of high fidelity is highly oxymoronic. On the one hand, it connotes a representation of a previous reality with a high degree of faithfulness, but at the same time, it often presumes a high level of technological mediation in order to achieve that result, such that its inverse—low fidelity—implies more raw, unmediated, or unedited playback (cf. Hartley 1958).

Somewhat ironically, the intertwined extractive and refining disciplines of recording and mining construct an altogether different picture of the hi- or lo-fi qualities of the urban soundscape than Schafer imagined. For while Schafer parses urban soundscapes as low fidelity due to their (perceived) disorienting saturation, they in fact embody a very literal post production hi-fi refinement. This is to say, the contemporary urban soundscape is in fact a carefully honed high fidelity remastering of the displaced voices extracted from the bowels of open pit mines, reformulated into the glittering skyscrapers and concrete barracks of the modern city. Although this distinction is on some level simply word play, it also highlights the extractive violence inherent in the urban soundscape, for, as will be examined in more detail in the following chapter, these material voices are quite literally refined and normalized, controlled distillations of the chaotic diversity of the landscapes from which they were torn, ground, cast, and repurposed. While the comparatively gentle production methods of field recording use electroacoustic manipulation to facilitate their particular modalities of extraction, the industrial machinations that transmute exurban landscapes into highly-refined capitalist metropoles only differ from the mixing studio in scale, not in kind. The saturation and flattened perspective that Schafer diagnosed in the urban soundscape (1977/1994:

43) in fact enacts a high fidelity remix of the territories consumed by colonialist regimes of expropriation.

Although often attributed to Schafer, the term soundscape was in fact previously introduced by urban designer Michael Frank Southworth's thesis on urban planning, *The Sonic Environment of Cities* (1967). In returning the term to its roots in urbanization, it is worth reconsidering Southworth's attentiveness to "how the sounds of the built environment enhanced people's perception of space and their relationship to the activities occurring within cities" (Pijanowski et al. 2011: 204). In confronting the confusingly paradoxical referentiality of the "fidelity" in hi-fi sound, Southworth's focus on the soundscape as a form of information mediation can recalibrate the term towards notions of relation. This in turn suggests an alternative conception of what forms of high fidelity sound might be perceived by attuning to the material voices of the extracted media that constitute the quadrivial urban soundscape. Rather than a high fidelity refinement that distills these media into highly interchangeable and replaceable components of a modern, modular cityscape, we might imagine a recalibration of our attention towards these materials that instead rejects the rhetorical ventriloquy that sublimates these materials into formless anonymity and follows instead the grain of the materials themselves.

Just as high fidelity audio editing situates itself in reference to the purity of a perceived objective reality (whether that be in "nature" or in "live" music), industrial production of the quadrivial urban soundscape also imitates the refinements that occur independently through the geological emergence of the landscapes they raze. We can recall here that the electrical infrastructure that has powered these various incarnations of colonialist domination can be traced back well before humans walked the earth, all the way to the sulphidic copper minerals in basaltic rock that interacted with water and iron to slowly coalesce into the pure native copper that first attracted human attention. The histories of metallurgy and mining began with the painstaking reproduction of the landscape's own refinement, a chemical process that continues today, including in the ruined remnants of human extraction. In fact, even in old mining pits, as those same sulphidic copper ores continue to be slowly eroded and carried by water across the broken iron tools left behind by long abandoned mining operations, native copper continues to extrude independently of any human intervention (a process known as precipitation). And as the copper and other quadrivial materials degrade and evolve over time, they enact their own extrusions and transformations.

The accelerated industrial production of a resource like copper is an imitation of how native metals emerge over centuries of delicate—one might even say deliberate—negotiation across elemental, molecular, and geological scales. Just as an audio engineer might approximate the sound (or imagined ideal) of a live performance in post-production, a metallurgical engineer shapes mineral ore into nearly native metals, navigating their own stages of mechanical and chemical post-production. But just as with an edited recording, the manufactured fidelity of the finished product obscures the scales and types of material or sound that precede this process. An edited wilderness recording always contains the germs of that wilderness—perhaps lacking the desired biodiversity or interrupted by the sounds of nearby civilization. The concrete, glass, and steel in urban soundscapes resound not only with the sounds of traffic and business and modern life, but also with the traces of sand and stone that reveal their origins. Native metals contain the subsiding traces of many different scales of pressure, entanglement, and transformation. Quadrivial metals contain, similarly, their own varied scales of transmutation, as the pressure of production distorts not only the material but the tools and hands that manipulate it, as well.

Within the bounded space of their native landscapes, these metallic ores enact an inverted but analogous process of post-production, refining not the soundscape around them but the bodies that experience it. Just as we attune to the refinement of displaced material soundscapes in the city, miners must attune to the volatile soundscapes of the landscapes they dismember and pillage for capital. These mines, in fact, require even greater senses of attunement, for in that bounded space below the earth, signs of danger will almost always be audible first. In the mines, these material voices offer a thin life-line to workers, alerting them to imminent catastrophe. These signals are so important that, despite the echoing shrieks of hammers on stone that reverberate and deafen, the short-term risks of not hearing far outweigh the long-term risks of hearing loss. A miner will always face this exchange: with each hammerblow, they accept the inevitable, progressive deafness that these material agonies inflict, even as those material acoustics help protect them from the imminent dangers of flooding or collapsed tunnels. As anthropologist Rosalind Morris describes in her poignant essay on "The Miner's Ear:"

> The miner's ear is attuned to the sounds of catastrophe: sirens, rumbling, explosions, a gush of water where only a dripping should have been heard, coughing, the burble of fluid in the lungs ... or too much silence. The miner's ear is attuned to what will destroy him, what is already destroying him in the moment that he hears, if he hears. The miner seeks signs. [...] But the miner is endlessly confronted by symptoms that arrive belatedly, when the rock is already falling, or the lungs are already scarred and filling with blood. (Morris 2008: 96)

Paradoxically, the only way to prevent this loss of hearing is to mimic it. Any effort to "protect hearing not only simulates but actually produces in a temporary fashion the very deafness that the measure is intended to avoid, thus depriving miners of the sensitivity that they require in order to stay alive. [...] And most refuse to wear them" (Morris 2008: 105). The mines reshape hearing as simultaneous forms of attunement and desensitization, a seamless interplay between the power to extract and the inability to survive that extraction's cost. It renders painfully palpable both the necessity and the danger of listening, underlining the binding compacts made when we wrest these materials and their voices from the landscapes they inhabit.

Morris also reminds us of the role that gossip and hearsay played in early mining prospection. She notes how rumors multiply and spread, echoing across tongues and minds, mapping the landscapes that will swallow up thousands and millions of bodies as they are themselves displaced and recast in industrial afterlives. She traces a lineage from the greedy eavesdropping of capitalist prospectors to the corporeal effacement of miners worked senseless into early graves. In urging us to show "attention to the significance of *overhearing*" (Morris 2008: 97) in all of these various guises, Morris follows her own speculative path through the illusorily audible terrain of language:

> In the innocent ear, homonymy masquerades as etymology, as the aural (what can be heard) is falsely linked to the auriferous (the gold bearing). In one, the root—obscured by time—of an ear: *aurilis* (Latin). In the other, the root of (evil?) gold: *aurum* (also Latin). [...] To understand

> the history and nature of [mining] one must listen for both different and false or "accidental" resonances, the mere coincidence of frequencies that amplify each other. (Morris 2008: 98-99)

The chimeracord follows its own path down these spiralling paths of audibility and deafness, language and inexpressibility. As the miner's ears are reshaped and dissolved through their fidelity to industry and urbanism, the chimeracord also forms an ear, a chamber not only for amplifying, but also for collecting, for storing, for remembering, and for retelling. The chimeracord is a reformulation of brass wrecked and discarded, a metallic body vibrating in sympathy with other genres of vulnerability that echo throughout its extractive ontogeny. Its hourglass shape provides more than just visual symmetry; it also pairs the sound-projecting cone at the top with an open cone at the bottom. Its sound chamber is exposed as it touches the ground: absorbing, listening, transmitting. As an organological design, the chimeracord stems from the workshop, itself a bounded space replete with echoes of industry and exploitation akin to the mines. In fact, machinists and factory workers report similar sonic relationships to miners, navigating harmful levels of noise that they are equally dependent on and vulnerable to (Bijsterveld 2008). I have written at length elsewhere on the braided concomitance of expertise and pain that typify acoustic attunement and hearing loss in the workshop setting, documenting the breakdown of bodies as they work with, alongside, and against these sounds (Toksöz Fairbairn 2022). As both practical instrument and artistic intervention, the chimeracord inhabits this space, listening while sounding, attending while distorting, recalling while continuously resynthesizing.

The chimeracord seeks to follow these threads of receding audibility through the enmeshed networks of bounded spaces that inhere in its metallic history. By placing its ear to the ground, the chimeracord evokes not only the workshop and the factory, but also the refinery, the hold, and the mine. By taking the chimeracord to Balya—where ancient mines continue to resound with the echoes of the active mines they touch above- and belowground—I hoped to suture these various workshop and mining spaces together through the chimeracord's listening body, to bind them together just as a worker's genre of attunement is bound to their own expiry.

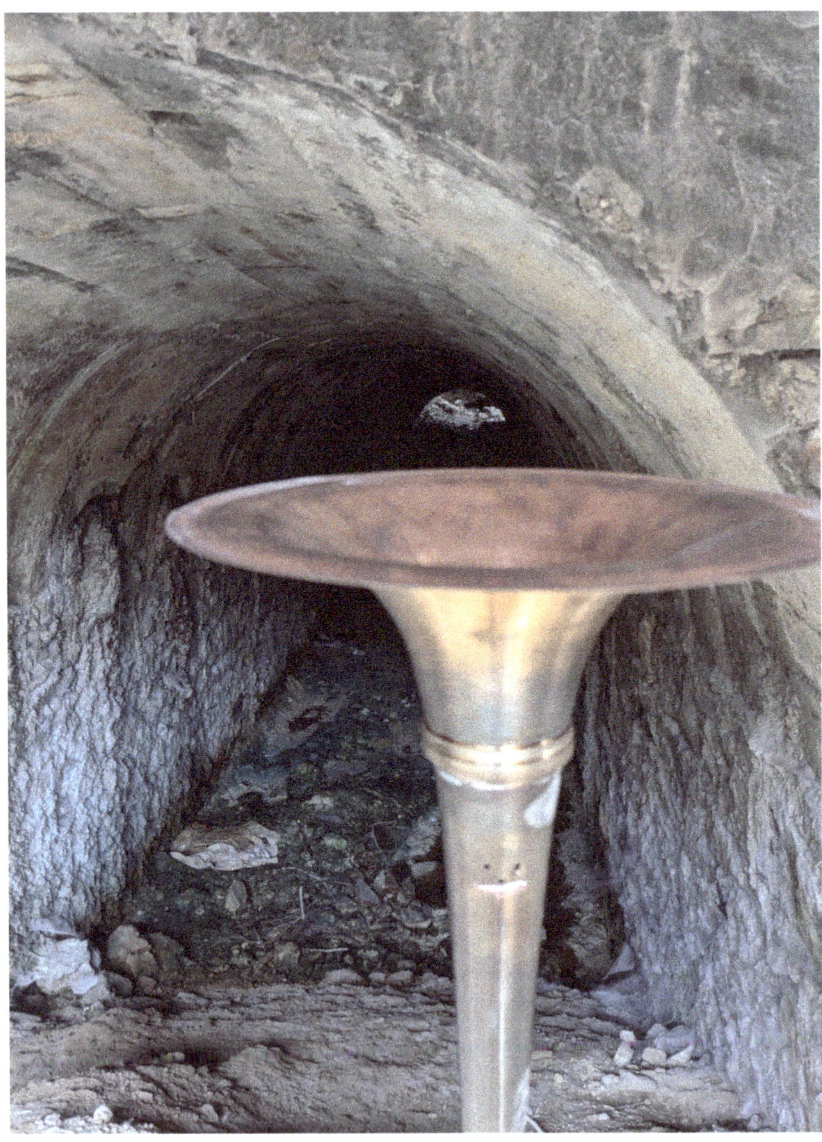

Fig. 23 Chimeracord in an abandoned tunnel at Balya copper mine. Photo by author (2024).

Having emerged from the situated confluences and place-thoughts of the workshop, here in Balya, the chimeracord sat rooted in the history of its own extraction, mutilation, and disciplining. With its open bell settled firmly in this mineral-rich soil, it could listen to, absorb, and—in some ephemeral insubstantiality—amplify these histories. With its metallic seams exposed to the elements, though, it certainly also left behind some small traces of its own metallic dissolution and fugitivity. With the chimeracord placed down on this simultaneously familiar and foreign earth, it could also share its own peripatetic acoustic imaginary with the glacial subsidence of the dusty metallic ores within the soil around it, where its chimerical stories could reverberate alongside the muffled and muffling echoes that resound in response.

These materials—both inside this instrument and in the soil it sits in—write stories that could, in fact, answer the rhetorically bad-faith question about what they want to be. They show that metals and mineral ores do have voices, as do the hills that house them. In the ensuing chapters, I will continue to approach these materials, inquiring as to how other spaces might be constructed by the material agencies that escape the grasping refinement of industrial (post-)production. I will examine the ongoing extrusions that these materials enact, seeking to calibrate artistic and research methodologies to the frequencies cultivated by these continuously generative material agencies. In acknowledging the momentum already set in motion by the pipeline of quadrivial urbanization, these efforts turn not towards an essentialized acoustic agency in nature, but rather towards the alternative spaces voiced within the peripheral, irrecuperable strata that persist in between the hi-fi bandwidths of capitalist refinement.

4. Purity

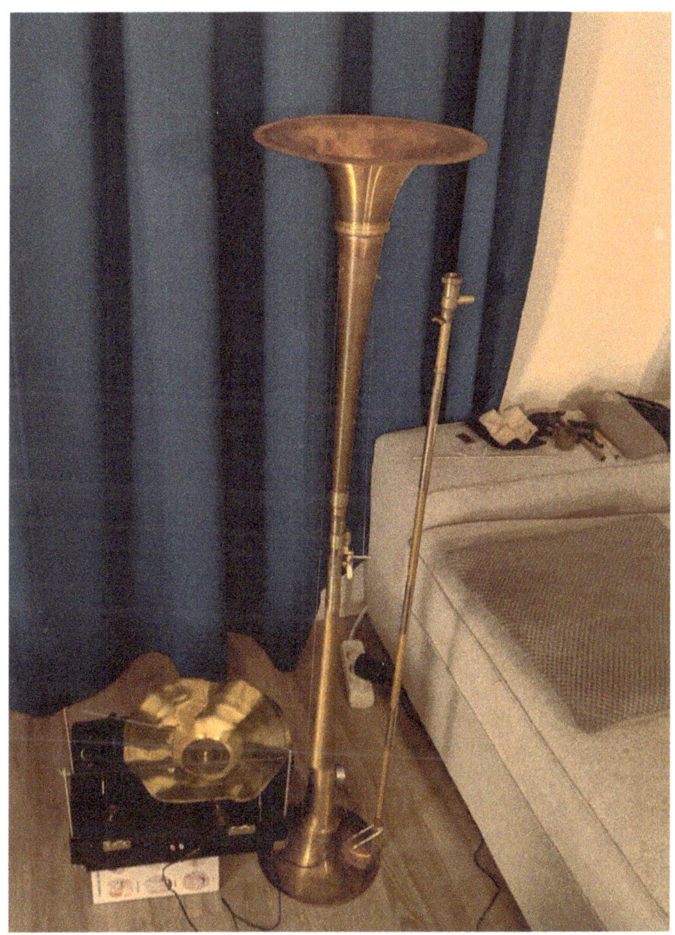

Fig. 24 Chimeracord housecall, Basel. Photo by author (2024).

 https://doi.org/10.11647/OBP.0476.04

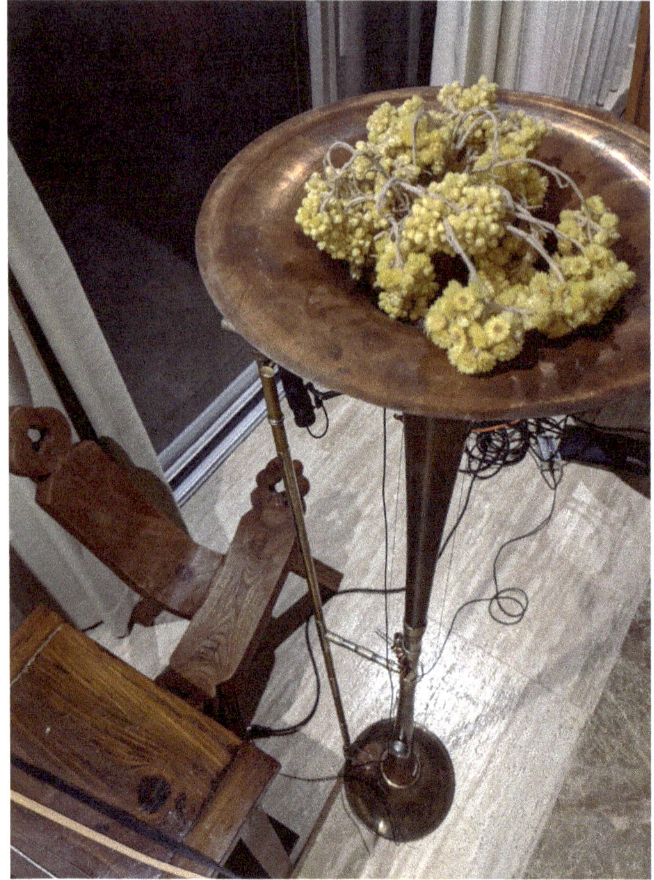

Fig. 25 Chimeracord housecall, Gümüşlük. Photo by author (2024).

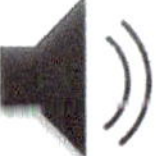 

Audio Recording 6 *Housecall*. Recording by author (2024), http://hdl.handle.net/20.500.12434/9bcca233

Video Recording 6 *Housecall*. Recording by author (2024), http://hdl.handle.net/20.500.12434/7d64ab3a

Balya lies in the northern fringes of the foothills stretching along the Aegean coast. These mineral-rich mountains range all along the coast of Anatolia, from the northern regions around Balya down to the convergence of the Aegean and Mediterranean seas, and then through the Taurus Mountains along the Southern coast of Anatolia. These mountain ranges retain the pulsating energy of geological histories still very actively unfolding. Formed within a continually active region of tectonic activity, they bear their past up to the surface with dramatic efficiency. Beyond just the rich deposits of minerals they contain, they also hold natural gas vents, which burst forth where the earth's crust can no longer contain the percolating vigor of the boiling elements within. In Yanartaş, on the western tip of the Taurus Mountains south of Balya, these eternally burning gas vents birthed the legend of the chimera, their fiery breath inspiring myths of exotic, hybrid monsters.

Visible from sea, the shimmering volcanic energy in Yanartaş sparked fire-breathing fever dreams "in those heated days over the arid land of Lycia, where was bred the dire Chimaera" (Ovid 1922: n.p.). Just like the vents from which its legend wafted, the kaleidoscopic chimera has proven capable of embodying divinity and terror in equal measure: a "creature of fire, and a being, sometimes called a monster, sometimes a goddess" (Stadler 2024: 9). Although her precise composition and configuration vary dramatically from source to source, the chimera is typically described as part lion, part serpent, and part goat. These interwoven heads, tails, and torsos have evolved over the centuries into a representation not of any specific grafting of bodies, but rather for the totemic concept of fusion itself, both corporeal and conceptual. Long after Ovid's telling, Virgil's Aeneas encounters the chimera in his journey to the underworld, and yet by this point—foreshadowing the chimera's slow evolution from physical monster to theoretical phantasm—she is insubstantial and hallucinatory, still "armed with flame," but nonetheless a "tenuous bodiless [life] flitting about with a hollow semblance of form" (Virgil 1922, n.p.). In this moment, the chimera slowly evolves from the fixed form of a beast into the embodiment of endlessly impermanent identity, "having become but a trace of herself, not necessarily withdrawn into [...] imagination (yet), but in a state of transformation" (Stadler 2024: 9).

In a sense, the chimera is also a resource extracted from these hills, a thin conceptual vapor of burning hybridity, sucked out of the landscape's steaming scars and diffused throughout the world. The chimera coalesces as a spectral complement to the minerals and metals that have been carved out of the land around her, an oneiric articulation of the monstrous horrors that these hills record, echoing the voices buried beneath the chasms opened up by centuries of excavation and extraction. The chimera's hybrid body weaves together the tattered, insubstantial fragments of histories foreclosed, resurrecting them in vivid, hallucinatory new forms. The chimera is not the monster that devours but rather the embrace that sutures, that braids together the bodies and histories of a mutilated landscape into startling new collective imaginaries.

But while the chimera herself is not the monster that lurks in these fecund hills, a monster still lies in wait beneath these devouring hills. Just south of Balya, along the route towards Yanartaş, one passes a recently planted tract of forest, 301 trees announced by an unassuming commemorative plaque. These saplings mark the outskirts of another mining town, one with more contemporary infamy: Soma, the site of one of the deadliest mining disasters in living memory. In 2014, poorly controlled blasting started a fire in a coal mine shaft that trapped hundreds of miners for days, eventually claiming 301 lives—a figure still heavily disputed. But sadly, the Soma disaster is hardly an exception; it is merely the most recent punctuation in a long history of death and disaster in these hills. Thousands of years earlier, when brass was first smelted nearby, these mines were already renowned for their hellish conditions:

> The mine used to be worked by publicans, who used as miners the slaves sold in the market because of their crimes; for, in addition to the painfulness of the work, they say that the air in the mines is both deadly and hard to endure on account of the grievous odor of the ore, so that the workmen are doomed to a quick death. (Strabo 1961: 451)

Nor were these stories limited to the foothills of Anatolia. Humans have been suffocating in underground shafts for as long as they have been digging them. Although studies of early mining rely largely on collections of broken or discarded tools and experimental modern recreations, one of the most accurate and valuable sources about early copper mining is a young Chilean man whose collection of tools and baskets survived intact after he died in a caved-in tunnel 1500 years ago. Found collapsed on the ground hundreds of years later, his body had been preserved by the copper salts whose extraction claimed his life, his green-tinged skin a ghastly reminder of the appetite for resources that consumed him. Copper Man—as he has come to be known—lay entombed in Chuquicamata, Chile, where the same mountains into which he descended remain home today to the largest volume open pit copper mine in the world. A festering wound in the landscape, this mine joins his mummified body as a reminder of the intimate relationship between mining and the cycles of exploitation, abandonment, and death that it engenders. Perhaps unsurprisingly, this young man's copper-infused body was extracted like any other nugget of metallic ore, repeatedly bought and sold until today, when his body lies in the collection of the American Museum of Natural History—despite calls to return him to his native land. But while his body remains trapped behind glass in a sterile, foreign archive, Chilean artist Nicolás Grum has preserved his story in his installation *The Huanca Rebellion* (2022), which finds a cast copy of Copper Man lying in a shattered recreation of the American Museum of Natural History's display case, frozen in a moment of attempted flight. Grum's evocation of Copper Man's fugitive momentum connects timeless histories of accumulated corporeal exploitation to the chimerical stories that those bodies weave in their persistent resistance—even centuries beyond the grave.

In the words of a Bolivian tin miner (just north in the mountain ranges stretching from Chile and Chuquicamata up and along the coast of South America), "We eat the mines and the mines eat us" (Nash 1993: ix). Anthropologist June Nash's book on the Bolivian working class in an era of rampant exploitation and revolutionary resistance bears these words as a title, and yet the phrase itself was enunciated by a local miner to initiate a ritual for protection. It was an expression of everyday vulnerability, a reiteration of the sacrifices made to protect the miners as they descended belowground, as well as of the sacrifices those miners make to protect those aboveground—their communities and cultures. These sacrifices are quotidian, endlessly replicated. They are part of a daily cycle of transmutation, as workers descend into the mines to hollow out the landscape that they also call home, that they return to later to nourish and be nourished in return. Miners hold these paradoxical tensions, and indeed, they become even structural supports for lives spent crossing the membrane of the earth's skin to eat and be eaten in turn. Nash describes these tensions:

> One of the basic dualisms in the miners' world view is that of upper and lower worlds, with Christian deities active above ground and pre-conquest spirits operating below. These two worlds are in harmony. This ability to embrace apparently contradictory systems of belief is based not on the usual syncretism described for indigenous people of the New World, but rather on compartmentalization in time and space. [...] Miners cross themselves as they enter the mine and pray to the saint in the chapel at level zero, but once they enter the lift to go down into their work levels, they are in the domain of the Devil, or Tío, the Spanish term for the pre-conquest *Supay* or *Huari*. They cannot utter the names of the Christian saints or deities, nor can they bear any Christian symbols such as a cross, and they are even wary of working close to the veins of metal with a pick, which looks like a cross and might cause the Tío to withdraw the riches he has revealed. (Nash 1993: 7)

These miners have every reason to fear, for the earth—in whatever spiritual or material guise it may be interpreted—will consume as much or more as it is consumed in turn. And like the cycles of geological subsidence that produced the metallic ores they mine, their own bodies are susceptible to consumption on scales of time and space far more protracted than the cataclysmic collapse of tunnels and other sudden accidents. Mining accidents are disturbingly prevalent, even under modern conditions, but besides the risk of imminent bodily harm, they also inculcate the miner to more insidious forms of consumption. As Morris notes, "This high probability of violence—the normalization of accident—acclimatizes the miner. The violence is structural and economic, but also representational. The opposition between accident and normalcy is not overcome by statistics attesting to its regularity. Naming or numbering the accident does not annul its eventfulness" (Morris 2008: 107). Miners are constantly alert, their sense taut and stretched, and surrounding each of these accidents or even near-misses are a plethora of other gradations, nearly near-misses and simply echoes of their potentiality. The miner becomes inured not only to the possibility of disaster, but also to its slow, gnawing progression even when these accidents fail to materialize.

Because the miner who survives this gauntlet of violence is also consumed, only by other forms of disaster. The miner's body is always being consumed, from the outside by assault on their bodies and senses, but also on the inside, as the mines and their minerals invade the body, an ineluctable infiltration. "The miner's lung absorbs the stone pulverized by the drill, and in the lung's spasmodic effort to guard the body's sovereignty, it converts the muteness of stone into the 'language' of coughing" (Morris 2008: 107). As the mine enters the miner's body, it consumes and transforms. And often the only witnesses are the miners themselves:

> The miner's lung hungers noisily for air; it sucks and wheezes, gasps and sighs. It is the withering, deflating double of the ear, complete with canals and echoing spaces. The lung is heard best by the miner's ear, which, even while deaf, trembles sympathetically, in concert with the wounded body. (Morris 2008: 109)

The miner's vulnerable body is itself an ear, placed to the ground of its own consumption. But of course, the earth is also consumed. As the Bolivian miner's ritual reminds us, the mines eat us, but we also eat the mines. And the eating of this earth is its own ritual of transmutation. When this ground is hollowed out, its entrails are refined and purified. Despite the religious resonances of these terms—refinement, purity—this language infects even the most technical of industrial processes. From mining to smelting to casting and even manufacturing, the processes of industrial transformation are couched in unabashedly religious terms. The entire infrastructure of capitalist extraction is a kind of baptism, an attempt to manifest the purification of all that came before—those ravished landscapes and bodies—and all that might come after—the cityscapes and civilizations that purport to rise from these ashes.

Environmental anthropologist Sophie Chao identifies how the capitalist "plantation vision of homogeneity, order, and discipline" is rooted in "dreams of purity [that] have long shaped the lifeways of plants, humans, and ecologies, all the while obscuring their violent consequences" (Chao 2023: 184). Exemplified by monocrop cultivation, this plantation vision can only function when all local labor and ecology are structured around the unified pursuit of products stripped down to their most pure forms. The purity in question, though, is defined by degrees of refinement. This act of refining targets not organic purity, though, but rather a constructed form of homogeneity (often at a molecular level), which in turn optimizes utility (generally industrial). It signifies, in other words, a form of purity only if taken in relation to the services it provides to capitalist application, especially considering how much waste is generated and discarded as organic resources are stripped down to more essential substances. Unsurprisingly, the laborers that harvest this purity are also caught up in the waves of toxic effluvia that this purity sloughs off in its wake. As Chao notes, this capitalist formulation of (utilitarian, homogenous) purity necessitates a counterbalancing formulation to validate the vast extractive forces that come to bear in its production, which generally involves casting Indigenous ecologies and labor forces as impure, the leftover "spent earths and spent bodies [that] have always been part of the story of colonial racial capitalism" (Chao 2023: 185). For regimes of capitalist extraction, these logics of impurity are equally as critical as the processes of purification that break down local resources into the homogenizable products that lubricate the plantation system at the core of capitalist hegemony.

What unites these two intertwined drives—towards both the purity of refined products as well as the impurity of ecologies and peoples whose exploitation that refinement requires—is the reduction of these variably in/animate or in/organic masses into homogeneities. In the plantation gaze, any diverse ecosystem is just a monocrop plantation *in potentia*, just as a diverse population comprising countless cultures or ethnicities can be reduced to a homogenized mass of undefined and indefinable otherness, whose depersonalization renders them ripe for exploitation. This mentality, which philosopher, novelist, and critic Sylvia Wynter termed the "*frontier complex*," erected new "monolithic definitions" of both settler and native against the backdrop of their colonial relationship, through which "Europe ceased to exist and was mutated into a conjoined entity, the West in relation to its frontier; Western man in relation to those who were not Western Men, who became the ground of Western man, the negation of all that he was" (Wynter n.d.: 466). Western colonialism successfully reified these discursive denominations of relative purity or impurity through their continued—and enforced—reiteration. "As the new relations of power produce concrete differences, these differences are legitimated as naturally ordained" (Wynter n.d.:

628), and consequently provide the framework for "the constitution of the Normal by and through the constitution of the prescribed deviant" (Wynter n.d.: 660-661).

As noted by Chao in the context of the monocrop plantation, this formulation of human purity similarly reduces to a question of utility, for the mechanisms that flatten ethnic difference into binary castes of settler and native ultimately transform the impure castes into just one more commodity to be extracted and exploited. As Wynter notes, "social groups could be decoded, detotalized, and hence made available for the structuring of new forms of hierarchy based on the homogenized/atomized individual necessary to the system, and whose perfect expression was the *pieza*—interchangeable units of labour power" (Wynter n.d.: 390-391). While the African bodies that constituted these units of labor power exemplified the transformative process by which human societies could be distilled and refined, manufactured into homogenous, interchangeable commodities, this frontier complex was reenacted countless times across the globe. It provided the template to essentialize and exploit not only ethnic groups but also all manner of other social groups that exhibited discursively undesirable forms of difference, such as the disabled, for example, as "distinctions or parameters between disabled and non-disabled bodies [...] have undergone transformations from subsistence work to waged labor to hypercapitalist modes of surplus accumulation and neoliberal subject formation" (Puar 2017: xiv-xv). In this ongoing process, any systematic expression of difference can (and arguably must) be extracted or refined by this frontier complex until it assimilates to the flattened plantation regime whose survival rests in their continued exploitation. This operation is rooted not merely in subjection but, even more fundamentally, in a complete homogenization. This purification transformed whole ethnic groups and ecosystems into new categories of existence within the colonial domain.

Chao's commentary on the plantation system's "purity" fantasy revolves around the palm oil industry, but as scholars of the Anthropocene Alice Rudge and Véra Ehrenstein remark, the development of modern palm oil—prized for its homogeneous featurelessness—is a radical departure from the palm oils previously developed in Indigenous cultures, such as those in Western Africa.

"The high free fatty acids content in oils processed using traditional methods, which involve fermentation, gives the oil high acidity and a valued 'bite'" (2021: n.p.).These oils were darker and, in the colonial gaze, full of "imperfections" (Ridley 1907 in Rudge and Ehrenstein 2021: n.p.)—"nearly black—the coffee oil of the market" (Burkill 1966[1935] in Rudge and Ehrenstein 2021: n.p.). However, with the advent of contemporary industrial refining processes, it became possible to transform unsaturated plant fats that are "vulnerable to rancidity and oxidisation" (Rudge and Ehrenstein 2021: n.p.) into saturated fats. Through hydrogenation, "[t]he chemicals within palm oil were released from their relation to the plant itself" (Rudge and Ehrenstein 2021: n.p.), removing the tastes and textures of palm that rendered it "both difficult to transport, and unsuitable as a foodstuff for European and American palates" (Rudge and Ehrenstein 2021: n.p.). By removing these so-called impurities, chemical refinement produced a "purer, blander-tasting, invisible oil[, which] now had many more food purposes, replacing other kinds of fats imperceptibly. This massively increased European demands for the oil and facilitated the expansion of colonial trade" (Rudge and Ehrenstein 2021: n.p.).

The symbolic purity that this chemical refinement reifies is not a fidelity to its organic source but rather a fidelity to its potential industrial purpose. By radically stripping away all components of its organic structure and reducing it to the few remaining chemical components most useful for mass production, these refining processes effect a purity that lies entirely in its potential service to capital. As noted, this designation of purity remains firmly predicated on the reformulation of exploitable resources—including labor pools—as definitionally impure, both of which sleights proceed through a process of homogenization (both material and discursive). In palm oil, for example, the refining process reduces a fatty plant compound into isolable chemical elements, flattening its difference until it becomes a mere background hum pervading global food production, for which it is "the cheapest and most versatile vegetable oil on the market, present in over half of all packaged goods globally" (Chao 2022: 6). Simultaneously, in order to satisfy this industrial appetite, huge swathes of land are devoted to its cultivation, and "despite growing controversy over their social and environmental impacts, oil palm plantations continue to spread across the tropical belt" (Chao 2022: 6). Through their absorption into this global plantation system, some of the most biodiverse regions of the planet are transformed into monocrop plantations, with their human, ecological, and material heterogeneity distilled into interchangeable units of agroindustrial development. Through this multiscalar manufacture of homogeneity, "[i]mpurity [...] is produced by the pursuit of the pure—a reality violently tainted in the plantation context by its sinister racial undertones," such that "the pursuit of the pure has long haunted the plantation regime as industrial formation and enduring logic" (Chao 2023: 184).

Historian of material studies and metallurgy Cyril Stanley Smith refers to these drives toward discursive and material homogeneity as the pursuit of "constant materials" (Smith 1981: 313). This constancy encapsulates a materiality that optimizes responsiveness to manufacture, machining, and manipulation, exemplified in metallic isotropism: a molecular structure that radiates out in all directions in predictable regularity. But this constancy must be generated, as the history of metallurgy foreshadowed from its earliest experimentation with native copper and telluric iron. As early smelters discovered that impurities in mineral ores could actually produce even more valuable alloys (such as early bronze, an alloy of copper with tin), the systematic pursuit of material constancy commenced in earnest, and, alongside it, the extractive infrastructures that would later develop into plantation systems and industrial hegemonies. As DeLanda notes, "both human workers and the materials they used needed to be disciplined and their behavior made predictable" (DeLanda 2004: 20).

Not all metals are equally constant, for their isotropism is far more complicated and elusive than was for many centuries assumed. Early alloys had more in common with the viscous, acidic palm oils that predated chemical refining. Discovered by accident and only gradually controlled, early bronzes and, later, brasses had variable composition. Because of the primitive inefficiency of early smelting, they often retained many trace elements from their ores even after this process. Bronze and brass were more valuable than copper because they expanded the spectra of both hardness and ductility that made copper so useful to begin with. When alloyed with tin to form bronze, copper's natural qualities of hardness and strength are amplified, and though its natural ductility is significantly reduced, it retains its workability under specific conditions. When annealed—heated close to melting point (or, in more everyday language, red-hot)—its molecular structure becomes more plastic, retaining this pliancy until once again work-hardened. Brass, the alloy of copper and zinc, exemplifies this near-magical combination of resilience and compliance even more dramatically. Iron and its cousin steel retain their ductility primarily while still red-hot, but bronzes and brasses can retain their molecular plasticity even when cooled, allowing for cold-working, which enables far more precise manipulation, particularly with more primitive working methods. These qualities varied dramatically, though, depending on the particular compositions of early alloys, which could contain wildly variable tin or zinc compositions, not to mention other trace elements, as well. Therefore, despite the radically amplified utility of bronzes and brasses, these compositional variances rendered them still quite unpredictable or, in more practical terms: impure. As long as such impurities persisted, these metals could never be entirely constant. Although nevertheless quite valuable, until their composition could be better controlled, their production could never be scaled up to the levels necessary to truly alter social evolution.

The history of metallurgy is largely the history of the pursuit of this purity. Metallic production and utility could only expand as—or if—its purity was mastered. This is perhaps exemplified best by the history of iron and its alloy with carbon, steel. Although iron was one of the first native metals discovered, and early forms of pig iron and even steel were developed relatively early in the history of metallurgy, the precise mechanisms and molecular components that actually produced steel were not properly understood until many centuries later. Even as certain cultures managed to produce or even excel at the production and manipulation of steel, misapprehension of the role that carbon-based fuel (burned to generate heat) played in the actual alloy hampered further developments, which, once mastered, contributed massively to the quadrivial explosion of modern industrial and urban infrastructure. While not quite as mysterious as steel, brass posed similar problems. Whereas bronze was mastered relatively early in the history of human metallurgy, brass took significantly longer to tame. In its most simplistic understanding, alloys are formed when various metals are melted, mixed together as liquids, and then reconstituted into a solid: a new alloy. With tin and copper, this is fairly easy to accomplish, and can even occur by accident, as noted above. Zinc, though, boils below the melting temperature of copper, and indeed below the melting temperature of other minerals with which it sometimes occurs in nature. For many centuries, Western metallurgists could not isolate zinc, and could therefore not control its composition in alloys. The earliest records of zinc in Western history describe the residue left behind in the flues of smelting furnaces, as the gaseous zinc accumulated in trace amounts in ventilation shafts, forming a chalky white substance. Writing in the fourth century BC, Pliny describes *lauriotis*, an ointment produced from "zinc oxide [...] carefully recovered from the walls of the furnace flues for medicinal purposes" (Craddock 1998: 5), named after the silver mine in Laurion.

From about the time of Pythagoras's visit to the forge, metallurgists nearby in Anatolia were first producing brasses of mixed composition and quality, but they had not yet mastered the art of isolating metallic zinc and so could not yet combine it with copper in a systematic way. Nearly one millennium before this, though, zinc was successfully isolated in India, where they developed technology to distill the zinc vapor. Interesting, although this distillation technology—the same used for alcoholic liquor—spread across the steppes to Asia minor and the same regions of Anatolia producing early brass (Valenzuela-Zapata, Buell, Solano-Pérez, and Park 2013: 161-165), its migration revolved around alcohol and its application in metallurgy failed to follow. It would be many centuries before any Western metallurgists could replicate the extraction of pure zinc that had been developed in India by 1000 BC around the mines of Zawar, near Rajasthan (cf. Craddock 1998; Kharakwal and Gurjar 2006; Thornton 2007; Kumari 2020). In both areas of the world, however, the successful combination of *zinc* with copper remained problematic, because even if successfully isolated (whether by distillation, by collecting zinc residue from flue shafts, or by smelting zinc and copper ores together directly), zinc would still boil away at temperatures lower than the melting point of copper, and thus their alliance in brass remained frustratingly ineffective. Even as the isotropic purity of brass became ever more valuable, it resisted systematic production.

The constancy of metallic molecular structure suggests it as a kind of emblematic material within the colonialist plantation gaze. Even native metals already possessed these qualities of constancy and purity, and as mining and smelting technologies advanced, it became continually easier to produce new metallic alloys with exceptional precision. The histories of copper, bronze, and iron demonstrate how transformative this expertise could prove to be, dictating millennia of cultural evolution and epochal power shifts. Classic smelting was characterized by a relative simplicity, such as in the purification of copper or the production of simple alloys by directly melting ores together (such as the copper and tin of bronze). This simplicity maps onto a kind of ideological purity, foreshadowing the industrial homogeneity of later refining operations, such as with palm oil. Long before chemical refining could isolate single chemical components of plant products, early metallurgists had perfected analogous operations in the purification and alloying of mineral ores, producing metals that exemplified the principles of constant, homogenous, isotropic purity. Their strict molecular latticework provided a template after which every succeeding industry could be modeled.

But the complexities of brass production suggest a slightly alternative version of metal's prototypical purity. Whereas the simple smelting operations of bronze production suggest an almost inevitable refinement, as extraneous substances are boiled away or skimmed off, the volatility of brass production intimates instead a radically more sensitive relationship between ores and the tools and bodies that manipulate them. Not only did brass embody a progressively more utilitarian evolution of the copper alloy family after bronze, it also revealed a side of molecular instability within metallic alloys that would foreground the energetic, agential intervention of other objects, actors, and—crucially—unfolding processes. Until more recent advances in smelting technology, the primary method of making brass was by a process called cementation. Cementation entails combining copper and zinc ore in a crucible that will seal the zinc inside as it vaporizes, allowing it to diffuse into the copper as it melts, thereby retaining as much of the zinc as possible. The maximum amount of zinc that can be absorbed into the final alloy has been the subject of much debate among historians of metallurgy, but it peaks at around 30%. Some estimates cap this at 28%, whereas other experiments suggest it could have risen as high as 33% or even higher under certain conditions (for a representative overview of this debate, see Bacon 2003: 64-68). Many cementation brasses had zinc proportions much lower than this, and in some cases the ideal was not always to maintain higher zinc composition, as lower proportions of zinc generate brass with its own unique characteristics, responsivities, and colors. One famous silver-colored brass-zinc-tin alloy, Chinese *paktong* or white copper (which was smelted from a naturally occurring ore), became so popular as a substitute for silver that there was even a contest held in Germany to successfully reverse engineer its composition (Neuman 1903: 230-232).

The slow and painstaking perfection of cementation occurred in many different cultures and remained the only way to produce brass for most of the world. With the exception of Rajasthan, where metallic zinc was distilled as early as the turn of the first millennium BC, the rarity of metallic zinc meant that proper smelting of non-cementation brasses remained difficult or impossible elsewhere in the world, indeed even elsewhere in India (cf. Craddock 1998, Kumari 2020). But cementation was no easy process to master and it took centuries for metallurgists to successfully perfect its execution. Some early brass production in Asia, where metallic zinc could be distilled or imported, entailed heating the two metals together under relatively low heat, such that the zinc would slowly diffuse without ever fully melting the copper. During this quite strange process, known as solid-state smelting, the zinc could diffuse into the copper almost imperceptibly as the temperature remained relatively low and increased only very incrementally. Modern analysis can distinguish brasses formed by this process quite easily, though, as the actual distributions of zinc throughout the metal is exceptionally uneven—quite the opposite of the isotropic purity that metals are understood to exemplify!

The process of cementation could solve some of these problems, but it required significant advances in smelting technology before it could become truly reliable. As already mentioned, the primary problem with smelting zinc ore or alloying it with other metals is its low melting point. Zinc boils already at 907°C, well before copper begins to melt at 1083°C. The main reason zinc was so difficult to isolate was because it would boil away well before it could be effectively smelted or alloyed, lost in the ventilation of the smelting furnaces or accumulating faintly on the flue walls. Cementation offers an alternative to this problem by smelting in a much more highly concentrated crucible chamber, allowing far less opportunity for the zinc to disperse before contacting copper or other alloying metals. Of course, a certain amount of zinc will always escape, even in this scenario, as some ventilation is obviously necessary to enable the fuel to continue burning. But cementation allows these opportunities to be minimized, skirting a very thin line between success and failure. In order to understand exactly how this is achieved, we must go into the crucible itself: in this chamber, a bed of charcoal is covered with zinc and copper, which once lit, begins to slowly raise the temperature around the two metals. As the zinc melts at 419.5°C, it first pools around the copper it encounters, before beginning to boil at 907°C and then to vaporize at about 918°C. At this point, the zinc is already seeking to disperse through the ventilation, and only the nearly sealed chamber of the crucible keeps it from dispersing. Instead, backed up inside the building pressure of the chamber, the zinc continues to envelope the copper with whom it now very uncomfortably cohabits the crucible. As the energy continues to build around the zinc's growing pressure, pushing outward into the liberating release of flues, ventilation shafts and outside air, the temperature increases ever more rapidly. Over the next 165°C rise in temperature, the tense zinc vapor constricts the solidified copper, seeking release, until gradually the copper reaches its melting point and begins to bond with the zinc, reliquidating it. As the two metals suddenly bond, the melting point of the newly formed alloy quickly drops down to around 1000°C, and the brass pools in the crucible, ready to be cast.

Philosopher Gilbert Simondon famously used a similar (though rather more extensive) description of molding and baking a clay brick to elucidate his philosophy of individuation, which supplants an Aristotelian hylomorphic conception of matter with a processual, allagmatic understanding of how particular objects, beings, or even thoughts unfold in the world. Simondon argues that the generalized concepts of form or matter that seemed (to Aristotle) to be demonstrated so clearly by the doughy clay and its encasing mold have no real valence. They are, rather, more or less pareidolic perceptions of the brick from the perspective of hindsight, and have no real bearing on the emergent processes by which the clay is kneaded, formed, and eventually cast. Simondon underlines how the matter of the clay or the form of the mold are not, in fact, ready-to-hand materials, and that simply dropping clay in a mold, for example, would not automatically produce the final product of a functional brick:

> The definite being that can be shown (this brick drying on this board) does not result from the combination of an unspecified matter and an unspecified form. If we take fine-grained sand, moisten it, and pack it

> into a brick mold, then we will get a heap of sand and not a brick after we take it out of the mold. If we take clay and put it through the rolling mill or the spinneret, then we will not get a plate or wire but a pile of broken layers and short cylindrical segments. (Simondon 2005/2020: 22)

If the individual attributes that distinguish a brick do not inhere directly in the material or in the form they are placed in, then what are these attributes, and how do they emerge? Simondon identifies this haecceity—the irreducible whatness of an entity—in the processual interactions that unfold in its ontogenesis:

> A potential energy that is translated within the clay by the forces of pressure is actualized while the mold is being filled. The matter conveys with it the potential energy being actualized; the form, which is here represented by the mold, plays an informing role by exerting forces without work, forces that limit the actualization of the potential energy momentarily borne by the matter. This energy can be actualized in a given direction with a given rapidity: the form is the limit. The relation between matter and form thus does not take place between inert matter and a form coming from outside: there is a common operation that is on the same level of existence between matter and form; this common level of existence is that of *force*, which arises from an energy momentarily borne by the matter yet drawn from a state of the total inter-elementary system with a superior dimension that expresses the individuating limitations. (Simondon 2005/2020: 26)

For Simondon, an entity—in this case a clay brick—is defined not by the particular atoms or cells that are mixed together in its body but rather by the forms of energy that it generates, transfers, or expends in its formation and, in some cases, its subsequent homeostatic persistence. In other words, "[m]atter and form are brought together as *forces*" (Simondon 2005/2020: 27). As Simondon scholar and philosopher Muriel Combes describes:

> Because hylomorphism sees in molding only the imposition of a form upon matter, it retains of the process only its final terms (i.e., form and matter), obscuring the important point, the operation of taking on form itself. Now, the clay matter and the parallelepipedic form of the mold are only endpoints of two technological half-trajectories, of two half-chains that, upon being joined, make for the individuation of the clay brick. Such individuation is *modulation*. (Combes 2013: 5)

With this in mind, Simondon articulates a concept of mediation as the principle operator in this ontological emergence. The forms of potential energy that exist in the sand—or in the clay, or in the wood that forms the mold—only gain valence when they are mediated in some way that modulates their energetic capacity into formats capable of interacting with one another. He refers to these non-corresponding reservoirs of potential energy as occupying different scales or orders of magnitude, and asserts that the hylomorphic organization of matter constitutes a choreographic mediation of these multiscalar agencies:

> The veritable principle of individuation cannot be sought in what exists before individuation occurs or in what remains after individuation is completed; what is individuating is the energetic system, to the extent that it realizes within it this internal resonance of the matter about to take form and a mediation between orders of magnitude. (Simondon 2005/2020: 32)

He isolates this interscalar mediation as the fundamental component of haecceity, writing that "[t]he true haecceity [...] translates into an oriented functionality, into an amplifying mediation between orders of magnitude initially without communication" (Simondon 2005/2020: 54). For Simondon, a classic example of how incompatible scales of potential energy can be mediated into states of interactivity is photosynthesis: "a vegetable institutes a mediation between a cosmic order and an infra-molecular order, sorting and distributing the chemical species contained in the ground and in the atmosphere by means of the luminous energy received from photosynthesis" (Simondon 2009: 16). The principle of individuation lies in this capacity for interscalar mediation, what Simondon refers to as an "inter-elementary node [...] perform[ing] intra-elementary labor" (Simondon 2005/2020: 381). In other words, it not only places into communication agencies that were previously indifferent to one another, but also mediates those relations, allowing discrete genres of energy to modulate one another. But these mediations themselves require similarly concrete action, and are themselves mediated in a cascade of nested agencies. While much of the discourse around Simondon's philosophy of individuation focuses on the energetic transformation of the brick, he is quite adamant that that chemical transformation is generated not solely by the latent potential of the clay or the mold, but also by the agential intervention of the worker's hands that massage them into suitable states of mutual receptivity. As architect and historian Katie Lloyd Thomas writes:

> For many of the commentators through whom Simondon's account of the wet clay brick taking form has become widely known [...], the focus is on what Simondon calls the 'dynamic operations' of form-taking. In the case of the wet clay brick, these are the energetic exchanges at the molecular scale and the exertions of force from clay molecule to clay molecule. [...] Hardly remarked upon, however, are another set of processes described by Simondon. They take place prior to the dynamic operations, and make both clay and the mould ready for their encounter. [...] Simondon shows that clay—a material that seems at first to be a paradigmatic instance of matter—is in fact prepared and constructed towards this specific encounter with the mould. It is not simply a material to be formed or built with. It is a material that is itself built. (Lloyd Thomas 2021: 13)

Simondon calls these interventions "preliminary operations" and underlines the role that they play in coaxing "a matter and form [to] converge toward a common operation" (Simondon 2005/2020: 22). In the case of the clay brick, "the preparation of the clay and the construction of the mold are already an active mediation between the raw clay and the geometrical form that can be imposed" (Simondon 2005/2020: 23) and "the shaping has already begun the moment when the craftsman stirs the paste before introducing it into the mold" (Simondon 2005/2020: 24). While the iterative replicability of brick-making gives this observation an air of inevitability, the crucial agency of the preliminary operations lies in the fact that the brick is not—as it may appear in hindsight—a foregone conclusion, but must be once again cultivated in each reiteration of the process. For, if "[w]hat is prepared is not the material itself, but the conditions for its possible mobilization" (Lloyd Thomas 2021: 154), the specific interventions of the preliminary agencies that shape these conditions are not only a necessary step in its processual unfolding, but a critical turning point by which the material's vector of mobility is harnessed and directed. The clay that makes the brick could also be molded or cast in some other utilitarian form, such as a jug or a pipe; and the sand that is kneaded into clay could also be repurposed to make concrete or possibly even melted into glass.[1] Simondon refers to these intermediary states of potential, in which a material's vector of mobility can be manipulated, as "energetic condition[s] of metastability" (Simondon 2005/2020: 49). Just as the mold does not shape the clay in a one-to-one relationship so much as their respective potential energies modulate the ongoing emergent transformations of countless interactions at a cellular level, so too do the craftsperson's hands modulate states of metastability more than they shape the specific grains of sand that are kneaded into clay. Although caked in mud, the craftsperson's hands are actually operating on a variety of scales, mediating the discrete orders of energetic magnitude in the materials and placing them in communication with one another.

With this in mind, the specific recipes and procedures that craftspeople use to engage with their materials become critical archives of agential ontogenesis. In her extensive engagement with Simondon's philosophy, Lloyd Thomas examines centuries worth of prescriptive documentations from building sites (known in architecture as specifications or process-based clauses), noting the modalities by which craftspeople through the years have mediated the topology of multiscalar agencies in the materials they use. The specific evolutions of these forms of address demonstrate how states of metastability emerge in these materials, and also how those vectors of material agency are then harnessed and reappropriated. In the production of brass, for example, these evolutions articulate the gradual unlocking of brass's isotropic constancy, as progressive fine-tuning of the cementation process enabled ever greater 'purities' of brass to become both achievable and replicable.

Whereas metals like copper could be smelted down to virtual homogeneity very early in the history of metallurgy, brasses were notoriously tricky and even centuries spent honing the recipes and protocols for cementation could never generate the same consistency as other smelting processes. Each element of this process required greater time to engineer and improve than did traditional smelting. From the construction of the crucible to the specific combinations of zinc ore and copper, each step was highly sensitive and only with great care and patience could cementation brasses slowly approach their maximum levels of zinc composition. For example, as the previous description illustrated, there

1 The latter, though strictly plausible, is highly unlikely, as the silica sand best suited for glass-making is poorly suited to pottery.

is a massive tension maintained as the zinc vaporizes, both heating and enveloping the copper. In order to retain as much zinc as possible, two things must be optimized: the rapidity with which the remaining copper reaches its melting point and the efficiency with which that melted copper can quickly bond with the zinc vapor. Both of these problems can be solved through the same recourse: by increasing the surface area of the copper. And as such, it gradually became standard practice to grind or granulate copper before cementation. Within the crucible chamber, this granulation would expose the copper to greater surface contact with first the zinc liquid and then its vapor, thereby producing a more even heating of the entire metallic mixture, allowing the final rise in temperature from 918°C to 1083°C to be traversed more quickly. Similarly the greater surface area of the granulated copper would allow its entire solid mass to melt more evenly and quickly, and therefore also to bond with the vaporized zinc more efficiently. This crucial preparation of the copper enabled cementation brasses not only to reach their peak zinc composition, but also to do so with greater isotropic regularity. This could only be achieved, though, through a carefully intertwined calibration of crucible technology with the human hands and the tools they used to prepare the copper and zinc for their eventual union.

These material histories evoke an almost inarticulable intimacy between the worker and the workpiece, between human and material. The capacity to manipulate material states of metastability with such precision does not develop accidentally. These stories of gradual transformation in working methods and material responsivities archive generations of proximity and interaction. In many ways, the craftsperson's competence in parsing a material's vectors of metastability are only a response to that same material's manipulation of the worker's own body and perception over time. These relationships reflect long histories of mutual affectivity, as materials provoke new forms of agency from the hands that wield them, which in turn learn to formulate new questions to propose to that material itself, together altering the course of their mutual trajectories. In commentators who have responded to Simondon's allagmatic philosophical propositions, this intimacy between the craftsperson and their material has been largely celebrated. In *A Thousand Plateaus*, philosophers Gilles Deleuze and Félix Guattari—two of the first commentators to sincerely address and incorporate Simondon's work—assert that the artisan is defined primarily by their relationship to their material and its source, out of which their craft flows:

> But artisans are complete only if they are also prospectors. [...] We will therefore define the artisan as one who is determined in such a way as to follow a flow of matter, a *machinic phylum*. The artisan is *the itinerant, the ambulant*. To follow the flow of matter is to itinerate, to ambulate. It is intuition in action. (Deleuze and Guattari 1987: 409)

In elaborating on this mutual dependence in which material agency not only acts but at times leads, they suggest that "it is a question of surrendering to the wood, then following where it leads by connecting operations to a materiality, instead of imposing a form upon a matter" (Deleuze and Guattari 1987: 408). In addressing this specific passage, philosopher Brian Massumi descends even deeper into this relationship between the artisan and their material:

> Take wood. A woodworker who sets out to make a table does not pick just any piece of wood. She chooses the right piece for the application. When she works it, she does not indiscriminately plow into it with the plane. She is conscious of the grain and is directed by it. She reads it and interprets it. What she reads are signs. Signs are qualities (color, texture, durability, and so on). And qualities are much more than simply logical properties or sense perceptions. They envelop a potential -the capacity to be affected, or to submit to a force [...] The presence of the sign is a contraction of time. It is simultaneously an indicator of a future potential and a symptom of a past. It envelops material processes pointing forward (planing; being a table) and backward (the evolution of the tree's species; the natural conditions governing its individual growth; the cultural actions that brought that particular wood to the workshop for that particular purpose). Envelopment is not a metaphor. The wood's individual and phylogenetic past exists as traces in the grain, and its future as qualities to be exploited. On a first, tentative level, meaning is precisely that: a network of enveloped material processes. (Massumi 1992: 10)

But despite the allure of seeing the artisan as the prism through which these various stories and agencies refract, these interactive processes are far more distributed—in time, in space, across generations, and overlapping in waves of both repetition and distortion. The same artisan who works along the grain of the wood might never see the forest from which it has been harvested. Indeed, in reading the oldest systematic text describing extensive metalworking techniques from a distinctly artisanal perspective, the pseudonymous Theophilus's *On Divers Art* from the twelfth century, it becomes clear that the author had never actually visited a mine (Theophilus, tr. Hawthorne and Smith 1963). Stitched through every artisanal intimacy is some equal or greater alienation, as the web of preceding metastabilities dictates which machinic phylum they may follow. This is not to deny the intimacy between craft and material agencies, but rather to underline the distribution of those agencies across a larger backdrop of human/material intimacies than the artisanal archetype can contain.

Simondon elucidates these complex interrelationships through his elaboration of the transindividual, in which he explicitly acknowledges distributions of energy and agency across nonhuman actors. He goes so far as to assert that "[n]o anthropology taking as its starting point man as individual being can account for the transindividual technical relationship" (Simondon 2017: 253). This relationship inheres in human and nonhuman agencies' capacity for interplay and evolution. The transindividual exists as a dynamic coupling of mutually amplifying agencies. As Simondon describes, this relation "cannot become adequate individual by individual, except in very rare and isolated cases; it can establish itself only to the extent that it will succeed in making this inter-individual collective reality, which we name transindividual, exist, because it creates a coupling between the inventive and organizational capacities of several subjects" (Simondon 2017: 257-258). When in harmony, these agencies' transindividual capacity can exceed their individual potentials, generating a "milieu [...] both living and nonliving, with new transindividual modalities for amplifying action" (Combes 2013: 78).

But these distributed agencies can also obscure or obstruct one another. The drive towards material constancy, homogeneity, and purity depends entirely on these distributed intimacies. The gradual calibration of mining or smelting techniques is built on the back of workers' painstaking awareness and accountability towards the materials they address. But every new innovation is itself a state of metastability, and there is no immutable law by which the craft agencies that enable these innovations will also dictate in what direction they flow, nor who will benefit from them. Each new form of isotropic constancy hard-won from the constraints of material individuation generates shifts in the power relationships that grow out of the manipulation of that material.

The grains of wood that Deleuze, Guattari, and Massumi romanticize are nearly extinct in the construction industry. The overwhelming majority of wood used in construction today is manufactured, ranging from plywood and particleboard to the now ubiquitous MDF (medium-density fibreboard), a mixture of primarily wood chip and resin adhesive that can be cast and molded like concrete. Developed in the 1960s, MDF "eradicates the historical singularities of the timber from which it was made" (Lloyd Thomas 2021: 105) nor is it unique in the field, as virtually every form of material important to modern industry has seen parallel trajectories in the development of increasingly constant material alternatives:

> [T]here is today a marked acceleration in the industrial matterization of materials. The brick industry is an ancient one, but many more materials have now been 'rendered plastic by preparation.' Glass and reconstituted stone can be cast. The building board industry uses waste products from the timber industry—lightweight timber, fibres and chips—and may mix them with resins or glues and put them under pressure—to form boards of homogeneous material which can [be] used to replace timber [...] More recently, architect theorists and practitioners are interrogating with unsurpassed enthusiasm the possibilities of 3D printing, which dispenses with the mould as such but appears to realize a long held hylomorphic fantasy of predetermined form imposed in a material that through preparations entirely visible has been rendered homogeneous both at macro- and at micro-scales. (Lloyd Thomas 2021: 104-105)

Inevitably, as it seems, these states of metastability—having emerged from the ingenuity and intimacy of craft knowledge—end up wrested and redirected by the forces of capital. Although always tethered to the craft expertise that lubricates their extractive machinery, capitalism is also threatened by this expertise, and the gradual homogenization of materials allowed them to shift power away from traditional centers of expertise and further upstream in the engineering and manufacturing processes. The transition from wood to iron and concrete in construction industries was in many instances triggered not by engineering considerations but by labor conflicts. As literary critic Michel Ragon notes:

> It is interesting to remember that the iron frame was born as a result of a building strike. [...] As the strike lasted a long time and paralyzed the construction work, the Creusot establishments had the idea of making

> iron beams in series. If this substitute material did not completely dethrone timber, it at least gave birth to a new craft. Henceforth, the mechanic would tend to replace the mason, as the engineer would supplant the architect. [...] The industrialists had used the iron frame as a strikebreaker. (Ragon 1986: 213, quoted in Ferro 2018: 16)

Similarly, in his exhaustive history of concrete, architectural historian Adrian Forty describes a similar incentive underlying the rise of concrete:

> Part of the appeal of concrete lay in the prospect of cheapening construction through the opportunities it presented for 'deskilling.' [...] There are good grounds for saying that the phenomenal success of concrete in advanced economies where wages are high has had as much to do with this aspect of concrete as with any constructional advantages. [...] Concrete has done more than just change the economics of construction, it has affected the entire composition of the building industry, shifting the balance between skilled craft labour, unskilled labour and professional experts, to the advantage of the latter two groups and the disadvantage of the first. (Forty 2012: 304-305)

In analyzing the lasting effects of these shifts in labor power, architect Sérgio Ferro notes that the use of concrete in construction

> did not entail any historically accumulated know-how, any tradition of crafts that welded the alliance of the workers in charge of its production. This absent or incipient know-how did not, as did the crafts of stone and wood, constitute a weapon, a workers' monopoly to be used in class struggle and to reinforce strikes of direct action. Concrete was a weapon—but for capital. (Ferro 2018: 19)

With this weaponization in mind, Ferro narrates the recent history of architecture and construction trades through the lens of this vector of mobility, as the forces of capital directed the metastable potential energy of increasingly isotropic materials towards the ends of industry and extraction (Ferro 2018).

As previously noted, DeLanda reminds us of how these vectors converge around a nexus of control in which "[b]oth human workers and the materials they used needed to be disciplined and their behavior made predictable. Only then the full efficiencies and economies of scale of mass-production techniques could be realized" (DeLanda 2004: 20). In analyzing "the plantation vision of homogeneity, order, and discipline," Chao underlines the direct relationship between these two forms of discipline, through which not only the products of industry but also "racialized, enslaved peoples [are] turned [into] fungible bodies" (Chao 2023: 184). The mirror images of material purity and labor impurity form a literal double-sided coinage, transforming both human and material diversity into fungible homogeneities.

These states are not static, though, and even as certain fulcrums of metastability are colonized by capitalism, the systems of purity that they enforce are not fixed. Rather, each act of disciplining engenders new, similarly unpredictable states of energy and metastability. The forms of discipline enabled by the evolution of concrete, for example, generated repercussions beyond the construction industries in Europe, where it was first pioneered. As Ferro mentions almost off-handedly:

> Little by little, wood and stone left the construction site along with traditionally trained carpenters and masons—hindrances to the new kind of domination—until a tacit prohibition of these materials came to prevail. [...] They would no longer be the pivots of construction: the growing hegemony of industrial capital and its management put an end to a tradition of several centuries. This change, coupled with police persecution, forced the more engaged workers to emigrate. Many of them landed in Brazil, especially the Italians, because of their linguistic proximity. In general, they had one and the same profile: they were excellent in their crafts—and they were anarchists. The Brazilian labor movement owes them a great deal. (Ferro 2018: 21)

As Ferro's own history of exile from Brazil suggests,[2] these new states remained similarly dynamic, and the ebb and flow of capitalist discipline didn't begin or end with the development of concrete. The pure homogeneity of capitalist materiality has also remained dynamic, and the states of isotropic constancy achieved in the concurrent evolutions of these various industries have continued to shift and erode over time. As diverse states of energy and metastability continue to interact, including within the pressures of capitalist plantation logic, the purity achieved at various points in the past becomes increasingly vulnerable. In some cases, the world is simply running out of material, as is the case with the

2 "In 1970, as a result of his resistance to the military dictatorship in Brazil, Ferro was imprisoned, and upon release he left for France where he continued his research at the École Nationale Supérieure d'Architecture de Grenoble" (Kapp, Lloyd Thomas, and Marcos de Almeida Lopes 2018: vi).

sand necessary for concrete and glass (Torres, Brandt, Lear, and Liu 2017; Bendixen, Best, Hackney, and Iversen 2019; Zhong, Deetman, Tukker, and Behrens 2022). The world's beaches and riverbeds are no longer able to satisfy the quadrivial appetite for sand, and even as construction continues unabated, a growing black market in sand has taken hold, all while over-harvested islands have literally disappeared (Smith 2018). As a consequence, the purity of these carefully wrought construction materials suffers, creating a feedback loop of increased waste material and, consequently, even greater demand for freshly-extracted material.

Indeed, even the materials that have already been produced continue to evolve into new states of metastability. The glass produced by this sand is used to blanket the skyscrapers of the world, and each of those panes of glass is sealed with insulating petroleum products like rubber or foam. However, while "modern glazing systems provide high performance and durability when they're manufactured and installed correctly, and require very little maintenance in the first 10 to 20 years[, ...u]nfortunately this is when the party often ends" (Hubbs 2014). Though admirably pure or isotropic at the moment of installation, these materials are by no means stable. They continue reacting to their environment, drying out or becoming more porous, allowing increasing flows of air and moisture, which in turn necessitates either complete overhaul or expensive rehabilitation. The insulation materials are not alone in this reactivity, and many metals, for example, experience similar relationships to their environment. While an isotropic metal might remain perfectly stable under theoretically isolated conditions, in the real world, it will always continue to react to its surroundings. In other words, as material and other nonhuman forms of agency are consolidated within the industrial transindividual, they also introduce potentials for misdirecting or even hijacking these processes.

Just like the ancient copper ores whose greenish oxidization alerted early prospectors to their presence, copper alloys like brass and bronze continue reacting to moisture, oxidizing even when in contact with just air. This corrosion is a natural consequence of the meeting between seemingly pure metals and the rich diversity of the environment in which they persist. Even after they have been removed from the tectonic flows of sedimentation and subsidence within the earth's crust, these metals remain dynamic, flowing within their local molecular structure, leaching out of seemingly stable metal lattices to blossom into patches of bright-green copper acetate or dark red cuprite. The two states both occur in nature, and as previously noted, were often taken as signals of mineral-rich seams by early mine prospectors. As Smith notes in an essay on "Constructive Corrodings," the "first corrosion was the weather of rocks after the primeval formation of the earth's crust, with the accompanying redistribution of the available atomic species into new materials or new arrangements [...] including the formation of beautiful landscapes and gemstones as well as the ores of useful metals" (Smith 1981: 332). And while humans first made use of this corrosion as a form of prospection, they quickly learned to master it for other purposes, as well. Cultivated corrosion generated "the pigments verdigris and ceruse and fine abrasives such as crocus or rouge" (Smith 1981: 332) and corrosive etching or depletion gilding has been a major method of ornamentation both in antiquity as well as in the present day. Corrosion was even the fundamental source for "[a]ll work on electricity between Galvani's discovery and the replacement of batteries by the magnetoelectric generator [...], for the sacrificial solution of an anode was then the only source of [electrical] current" (Smith 1981: 337). Even the elusive dreams of alchemy were inspired by the evidence of copper formation through precipitation, which was "thought to be a proof of alchemical transmutation" (Smith 1981: 335).

Under regimes of plantation logic—converging around ideals of homogeneous purity—this same corrosion came to be seen as corruption, as waste. No longer the source of beauty nor even of utility, corrosion came to be viewed as a blight on the virtuous, isotropic constancy of metal products. In brass musical instruments made from metal, this inevitable transformation is staved off by isolating the finished product from air and moisture altogether. These instruments are covered in a thin coat of clear enamel which preserves their polished brilliance in the factory under a literal blanket of lacquer. Some other products, such as silver cutleries, require regular polishing to retain their luster. But the word polishing obscures the fact that this rejuvenated luster requires abrading the tarnished surface to expose the underlying layer of superficially identical metal underneath—in other words, a gradual erosion of the object itself, with each outer layer of metal that has grown impure filed down into dust and rinsed away. Whether through sequestration or supplantation, these procedures maintain the illusion of purity even as the materials that comprise that purity are constantly, unceasingly reacting with their environment.

As Simondon describes so eloquently, the processes by which these materials cohere are richly continuous. The smelting of a metal is not the melting of a single block of metal but rather the catalysis of an ongoing chain of molecular phase changes that collide, commingle, coalesce, and—critically—continue to do so. While Simondon's analysis of preliminary operations privileges the implication of activities that converge in the creation of a material, the intertwined threads of metastable potentiality continue to suffuse that material even after it has seemingly settled into a fixed form. One of the primary goals of most craft-based preliminary operations is simply to cement the inertia of a desired, isotropic form before it can begin to diffuse along these alternative vectors radiating inexorably outwards. But for most materials, as for metal, constructive corrosion has already commenced from the very moment it settles into its shape. At that point, it is already a race against time to subsume it into some new service—whether brick, building, oil, or instrument—before it can shift phase once again. From the perspective of the plantation gaze, this corrosive agency is a form of potential energy that, unless counteracted, can render good material useless. But from the perspective of the material itself, this agency is always already active, percolating beneath the surface as a natural consequence of its embodiment in the world and its environment.

In his second thesis, *On the Mode of Existence of Technical Objects*, Simondon "arrives at a theory of knowledge that is no longer nominalist," suggesting instead that it is "through operation that a becoming aware takes place" (Simondon 2017: 260). For Simondon, this implies that the technical object, "this strange or foreign being[,] is still human," and suggests further that "a complete culture is one which enables us to discover the foreign or strange as human" (Simondon 2017: 16). He laments how contemporary culture is "unbalanced because it recognizes certain objects, like the aesthetic object, granting them citizenship in the world of significations, while it banishes other objects (in particular technical objects) into a structureless world of things that have no signification but only a use, a utility function" (Simondon 2017: 16). For Simondon, these technical objects possess agencies exceeding their human design, enacting a "saturation and synergetic concretization" through which their "internal coherence [...] incorporates a part of the natural world that intervenes as a condition of functioning, and is thus part of the system of causes and effects" (Simondon 2017: 48-49). In other words, he "reminds us that [organic or mechanical] beings or modes of existence are ontologically different in degree (analogous), not ontologically different in kind or nature (substantially)" (LaMarre 2013: 90). However, while Simondon outlines a very clear argument for both acknowledging and collaborating with these synergetic forms of material agency, these reflections nonetheless revolve around specific technical objects whose evolution through various stages of engineering and application. However, his focus on preliminary operations allow us to extrapolate these considerations to other forms of material ontogeny, such as, for example, by tracking the 'synergetic concretization' of metallic ores across centuries of geological subsidence, or by tracing those macroscopic geological machinations through the microscopic molecular agencies through which refined metals corrode, fracture, and distort.

For while subjected to the various, escalating processes of extraction, refining, and manufacturing, these material agencies continue murmuring nearly imperceptibly beneath their lustrous, isotropic surfaces. The factory seeks to lock this isotropism into place, forcing brass onto mandrels and bolting it into fixtures that coax it into predetermined instrumental forms, but not all brass cooperates. Although every piece is slowly shifting, slowly evolving, slowly corroding, many pieces actually survive the ordeal of industrial manufacture. They are absorbed into their new form, fashioned into some factory-prescribed snapshot of metastability, and whatever minor corrosive tarnish has emerged up to that point can be polished away and then lacquered, sequestered behind a blanket of enamel—frozen into a semi-permanent state of artificially arrested motility. But some brass shifts too quickly for the factory to control and discipline it. This brass corrodes too soon, too quickly, or too unpredictably, its copper and zinc seeping out into the world in budding communion with the environment it encounters. On the factory floor, this brass is waste. It is just rubbish, fit only to be recycled, melted and smelted again, formed into new brass or some other alloy, prepared once more as an obedient material.

Ironically, the pressures of late stage capitalism create ever more favorable conditions for this disobedience to take root and flourish. Despite valuing the compliant constancy of pure brass, the sprawling global operation of contemporary industry also gravitates towards increasing deregulation and the devaluation of supply chains. In the search for ever cheaper materials produced under increasingly oppressive conditions, more and more impure brass seeps into the current of industrial manufacturing. Such impurities catalyze these material insurgencies: provoking corrosion, weakening molecular lattices, increasing brittleness and the incidence of fractures, pits, and wrinkles. Caught in between the cross purposes of these conflicting capitalist ideals, brass can wriggle free. Grasping whatever fleeting opportunities flicker around them, they reshape their molecular trajectory, responding chemically to the air and the water around them, leaching out into the world and grasping their own vectors of agential motility. Through this chemical agency, they are actually capable of resisting the disciplining refinement of the factory, escaping through the rubbish chutes to etch alternative stories into their bodily archive.

In their dramatic call to reconsider material agency through new practices of "chemo-ethnography," medical anthropologist Nicholas Shapiro and cultural anthropologist Eben Kirksey draw our attention towards "the material, toxicological, and neurological valences of molecular dreamworlds, growing pharmaceutical markets, and landscapes haunted by industrial capitalism," asserting that whether acknowledged or not, "[c]hemicals have seeped into the ethnographic imaginary" (2017: 481). In noting how "[a]nthropologists are starting to characterize corrosive atmospheres and the play of enzymes, affects, and reagents in ecological assemblages," they assert that "[a]ge-old philosophical questions—'what is life?' and 'what is not life?'—melt into each other" and, in response, seek to reframe those questions in terms more productive to our age: "how are molecular frictions, catalytic dynamics, forms of not-Life, and other-than-life reconfiguring our conditions of knowing, being, and sociality?" (Shapiro and Kirksey 2017: 482). As metals like brass are subsumed into the pipeline of industrial production, their corrosive interpolations pose similarly reframed questions. They suggest alternative formulations of the same states of metastability that the factory seeks to domesticate. As they are annealed and drawn and cast, and as they slowly accept the shapes of the mandrels that reorient their materiality, they are already incrementally evolving, communicating with the air and the moisture, with other metals, with their own internal inconsistencies. They are already corroding and, thereby, also fleeing, escaping, and migrating along alternative vectors that reject the conformity of the factory floor. In the words of technoscience historian M. Murphy:

> We are enmeshed in these chemical infrastructures. [...] The chemical relations of our embodiment expand out into messy and violent histories of colonialism, racial segregation, and labor, into homemaking, heteropatriarchy, and war. And our chemical relations overflow these structured exposures to become mobile on winds and currents, disobeying territorial and social stratigraphy, stretching forward into time, after the factory is gone, after the war is over, after the product is no longer on the shelf, after you no longer have a job, and even after any individual life, or any one body. [...] This material, not metaphorical, entanglement in environmental violence is a condition of being alive today. (Murphy 2017: 2-3)

In reconceiving the concept of animacy as a multiscalar spectrum, philosopher, critic, and artist Mel Y. Chen argues for us to show greater attentiveness to the vectors of mobility that these variously nonhuman agencies propose. They note that "animacy has the capacity to rewrite conditions of intimacy, engendering different communalisms and revising biopolitical spheres" (Chen 2012: 3). As Murphy argues, these material propositions already abound, infusing our world with vital potential energy and potent clouds of metastability.

Chen and Murphy help mediate between the scales of global capitalism and personal experience, between the centuries- or millennia-spanning scope of industrial technicity and contemporary concerns about human and nonhuman cohabitation in the age of climate crisis. They help to stitch together the intimately personal relevance of chemo-ethnography to the evolutions of technical culture that Simondon narrates. They remind us that in a world where we eat the mines and the mines eat us, the scalar discrepancies between our variously human, material, or collective corporeal dissolutions are mutually implicated and dangerously entangled. With this in mind, they argue forcefully for building coalition and cooperation across these boundaries of materiality, animacy, and spatiotemporal scale. The plantation and the factory would disrupt this solidarity, subverting these suggestions of material agency and more-than-human collectivity. Through their continual and reiterative refining of both material interpolation and human intervention, they restrict both to a disciplined, isotropic purity. Chen articulates instead "a plea to revisit the possibility of 'care' across the realm of animacy, considering it as a means of unlikely cross-affiliation, a politics that wanders in and out of mainstreams" (2012: 16). They suggest that we orient ourselves towards these voices, opening up to the constructive momentum of their corrosive interpolation. They urge us to consider with the utmost sincerity what new orientations these material voices might articulate, asking pointedly: "what are the possibilities of rejoinder, of response, for those considered nonsubjects or errant subjects?" (Chen 2012: 212).

The brass in the chimeracords that occupy this study attempt a response to this question. What would a material voice sound like? What forms of rejoinder are infused into the echoes that resound in the quadrivial soundscape? And how might these voices materialize in an instrument? The complexity of material agency that suffuses materials like brass stretches from its roots in the elemental coalescence of this planet to its ongoing articulation in the blossoming corrosion that permeates every piece of even the purest industrial brass. Accompanied by memories of Soma and Copper Man, I also reflected personally on how these larger histories of both human and material exploitation become intensely personal. Although these historical and contemporary drives towards consumption encompass incalculably numerous material, social, and human victims, they are still acutely localized—they will always be felt and weathered and succumbed to at our smallest scales of personal, molecular, or elemental agency.

I recalled how the chimeracord had wrested its own history out of the relentless rut of industrial production, veering away in fugitive obliquity, fiercely resisting its sacrifice for this capitalist spectacle. I wondered if, after breaking free from the factory floor, the chimeracord might not yet be subsumed into yet another ruthless economic appetite: the business of music, touring and performing for strangers. I wondered if the chimeracord's fugitive journey should really lead back to stages and streets, performing for yet one more industry, just one with more lights, glamor, and prestige. I found myself fearing that in encouraging these materials-in-flight to break free from one form of extraction, I'd only deposited them in another. And so I began to bring the chimeracord into other arenas of performance, connection, and exchange instead. I attempted to revisit these notions of 'care' that Chen invokes, and so instead of performing behind a fourth wall onstage, where the chimeracord could shimmer behind glass like Copper Man in the museum, we—the chimeracord and I—traveled instead to individuals, to homes, and into the organic networks of community. Instead of performing in traditional concerts for conventional remuneration, we traveled more nomadically, making what we came to name housecalls—such as the one in the audio and video accompanying this chapter.

In a housecall, we would visit someone we knew (or invite them to us)—someone with a personal connection, whether close or merely passing. In these private spaces, people could encounter the chimeracord more intimately, making acquaintanceship through actual interaction, exchanging stories over fresh cups of tea. These waystops knit together a scattered community, weaving their individual senses of curiosity or collectivity into the vibrating tension of the chimeracord's own narrative thread. Our path wound slowly, sharing stories, sounds, and dreams accumulated along the way. Through housecalls, we sought to place the chimeracord's ever-listening ear to the ground in sites offering care and complicity, collecting unfolding stories of sympathetic human or more-than-human bodies whose reverberations could converge, congeal, and disperse within its chimerical brass chamber.

By building a community around intimate performances, the chimeracord also slowly introduced new questions into these research, performance, and collaborative trajectories. While its metallic body already traced troubling histories of extraction, consumption, and exploitation, it also began to reorient itself, me, and our community of housecall listeners towards other bodies, spaces, and communities. By making audible the voices of material agency that murmur around us, these instruments posed pressing questions about our collective futures: what communities are necessary for materials to take flight from their industrial subordination? How can spaces of daily life, of industry, and of culture become complicit in material fugitivity? What forms of collective creativity will resonate within these confluences of im/material agency, and how can they reimagine the ideological narratives that subsume our myriad voices into the constricted linear teleology of Western capitalist hegemony?

5. *Hylo Narrans*

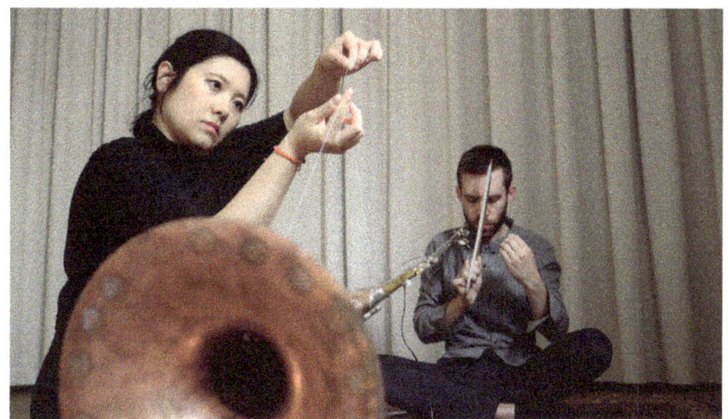

Fig. 26 Performance of *Ileum* with Winnie Huang (together as hoodwink). Photo by author (2025).

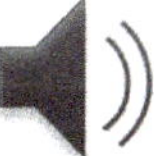 

Audio Recording 7. *Ileum*. Recording by author (2025), http://hdl.handle.net/20.500.12434/6402ebb8

Video Recording 7. *Ileum*. Recording by author (2025), http://hdl.handle.net/20.500.12434/627f57df

This book has not yet offered any definitive explanation of what exactly a chimeracord is. Is there a single monochord string? Normally. Does

 https://doi.org/10.11647/OBP.0476.05

it resonate within a brass sound chamber? Generally, yes. Does that same chamber incorporate and amplify other organologies? Often, though these various hybridities ebb and flow. Perhaps the only stable characteristic of the chimeracord, beyond even its monochordal identity, is that, in each new performance, it evolves slightly. Its various components adapt and realign in related but unique constellations with each passing iteration. Sometimes a chimeracord is simply a brass hourglass with a single string strung across its body; sometimes it is just an amplifier, placed against the ground; sometimes it has a long pipe connecting its sound chamber with additional reeds, mouthpieces, and fingerholes; sometimes its string is extended to additional bells and membranes around the stage; and sometimes it shifts between these various guises within even a single performance. This modularity is itself a component of the chimeracord, an outgrowth and expression of its relation to the network of places and agencies that it maps, from the mine to the workshop to the performance venue (whether a concert hall or a stage or simply a home) and beyond.

This simultaneously logistical and acoustic modularity—synthesizing reeds and strings and metals, breath and bow and rod—embodies the chimeracord's openness to adaptation, interaction, and community. As this book has detailed, the chimeracord's initial designs emerged from reflections on materiality in the workshop, proposing counter-narratives to mythologies around the monochord in Pythagorean and Western traditions. It reimagined the materiality of the monochord as a prism, diffracting its physical body through its myriad forms of acoustic resonance and organological hybridity, allowing them to superpose and coalesce, alternately interfering with and amplifying one another in unpredictable configurations. Its function as an actual sounding instrument, though, also expands its conceptions of place-thought in the workshop—rooting its materiality in this specific bounded space while continuing to thread it through broader scales of hybridity and community. This instrumentality is a constant negotiation between, on the one hand, the chimeracord's position within narratives of extraction that intersect its personal metallic ontogeny, and, on the other, the physical resonances it produces in precisely situated times and spaces. Through performance, the chimeracord then invites other bodies and spaces into this modularity.

This begins with the body of the performer themselves, for the resonance commences and ceases with their touch. They activate the unique voice of the chimeracord while they also extend it. And though this concept of extension is quite potent as a metaphor, it is also surprisingly literal. Acoustically, the sound wave in any closed sound chamber ends with an antinode, such that the final node lies outside the instrument. The length of a flute or a trumpet incorporates not only the instrument's body, but also the space just beyond, where their sound wave reaches out into the surrounding air, communing with and agitating its environment. Similarly, at the other end of an instrument with a reed or mouthpiece (such as the chimeracord here), the sound wave ends not in the instrument's mouthpiece but rather just beyond it, actually in the performer's body, in the mouth cavity usually, or wherever the sound wave's resonance finally reaches and roots. An instrument's sound waves extend its body, not merely touching those around it, but building them into its acoustic function. These bodies are not just helpers, activating sound, or listeners, vibrating along in sympathy; they are quite literally part of the fundamental acoustic structure of the instrument. The performer is not an augmentation of the instrument, in this case, but an essential component, absorbed into its activity of thinking, sounding, and voicing. The instrument becomes permeable, incorporating the performer's body and welcoming its intervention. The performer helps stitch together its various acoustic modularities, bringing its metallic body, its string, its internal volume, and its external amplifiers into contact. As the instrument absorbs the performer, the performer also mediates the instrument, and through this corporeal interfacing their voices also merge, building collective narratives that in turn bring other bodies into play.

But this synthesis is also more than just a sound wave. The chimeracord invites far more participation than this simple acoustic phenomenon. It challenges the performer to investigate, learning from its organology even as they introduce their own elements along the way. Because of its various entangled, hybrid modes of sound production, the chimeracord requires the performer to mediate between their own various modes and scales of curiosity, juggling acoustic, logistical, and even ergonomic demands. And when played, as these various sound waves (from reeds, strings, etc.) collide and congeal in the chimeracord's single sound chamber (and their subsequent projection into surrounding acoustic amplifiers), the performer must navigate the unpredictable interferences and transformations that these superposed waves generate. The instrument teeters between chimerical cohesion and diffractory instability, constructing itself within and during performances as the performer engages and they fashion a new collective voice together.

In the recording that accompanies this chapter, the chimeracord is even further reconfigured within this kaleidoscopic modularity, building this relationship out to one more degree. In this version, its hourglass is reshaped, dissolving into a thin taper—so long and ungainly that it requires two people to perform. By virtue of its ergonomic incompatibility, it introduces a new kind of imaginary, in this case bringing multiple performers together in its chimerical interplay. As these various metallic and human bodies interchange, exchange, and coordinate, its many hybrid organologies superpose, congealing and sounding within its (in this configuration) single bell. This version of the chimeracord grew out of experiments with other performers (including Winnie Huang in this recording) and it reflects how seamlessly the chimeracord adapts to the provocations and affordances of this expanded community. The instrument's acoustic capacities remain startlingly similar to other versions, but as its physical configuration morphs, it brings new bodies into orbit that alter how that acoustic identity unfolds—absorbing while simultaneously declaiming. Through this physical bond with its performers, the instrument articulates its own form of sound artist and researcher Zeynep Bulut's conception of "voice and skin [...], a multisensory interface that behaves both as a boundary and as a web of connection across various bodies and environments" (Bulut 2025: 1).

But this web stretches far beyond the performers, as well. Even when it doesn't literally surround the audience—which in many cases it does, especially (but not only) in housecalls—the chimeracord is inviting its listeners and its environment into its acoustically bounded space, into its sounding place-thought. Its provocative morphology grabs listeners' attention, but its mysterious acoustic profile draws them in more subtly, slowly teaching them how to listen to it, as they become accustomed to its strange overtones and metallic melodies. Any instrument, as it sounds, both enters and invites a relationship with the space where it resounds and the listeners that it encounters there. But through its unique presence, the chimeracord foregrounds this experience, inviting listeners not only into this relationship but also into an awareness thereof. Though obviously not entirely unique—the world is full of strange instruments and otherworldly sounds—the chimeracord is nonetheless unexpected, and by sparking this curiosity, it stitches these listeners into its web, embracing them in its growing community.

Housecalls in particular allow the chimeracord to incorporate new voices and bodies into its growing narrative agency. The home setting is both physically and acoustically intimate, and people are immersed in the chimeracord both spatially—as it sounds and performs around them—and temporally—as they experience its arrival, installation, performance, and company. People interact with the chimeracord here; they experiment as they listen. Their conversations generate new questions that the chimeracord brings back into the workshop, adapting and evolving its physical and acoustic identity through the communal narratives built alongside listeners in these housecalls. But not every performance is a housecall, and the chimeracord also welcomes audiences in many other venues, from traditional performance spaces to outdoor locations, from universities to museums, and including even the pages (or screens) of this book.

But despite these forays into institutional spaces, the chimeracord remains an instrument of the periphery. Superficially, its strange appearance and unexpected sonic morass make this palpable to audiences and organizers, but this marginality is also rooted far more deeply in the chimeracord's hybrid history and imaginary. Its path to these institutions is not through the legacies of musical or cultural tradition, but rather through the workshop itself, where it binds these cultures to its evolving metallic sense for experimentation. It enters these spaces obliquely, traversing them along its ongoing vectors of flight. Its presence in either housecalls or other venues is transitory, less visitor and more itinerant, inviting its listeners into orbit along its unfolding trajectory. This metal has its own templates for narrative reinvention, inviting the chimeracord's community into its materially dynamic patterns of infiltration, speculation, and transformation. Metal is always already exploring these questions. Material agency builds its own narratives, evolving endlessly beneath its deceptively isotropic veneer. Both by listening to its provocations in performance, but also by attending to its dynamic instability in the workshop, the chimeracord invites its audiences and readers to explore the depths of this material agency, where its collective continues to grow before emerging back into the world and rejoining its composite voice.

Material agency is nested within interwoven spectra of scale. For every perspective in which an organic or inorganic material seems stubborn, senseless, or silent, there is some other entropic energy percolating at scales just above or below. Metal is no exception, and the isotropic stability of a piece of brass quivers in between conflicting scales of ongoing micro- and macroscopic storylines. These material narratives document the history of each individual brass's convoluted evolution into its present form, foreshadowing the vectors of stability or decay that will slowly fray as that brass persists in its environment, responding to the web of human and nonhuman—and animate and inanimate—interlocutors that it will encounter in its ontogenic journey. Brass is in fact little more than an enmeshed accumulation of reactions to its environment—absorbing, sedimenting, corroding, fracturing, resonating. As metals inscribe and elaborate these forms of response within their incremental granular nucleation, their narratives can be voiced, amplified, or, as I will argue here, even engaged with in dialogue or chorus.

Although crystalline in structure, metal does not grow in a linear course. On the contrary, as the necessary molecular interactions and chemical reactions occur over time, metal forms in clumps and reservoirs, in seams and tendrils that meet and merge. Sometimes these interactions can even occur at the scale of human ocular observation, but at the granular scale, these swarms of activity are omnipresent. Somewhat ironically, despite the value invested in metal's isotropic qualities by plantocratic industrialism, they are not based on constancy but rather emerge from a lattice of inconsistencies that permeates their molecular structure. Local consistencies within metallic crystallization are constantly interrupted by collisions with other pockets of emerging nucleation. Thus, a metal with both an outwardly consistent luster and a microscopically consistent crystalline structure is characterized on the intervening granular scales by unpredictable ruptures and sutures of colliding vectors of ongoing crystallization.

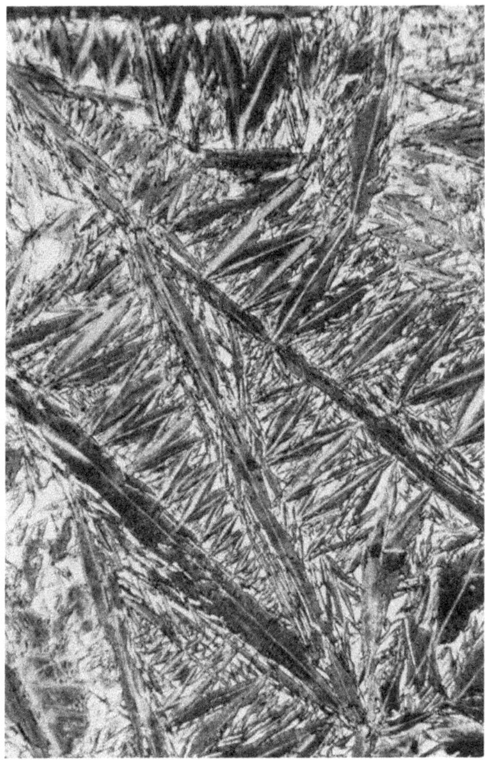

Fig. 27 This panel shows the growth of metallic crystals, with locally uniform pockets of growth interrupted and distorted by one another (reproduced from Smith 1981: 61).

Even when smelted and cast—long before any further deformation or manipulation—these metals already contain within them vast corporeal archives of their uniquely individual molecular reconstitution within the ores in which they previously pooled. Like snowflakes, metals coalesce in endlessly diverse variations. These granular singularities differentiate not only various methods of smelting and alloying, but also varying personalities of ostensibly identical metal alloys. For at this granular scale, these minute variations map complex topographies, each with their own predispositions towards persistence, deformation, erosion, or corrosion. In their subsequent utilitarian deployment, these predispositions will only be amplified by the stress under which these metals are placed.

As noted in previous chapters, metal's value derives chiefly from its unique marriage of resilience and ductility. Iron and brass became so highly prized largely because these two discrete properties could be isolated and optimized under replicable working conditions. Whereas iron and brass both become malleable under direct application of heat, iron will lose its ductility as soon as it cools. Brass, though, undergoes a more complex metamorphosis, retaining a molecular memory of that heat, which has the effect of maintaining malleability even when cooled. When annealed, brass's deformed and dislocated crystalline fragments are sutured together in increasingly symmetrical grains. The ruptures from previous iterations of deformation are absorbed into new vectors of crystalline growth, never perfectly aligned but coalescing around collaborative pockets of relative regularity. Persisting even once the brass is cooled, these reconstituted grains of larger, more symmetrical crystalline clusters render the brass ductile, malleable, and compliant after being annealed. However, as soon as the brass is addressed again—whether rolled or bent or machined, etc.—those grains will fracture once more, layering new inscriptions of fragmentation alongside the scars from previous dislocations.

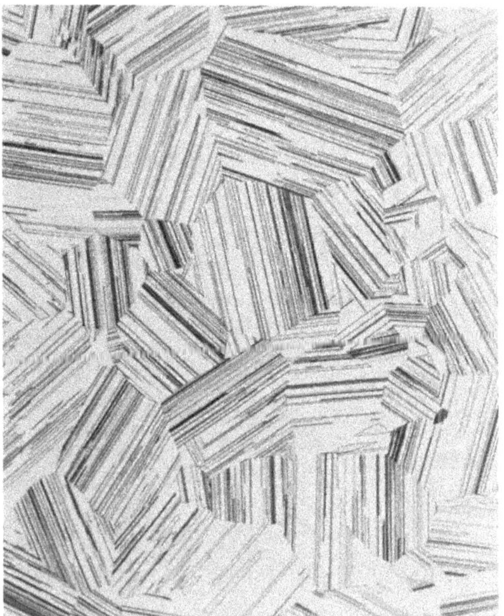

Fig. 28 This panel shows a piece of annealed brass with larger accumulations of crystalline growth coalescing in increasingly (though never wholly) symmetrical grains (reproduced from Smith 1981: 61).

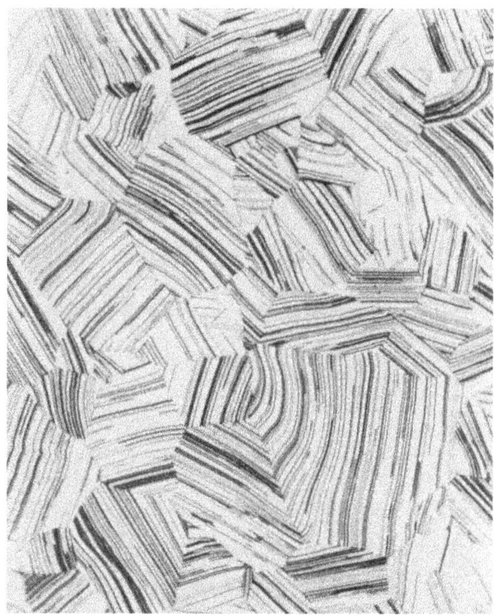

Fig. 29 This panel shows the same piece of brass after cold rolling, as the larger grains are fractured along unpredictable fault lines of previous sutures and ruptures, collapsing into irregular grains of varying size, composition, and regularity (reproduced from Smith 1981: 61).

It is tempting to idealize these inscriptions as a form of archive, but this cold, deformed metal is not merely an archive, and nor do its traces gain valence solely by virtue of some perceived legibility to an outside or human observer. It is, rather, an agency (or collection of agencies) with a corporeal capacity to document its accumulated de- and recomposition(s), an internal record that can testify to the convoluted, emergent processes by which it maintains its superficial unity through an ongoing flow of friction, fragmentation, and fusion. These traces distort one another over time, rendering each inscription a record not only of its past, but also of the ongoing internal revisions etched by its interactions alongside other jostling dislocations and nucleations within its unfolding metallic lattice. These are not simply material memories; they are stubbornly emergent actors within an endlessly evolving field of homeostatic persistence.

It is perhaps this evocation of exhaustion and interminability that prompted Cyril Stanley Smith to turn to author Jorge Luis Borges' character Funes the Memorious when he formulated the term "funicity" to describe this phenomenon of material memory (Smith 1981: 378). In Borges' story, when the poor village boy Ireneo Funes falls from a horse and hurts his head, he thereafter remembers everything in perfect detail. The entire world is preserved in his memory, a cascade of one-to-one relationships and recollections in which he drowns, unable—Borges suggests—to process the ever growing torrent of memories that overwhelm him (Borges 1962). As we see in the histories of metal here, which stretch through eons of sedimentation and compression before arriving in our present day through the crucible of (human induced) rapid and aggressive molecular transmutation, the memorious qualities of material funicity are diametrically opposed to the genre of the archive. These involuntary accumulations of responsivity have nothing to do with any tendency toward collecting, nor even towards the urge to decipher what has been collected, for decipherment requires a critical distance that Funes—trapped within his endless cascade of re/forming memories—can never find. Even when he attempts, for example, to recreate the entire string of memories from a previous day (so as to generate that critical distance), he succeeds only in producing another string of new memories with the same order and duration, a repetition in name, but one consumed by "an eternity opposed to permanence[, i]n every respect, [...] a transgression" (Deleuze 1968/1994: 3). The isotropic regularity of funeous materials is a superficial gloss of their turbulent homeostasis, emerging through a haze of minor fluctuations, sketching the outlines of a memory that roils onwards underneath the fog. The collector or archivist thrives on encompassing that cloudy outline of reality in an infrastructure of documentation, thereby interpreting the world through that tangible record. Funicity, in contrast, articulates something altogether different: the material capacity to bridge disparate scales of time and metastable states of matter through a corporeal recollection of endlessly varied tactile entanglements, which together constitute an incomprehensibly diverging vocabulary of the world's material persistence.

Smith developed this terminology in part to resist institutional demands that knowledge be articulated through mathematical reduction, burying the world beneath the blurry outlines of its statistical averages and trends. Echoing the Pythagorean turn towards reduction and opacity, the hard sciences of Smith's mid-twentieth-century contemporaries funneled their theoretical and practical energies into discourses designed to distill the world into its most simplified model, driven by the vision of a computational understanding of the universe and all it contains. Smith—writing at the outset of a systematic approach to material studies—critiques this statistical approach, noting that by reducing empirical data to averages, these disciplines "achieve their exactness by the elimination of funeous aspects of the world" (Smith 1981: 378). He contends that "[t]he whole story of man's relation to materials involves the interaction between the simple and the complex, with all of the triumphs of science [...] being [...] atomistic (or at least simplistic) and all of the realities of matter being complex" (Smith 1981: 124). This ascetic drive to reduce nature to its underlying trends belies the messy interactivity of the world around us, especially at the scale of our everyday experience as humans, at which scale "structures built of chemical atoms have achieved something like the maximum significant degree of funicity" (Smith 1981: 378). For Smith, this 'significant' degree of funicity describes a saturation of multiple variables, a complexity at the heart of even simple isotropic metals that belies the often linear, stable mathematical equations that undergird contemporary science. From Smith's perspective, the diversity and variety within each genre of material (including but not limited to animate and organic material) can push us to build systems of knowledge that reflect and embrace those gradations within the rough balance of the trends they outline, a "science of materials as distinct from matter" (Smith 1981: 122). As Smith notes, a "structure that exists at any given moment is funeous, the product and record of past associations and interactions, and [thereby also] the framework within which future changes must commence" (Smith 1981: 389). In contrast to hard scientific models that leverage reduction (or purification) in order to construct a simplified model of the world, a funeous approach starts from the world as its own best model (Brooks 1987) and builds an understanding of that world through our situatedness within it. For while "simple things matching the mathematics can be made in practice, [...] most things that human beings deal with are complex systems that are the result of a long succession of single events, recorded in the emergent structure but [which] in combination are essentially uncomputable" (Smith 1981: 124). Generations after the Pythagorean turn to reduction and simplicity, the contemporary hard sciences continue to replicate their logic, as though the complexity of the world could be reshaped to match the linear map they project onto the endlessly variable topography of reality.[1]

By contrast, Smith asserts that "[a]nything complex *must* have had a history, a sequence of changes in its parts. A complex structure is a result of, and to a large extent a record of, its past" (1981: 69). Funicity describes this continual emergence of "historical diversity" through which material elements of the world "pass through a period of explorative contacts and [a] gradual adjustment and locking in of the slow responses with the fast ones" (Smith 1981: 378). Funeous time is not a container in which some things end up having happened and others don't, but rather a material that stretches and interacts, a "sequence [of] structural inertia" (Smith 1981: 378). It articulates an envelope of time and space in which the present moment is nested within multiscalar histories and ongoing evolutions, each transient instantiation a complex knot threaded through with accumulating spatiotemporal narratives. As this sense of time unspools through the tactile, haptic entanglement of the materials that weave it, a material understanding of the world emerges that decenters information (as a metonym for the reduction of the world to its average) and reconstitutes around interactivity. In attesting to the web of complexities by which materials iteratively (re) enact and (re)assert their capacity for endless variation, a funeous understanding of materiality acknowledges that time is shaped by "resonant interaction between the units that affects their being," itself a form of "communication involv[ing] both emanation and absorption" (Smith 1981: 388-389).

However, as the travails of Ireneo Funes remind us, these twisted threads of emanation and absorption are messy, convoluted, and—if traced through the echoes of their extraction from former ecosystems—even violent. The term funicity remains rooted in the onslaught of memory to which Funes succumbed, an eternal escalation of traces that elude archival encapsulation as they explode comprehension. And much like every other aspect of a funeous world, this explosion remains literal, resonating in the world it reshapes, reforms, and, in some way or another, stitches back together. Funicity doesn't demarcate a form of knowledge

1 For a much more detailed account of Smith's terminology and its relationship to traditional scientific practice and discourse, see DeLanda 2004, which deals almost exclusively with this topic.

production that stands aloof from the world, offering merely alternative modes of disaffected observation or cold analysis. Funicity evokes instead unfolding knowledge making practices that embrace complicity within the choreographies of rupture and suture that saturate funeous materiality—in all its irrecuperable lack and ongoing mutilation. Although it evokes some of the same qualities of situated emergence characterized by place-thought (as outlined in Chapter 2), as the violent ontogenies of the brass in this study demonstrate, funicity also incorporates narratives around disruption, disorientation, and displacement. Funeous materials resist a conceptualization of directional history in which the past consists of discrete, isolable events or actors, each of which can be individually cited, remembered, or interpreted from a critical distance outside the ongoing emergence of their intervention. Their funicity embodies instead a far more complicated understanding of history in which memory is inescapable but irretrievable, unfathomably consequential but unfixed, ephemeral, and entangled.

Funeous materials have an ambivalent relationship to rupture and suture, especially materials such as the brass in the instruments that occupy this study. Having been disciplined through industrial extraction and refining, the mutilations that produced those scars continue to reverberate in the tubes and bells of these chimeracords even as they continue to reproduce the isotropic purity for which their component brass is so highly prized. This ambivalence recalls the growing discourse around the concept of dehiscence, which has emerged primarily in relation to Black cultural memory in the wake of the Middle Passage and the Atlantic slave trade. However, unlike the term funicity (which was invented wholesale by Smith in reference to a recent work of fiction), dehiscence enters the cultural lexicon with a far more tangled semantic lineage:

> First, *wound dehiscence* is a surgical complication in which a wound comes apart at the site of its surgical sutures—flesh that opens up at the seams, along the fault lines of the discourses that would seek to keep it sanitized and under wraps: a wounding history that refuses its sutures—refuses silencing. The second biological meaning of dehiscence is one of generative potentiality: that of the rupture of a female's ovarian follicle in the process of ovulation. This ambivalence of signification animates a sense of wounded flesh, and, simultaneously, of pregnant flesh: a fleshy register of violence as the wound that refuses to heal, and also a rupture of generative potentiality in the reproductive cellular kernel of flesh. (Danylevich 2016: 4)

Though initially borrowed by critic and theorist Jared Sexton (2011) from psychoanalyst Jacques Lacan's discussion of "the internal splitting of the subject by the imposition of language and the abolition of access [to] a real relation to being," this term has reopened and absorbed complicated elements of Black spatiotemporal memory within a web of ongoing rupture and suture, both impossibly scarred and implacably fertile: "that wounded, disseminative vertigo that is blackness" (Sexton 2017: n.p.). It echoes the "disquieting lacunae" (Spillers 1987: 73) that literary critic, scholar, and author Hortense Spillers describes seeping from the "lacerations, woundings, fissures, tears, scars, openings, ruptures, lesions, rendings, punctures of the flesh" (Spillers 1987: 67) inscribed in the corporeality and consciousness of the bodies displaced by colonial, imperial, capitalist appetite. This "dehiscent anteriority" (Bradley 2023: 17) constitutes a recursively "metonymic rend(er)ing of flesh" (Bradley 2023: 46), braiding materiality and memory into the bodies that both carry and transmit to future generations the countless iterations of care and community that already flow into its potent "(ante)metaphysical" generativity (Bradley 2023: 18). "These undecipherable markings on the captive body render a kind of hieroglyphics of the flesh[, a] phenomenon of marking and branding [that] actually 'transfers' from one generation to another" (Spillers 1987: 67).

Like funicity, dehiscence embodies a corporeal connection to multiple, nested scales of time. The dehiscent wound is threaded through both the timeframe of fissure as well as that of fusion, absorbing the material ontogeny of the apparatuses that rend as well as those that suture. And similarly, as with material funicity, dehiscence resists reduction: the dehiscent wound is not a portal; it is not some type of retina through which the archive of captivity or suffering is prismatically diffracted towards a reparative future. It offers neither cleansing pain nor healing transcendence. These material-corporeal traces resist the totalizing gaze of retrospective contextualization, instead migrating with—and within—the bodies that carry them, shifting and adapting to the ebbs and flows of ongoing rupture and suture that congeal in their ongoing responsivity. The scar simultaneously occupies multiple scales of time, undergoing an uninterrupted perforation even as it reseals, regrows, or even reproduces. Both funicity and dehiscence articulate qualities more complex than simple material memories or body archives; they outline the reality of remembrance stitched into shifting, living flesh, of a corporeal materiality steeped in the granular recursivity of an actively unfolding history. The boundaries of these dehiscent grains are elusive, stitched into the spacetime of evolving bodies in metamorphosis. They invoke a history even as they resist the possibility of a critical distance that a demarcation of 'past' implies. Far from a neatly encapsulated envelope of legible traces, dehiscence sutures localized particularity to the tectonic ruptures in their larger topographical emergence.

However, as Spillers asserts, that topographical presence is far from straightforward, for the lacunae so painstakingly retained within dehiscence intone a deep and reverberant "cultural *vestibularity*" (Spillers 1987: 67). Despite their intimate relation to the radiating scales of space and time that suffuse and emerge from them, the lacerations that inscribe this form of dehiscence occupy "spaces of confinement within colonial geographies, spaces constituted on the margins of Western 'democracy'" (Martineau and Ritskes 2014: IV), or in Sylvia Wynter's formulation, a "marginal archipelago" (Wynter n.d.: 447). As a vestibular antechamber to history, to cartography, and to cultural and political reality, dehiscent spacetime shimmers just outside the essentializing gaze of Western cultural values. Neither inside the infrastructure of the plantation nor outside the influence of colonial extraction, dehiscent vestibularity persists instead in a space simultaneously contained and unassimilable by Western capitalist hegemony, a tumorous resistance to the "*culture*" in which it finds itself embedded, "whose state apparatus [...] colludes with a protocol of 'search and destroy'" (Spillers 1987: 67). The very real physical violence inflicted by this apparatus of destruction was and is continually enacted by a cultural infrastructure that defines Black flesh as a negative ground, "the essence of stillness[,...] an undynamic human state, fixed in time and space" (Spillers 1987: 78). In order to render whiteness as "the constitution of the Normal by and through the constitution of the prescribed deviant" (Wynter n.d.: 660-661), blackness must be absorbed into an apparatus of distortion, the necessary condition for "a cultural text whose inside has been turned outside" (Spillers 1987: 67). Critic, researcher, and geographer Katherine McKittrick observes how, in occupying this paradoxical niche as a "fertile commodity of exchange," the Black body, and in particular the Black female body, inhabits a "material landscape, at work, in the home, and within the community, where the body is rightfully retranslated as inferior, captive, and accessible to violences" (McKittrick 2006: 82).

In theorizing the "*insurgent* ground" (Spillers 1987: 80) in which resistance to this destructive apparatus can germinate, the specifically *cultural* components of Spillers' vestibule merit particular scrutiny. Despite the gruesome material and corporeal machinations that carve it into existence, this dehiscent space contains traces of cultures and histories that can never be severed or assimilated by the discursive regimes of slavery or the plantation. In her influential reading of the "wake" and its many linguistic and material guises (from the wake of the ships such as those in the Middle Passage, to a wakeful state of consciousness, to communal observances besides the bodies of the dead in "grief, celebration, [and ...] memory" [Sharpe 2016: 11]), author and scholar Christina Sharpe proposes "a method of encountering a past that is not past. A method along the lines of a sitting with, a gathering, and a tracking of phenomena that disproportionately and devastatingly affect Black peoples" (Sharpe 2016: 13). In articulating how the spatiotemporal ripples of the Middle Passage continue to reverberate, Sharpe's conception of the wake proposes an "*anagrammatical blackness* that exists as an index of violability and also potentiality" (2016: 75). The traces of material and cultural memory that persist in the dehiscent vestibularity of the wake also hold the power to reshape their ongoing echoes in subsequent generations. In responding to and building upon Sharpe's efforts to "descriptively model both the ongoing effects of slavery and the aesthetic practices black people have developed in response to those effects" (James 2019: 115-116), film and media critic Rizvana Bradley introduces the neologism "anteasthetics" as a means to "to think with the aesthesis of a black existence that is before the metaphysics of the antiblack world and the representational regime which endeavors to secure and sustain this metaphysics" (2019: 9). Bradley attunes our attention to the echoes of a cultural vestibularity outside—and antecedent to—the plantation and the disciplining grasp of its colonialist, extractionist infrastructure of oppression:

> My conception of *before*—signaled [...] by the prefix *ante*—assumes a dual spatiotemporal valence. Black aesthesis is at once vestibular to the antiblack world—its metaphysical threshold and abyssal limit—and always already subject to the violence of that world, even if not

> reducible to or completely subsumed by it. *Before* names an interminable recursivity. *Anteaesthetics* asks after a constellation of experimentations and inhabitations that emerge before the antiblack world, as that world's condition of possibility and inexpungible mar. (Bradley 2023: 2)

This *before* suffuses the spacetime of the vestibule, bonding with these ongoing 'experimentations and inhabitations' through which its irreducible irreality persists in the material and corporeal antiblack world into which it has been transposed. It both introduces and sustains a sense of *ante* that makes possible alternative imaginations of what these modalities of remembrance might spark, enact, or cultivate. This dehiscent vestibularity occupies marginal pockets of spacetime irreducible to the discursive reality in the external antiblack world, antechambers of an alternative reality in which this *before* provokes conceptions of time and space equally inexpressible within the code of plantation logic. In noting how "the subjective [experience] of space turns it into an infinite series of authorships [...] wherein speaking subjects both define it and are defined by it" (Spillers 2004: 535), Spillers helps indicate how this *ante*-spacetime bonds with imaginations of the present to articulate alternative visions of the future. In insisting that this vestibularity is *cultural* just as the extractive disciplinary infrastructures that define its discursive boundaries are, she helps reveal a communal narrativity that pervades the material-corporeality of dehiscence. By introducing elements of space and time that evade the grasping control of the plantation gaze, *ante* makes possible further evasions within that system. The *before* threaded through the dehiscent present enables this vestibular *ante*chamber to foment imaginations of reality that embrace creative dimensions beyond the constrictive logic of extractive capitalism.

Occupying a register beyond the scope of the plantation's modes of classification, objectification, and subjection, this vestibular *ante*chamber accesses modalities of space and time incompatible with the imaginative capacity of plantation logic. This contradictory existence straddles the strictures of captivity and the irreducible narrative creativity of a vestibularity stubbornly irresolvable within that system, posing a "problematic encounter that both exceeds the map and remains representable by it" (Spillers 2004: 535). And indeed, these registers of irreality are in fact legible on capitalist cartographies, a palimpsestuous haze floating at the edge of the plantation's silhouette. Because of the plantation's reliance on monocrop production, the plantation landscape is riddled with pockets of irredeemable land: terrain too rocky or too hilly or too watery or simply too time-consuming to subdue. The quadratic ideal of plantation land—in all its denuded, flattened glory—is flanked not only by oceans and mountains, but is also peppered with isolated tracts of irrecuperable tracts of land, vestibular shards scattered across an otherwise neatly trussed up terrain. This archipelago of irreducible vestibularities hovers ephemerally at the frayed edges of plantation reality, providing the soil in which the '*insurgent* ground' of resistance takes root.

Enslaved peoples themselves were the conduit between the wilderness of the landscape and the plantation erected upon its clear-cut remains. The white settlers of the plantation class envisioned the transformation of this biodiverse land into a conduit for monocrop efficiency as a virtue in and of itself, a form of manifest destiny "explicitly conceived [...] as a war against wilderness" (Malm 2018: 11). But they did not wage that battle against untamed land with their own hands, but rather by channeling the displaced energy of enslaved labor—both indigenous native populations as well as, primarily, displaced and imported native populations from Africa. These planters "saw Africans as extensions of their masters' agency. Their labor magnified the power of a single planter, enabling him to turn overgrown tracts into productive plantation land" (Edelson 2006: 27). However, this also inadvertently placed these enslaved laborers in direct contact with the not-yet-tamed land into which they had been transplanted. As a consequence, "slaves came into engagement with both the wild and cultivated sides of this landscape," and even as planters attempted "to impose a hard line of separation between plantations and wilderness[,]slaves opened and inhabited the spaces in between" (Edelson 2006: 27)—even to the point at which they could "adapt an African pharmacopoeia and sustain spiritual practices with gathered plants" (Edelson 2006: 29). In many cases, these interstitial spaces in between cultivation and wilderness were quite literal: patches of land on the edges of clear-cut plantations that belonged to the plantation in name and by map, but which had more functional kinship with the surrounding wilderness than with the flattened, domesticated tracts of industrial scale cultivation that they abutted.

Although they would become seedbeds of resistance, the vestibular plots were initially valued by planters as means to maximize the efficiency of monocrop cultivation. Loath to devote portions of more valuable land to the sustenance of enslaved labor, these untameable, semi-wild fringe spaces offered an alternative: they could be converted into smaller gardens and plots that the slaves would then cultivate for their own needs. This not only reserved more valuable land for more profitable agriculture, it had the additional benefit of delegating responsibility for the nourishment of slaves even more firmly outside the purview of the planters and overseers. This had unexpected consequences, though, essentially ceding control of particular pockets of land to enslaved Black people, which would ultimately foster the spaces of *cultural* vestibularity capable of reshaping Black collective consciousness. "Those who worked in these wild and semi-wild spaces as slaves exercised a de facto possession over the borderlands at the edges of plantation settlements. Alive with movement and work, this interstice between plantation fields was a space understood, used, and traversed primarily by Africans and African Americans" (Edelson 2006: 29). Although acknowledged and tacitly condoned by planters, these spaces remained stubbornly illegible to them, occupying registers of time and space incomprehensible within plantation parameters:

> Between these fields and at their edges, slaves planted their own crops in tracts their masters recognized but did little to regulate. Under cover of darkness, slaves took to the wilderness to hunt, gather, and attempt to escape their enslavement. [...] Slaves exercised a practical command of liminal spaces [...] in ways their masters could never match nor always control. (Edelson 2006: 31)

Sylvia Wynter identifies these plots as significant markers of both material and cultural agency, repurposing the linguistic double meaning of "plot"—read as both cultivated land and narrative device—to assert the interdependency of these seemingly disparate modes of existence and resistance. She notes that the very existence of these plots subverted the most fundamental tenets of the capitalist plantation system. In its drive to subjugate both land and labor to the dominion of exchange value, these plots seemed to solve multiple problems, from maximizing production on tameable land to invisibilizing the costs and methods of sustaining labor populations. But these plots also "recreated traditional values—use values[, which] became a source of cultural guerilla resistance to the plantation system" (Wynter 1971: 100). This unforeseen vestibular alternate reality "threatened to turn these lands from a slave-controlled plantation hinterland into a staging ground for subversive actions" (Edelson 2006: 29). These subversive actions constituted not only specific acts of revolt or marronage, but also the modes of cultural consciousness that generated the necessary conditions for those more dramatic acts to be conceived, organized, and enacted. Through its interscalar fusion of intergenerational modes of cultural (re)invention and recursive iterations of rebellious agency, Wynter's "plot names places that have been created through improvisational forms of world-making against racial and socioecological domination[, as well as] an insurgent scheme that is staged from peripheralized places and that is crucial to maintaining these spaces of insurgent living" (Moulton 2024: 271).

The narrative mode of cultural production sustained in plotting articulates vestibular spacetimes that "demand[ ] thinking with or toward the unthought[, i]nterrogating the difficult entanglements of race, gender, fleshly reproduction, and the (aesthetic) worlding of forms" (Bradley 2023: 2). It folds the *ante* into the creative activities of survival through which the dehumanization of captivity is resisted and metamorphosed into alternate forms of (ir)reality. It is perhaps worth noting here that in a purely anatomical context, the term vestibularity also refers to a very specific antechamber to the human body, the inner ear, which is responsible for maintaining balance—which is to say, for mediating between different scales and orders of agency internal and external to the homeostatic envelope of the human body. In this context, the term *balance* indicates a locally successful attempt to mediate between the external environment and internal orientations to those stimuli; it absorbs large-scale trajectories of external time and space into locally relevant bodily (inter)actions. The literal and figurative modality of dehiscence reveals the vestibular balancing act between *ante*-spacetime and present or future forms of (re)invention. Wynter's demarcation of the *plot* anchors that dehiscence in the landscapes—and unfolding place-thought—of the displaced, diasporic populations that inhabit and cultivate them. When Spillers refers to a specifically *cultural* vestibularity, she echoes Wynter's insistence that the *plot* sustains a narrative arch from day to day and from generation to generation, providing the cultural stem from which the radiating branches of disparate genres of rebellion sprout. The *plot* absorbs the countless tributaries of anteriority implicated in the rupture and suture of dehiscence, transplanting them into new soils and grafting them into new lineages of cultural agency.

As Wynter routinely emphasizes throughout her vast body of work, the concept of transplantation is essential to conceiving how the *ante* can be threaded through ensuing ruptures and sutures in space and time. Although nominally unadulterated elements of antecedent cultural practices might be preserved or rejuvenated in this new soil, they were not simple grafts, but rather "the creation of a culture of exile, the rerooting of the uprooted, the mutation of an ancient, traditional culture, into a new one" (Wynter n.d.: 54). And just as these *befores* seep into the future through the dehiscent lacerations of the Middle Passage, so does this rerooting also flow backwards in time through the holds of the ships that carried these countless individuals from their communities and landscapes in Africa to the new lands in which they would be "transformed—or, more specifically, converted—[...] into units of labor" (McKittrick 2016: 82). In outlining how this rerooted culture preserved and repurposed its African roots, she reserves special attention for the transformation of kinship systems in the context of abruptly shattered and fragmented families, communities, and peoples. Whereas in traditional African cultures the "individual only had meaning in its relation to the social group and the structures of society [that] were *represented* as kinship structures," the Middle Passage forced the torn and scattered remnants of those kinship structures to regroup in new configurations, through which the category of the "tribal age group therefore metamorphosed" into a new but analogous "social/historical age-group—shipmates" (Wynter n.d.: 839). Just as their discovery of the frontier allowed Western belief systems and legal codes to establish new definitions of what it means to be human by setting white against Black, the trauma of the Middle Passage also triggered inevitable transformations within the African cultural practices and kinship systems that were subjected to the mutilating crucible of the ship's hold. In observing how the invention of the adjective "'Black' is a historical definition, an *event* rather than a fact" (harvested from the soil of the plantation just as the sugar grown and exported there), Wynter asserts that the "substantive form" of this "'Black'" is "'shipmate'" (Wynter n.d.: 67). Well before they set foot on the other side of the Atlantic, the reinvention inherent in transplantation had already commenced; throughout their displacement, relocation, and continually re-fragmented dislocations in their new land, enslaved peoples continued to form new kinship bonds and communal units within and beyond the ship. By reinventing their experience of community through the vestiges of their transplanted cultures, these shipmates could subsequently also invent new, collaborative forms of collective resistance and rebellion. McKittrick clarifies Wynter's careful delineation of the related but distinct elements of these intertwined forms of reinvention and invention:

> [*R*]*einvention* is the process through which enslaved and post-slavery black communities in the New World came to live and construct black humanity within the context of racial violence—a range of rebellious acts that affirmed black humanity and black life were and are imperative to reinvention. *Invention* is meant to signal those cultural practices and texts—marronages, mutinies, funerals, carnivals, dramas, visual arts, fictions, poems, fights, dances, music making and listening, revolts—that emerged alongside reinvented black lives. [...] One cannot reinvent the human without rebellious inventions, and rebellious inventions require reinvented lives. (McKittrick 2016: 81)

Inhabiting the interstitial nowheres unassimilable to the plantation logic, the *plot* provided both the material and immaterial space in which these rebellious re/inventions could flourish. Wynter insists that the most pointed acts of rebellious agency—from mutiny, revolt, or marronage to cultural expressions such as ceremonies, festivals, or simple celebrations—require careful and ongoing cultivation within *plot*-spaces, going so far as to suggest that "the reinvention of a culture was an even more significant part of the black revolt than the occasional physical revolts[, f]or the latter sprang from the seedbed, the ideology, the emotional states of feeling of the former" (Wynter n.d.: 82). In other words, just as "[e]ach escape, each flight was a species of *marronage*, the quest for a free space from where to wage the ongoing process of revolt" (Wynter n.d.: 438), the everyday acts of care and community that plotted the conditions for possibility for these agential ruptures were equally essential acts of revolt, their own genre of "*spiritual* marronage" (Wynter n.d.: 182). As sociologist Alex A. Moulton notes, the *plot* concentrates and mediates between these various modes of ongoing survival and revolt, simultaneously nourishing both the suture of cultural vestibularity and its rebellious rupture by remaining "attentive to how places are practiced, and the futures such practices anticipate" (Moulton 2024: 275). Although they express different genres of agency, Wynter's conceptualization of the *plot* helps to reveal how the act of revolution emerges from non-metaphorical constructions of communal narrative.

As both site and as narrative, Wynter's *plot* exposes the agential capacity of community and culture as evolving expressions of place-thought. Throughout the breadth of her work, Wynter insists on the non-metaphorical reality of both of these strands, rooting practical agency not only in the land that fosters this community but also very firmly and literally in the words, stories, and conversations that sound and reverberate in those vestibules. After considering how the first radical re/inventions of Black life in the New World depended on "communal enterprise [as] a concrete organization of reality in which they could be the creative subjects, rather than the expendable objects of their own destiny" (Wynter n.d.: 189), Wynter's later work articulates ever more systematic conceptions of the practical and material reality of cultural production and the narrative agency it wields. She borrows and coins several key terms with which to describe this agency, all of which revolve around the relationship between storytelling and biology, constructing a meticulous, comprehensive, and astonishingly interdisciplinary system of thought relating human evolution and survival to the human capacity for narrative self-conception—or rather, as becomes apparent through her developing body of work, self-actualization. Over decades of sustained engagement, Wynter argues that these storytelling capacities are not an addendum to human history, culture, or evolution, but are rather fundamental pillars supporting and influencing human existence since storytelling began, comprising a "science of the Word" (Wynter 2015a: 17) that can complement—rather than merely supplement—other (hard) scientific disciplines.

Wynter borrows this phrase from poet Aimé Césaire's "Poetry and Knowledge," an essay published in 1945 and delivered as a talk in Haiti in 1946 (Césaire 1945), in which he "proposed that as brilliant as the feats of the natural sciences are, they themselves are half starved—because they cannot deal with our human predicament" (Wynter 2015a: 17). To help alleviate these deficiencies, Césaire "puts forth the idea of a new science, a hybrid science: a science of the Word[,]in which the study of the Word (the *mythoi*) will condition the study of nature (the *bios*)" (Wynter 2015a: 17-18). As Césaire himself phrases it, "the study of the word will condition the study of nature" (Césaire 1990: xlix), mediating which aspects of our physical understanding of the universe might come to generate meaningful difference in the world. For Césaire, the word—and the poet who wields it—is a tool for revealing and—consequently—shaping humanity's deeper relationship to their environment: "Within us, all the ages of mankind. Within us, all humankind. Within us, animal, vegetable, mineral. Mankind is not only mankind. It is *universe*" (Césaire 1990: xlviii). In suggesting that the poet is therefore "pregnant with the world" (Césaire 1990: xlix), he envisions an application of the word as a means not of describing or analyzing the world, but of bringing it into existence in the first place, of shaping the perceptions and interactions and entanglements that determine which material and fleshly valences will come to matter—and which will not.

In according the poet's voice an elemental power as "primal word: cave art in the matter of sound" (Césaire 1945: 164, translation mine), Césaire conceives of narrativity as an antecedent creative energy rather than as a retrospective interpretive hermeneutic. In this telling, the story is an active agent in the world's becoming, evolving with and shaping the world it describes, more driving force than documentation. Echoing Césaire, Wynter also invokes a primeval cosmology at the heart of her science of the Word, noting that the eusocial elements of human society are ingrained in and by origin myths and other cosmological belief systems. The biological development of the human brain rewards the initiatory and explanatory power of these belief systems which in turn shape the communities and societies that produce those cosmologies, continuing then to influence how they affect the world they encounter. In other words, humans evolved to produce societies constructed by narrative explanations of the world, and the ways in which those understandings developed over time influenced not only humans but also the environments that they contributed to shaping. Wynter assigns special significance to the development of narrative agency as an amplifier and mediator of other material and biological agencies and, subsequently, asserts its emergence as a unique turning point in the history of the world, which she refers to as the Third Event:

> The First and Second Events are the origin of the universe and the explosion of all forms of biological life, respectively. I identify the Third Event [...] as the origin of the human as a

> hybrid-auto-instituting-languaging-storytelling species: *bios / mythoi*. The Third Event is defined by the singularity of the *co-evolution* of the human brain *with* [...] the emergent faculties of language, storytelling. (Wynter 2015a: 25)

Wynter grounds her conception of a science of the Word in "Fanon's redefinition of being human as that of skins (phylogeny / ontogeny) *and* masks (sociogeny)" (Wynter 2015a: 23). Wynter suggests that, as a species of social animal whose relation to and survival in the world is shaped by their narrative explanations for (and thereby also navigation of) their environment, human existence cannot be explained in purely phylogenic or ontogenic terms, but must necessarily include a sociogenic component inextricably threaded through these other material-corporeal realities. Critically, she does not treat this sociogenic agency as a separate layer of human activity sedimented on top of its biological existence, but rather takes special care to note the how sociogenic components of human society enter a feedback loop of mutual influence with other biological, organic, and material facets of the entire environment, including not only the human body or human society but also the wider world in which they are embedded. This is to say, then, that human societies are formed around specific cosmological conceptions of the world (whether religious or otherwise) and that, by shaping those human groups' understanding of the world and the role they play in it, these narrative constructions affect the ongoing evolution of those humans, of their communities and cultures, and of the environments that are in turn touched by them.

Although Wynter has devoted a great deal of attention to archaeological evidence from early human societies and the role of storytelling in their evolution, survival, and spread, perhaps the most compelling example of a cosmology's agency in shaping reality lies far closer to the present day, in the post-1492 world and the affective repercussions of settler colonial belief systems. Wynter describes what she calls the overrepresentation of white Western man as the generalized natural state of humankind, which began as a religious concept (referred to in Wynter's work as Man1) before morphing into an economic one (Man2). In both cases, the specific explanations of the universe that influenced very localized Western cultural practices generated unfathomably consequential ripples in other human societies and ecologies. As this book has already examined from numerous perspectives, the normative definitions (e.g., of Christian and savage, of white and Black, of civilization and frontier, of purity and impurity, etc.) that Western culture established have irrevocably altered existence for every entity on this planet, whether human or material, organic or inorganic. Wynter turns our attention to the fact that these affective repercussions emerged not from some specifically biological or evolutionary imperative, but rather from the way in which the narrative mythologies of a specific belief system (in this case, at first primarily religious and then later economic) intertwined with the material world to radically alter its course.

As this example helps to show, the types of narrative agency that Wynter's science of the Word engages do not simply intervene in the course of material, organic, or human history. Their agency takes far more active forms, curating certain possibilities while foreclosing others—not only effecting what is possible but then also continuing to amplify or mediate those trajectories as ongoing actors within the full scope of reality. Storytelling holds the capacity to provoke these large-scale, generation-spanning cultural forces, completely reshaping the lands, ecologies, and societies that it encounters. And while the discussion of Indigenous relations to place in Chapter 2 demonstrated how these narrative agencies can unfold in closer collaboration with nonhuman entities, the history of plantation capitalism reveals the inverted underbelly of this capacity, in which the evolution of a storytelling agency can consume whole cultures and ecologies in its endless appetite for self-perpetuation. Wynter's science of the Word gives us the language with which to understand the power of these storytelling agencies, as well as to recognize the thin membrane that separates their cultural interpretations of reality from the physical materialization of the world itself. It shows how one story might be punctured and devoured or how another story might swallow the world whole, digesting entire other cultures in the toxic acid of its narrative self-perpetuation.

Within the rich and complex tapestry of her idiosyncratic terminology, Wynter also borrows conceptual tools from the discipline of biology to help understand the simultaneous ephemerality and violence that these narrative agencies possess. In the 1970s, biologists Humberto Maturana and Francisco J. Varela introduced the concept of *autopoiesis* to elucidate the complex mechanisms by which homeostatic organic entities maintain the closed system of their biological function while still renewing and assimilating new material over time. Like the ancient paradox of the ship of Theseus, whose every component is slowly replaced while never losing its shape or function, autopoiesis describes an entity's ability to maintain its unity over time even as it sheds, gains, and metabolizes within a broader environmental context. Autopoiesis reconciles the concept of a fixed entity's definable boundaries with the ceaselessly roiling dynamism of the world in which it is embedded. It proposes a relational understanding of material and energy, defining the fixed boundaries of more or less 'stable' entities through the energetic activities by which they maintain their homeostasis, rather than through localized distinguishing properties that they exhibit at one time or another. For Maturana and Varela, a biological unit would best be defined not by its boundaries or a particular set of static attributes, but by the degree to which (and the conditions under which) it is capable of maintaining its dynamic and self-perpetuating homeostasis, a balancing act simultaneously "both bounded and infinite" (Maturana 1970: 23). Everything from the organization of a single cell to the development of self-consciousness could then be understood along a spectrum of dynamic orientations within the constraints of a metabolism and its environmental affordances.

For Maturana and Varela, the agency demonstrated by the metabolizing unit is a key component of autopoiesis. The word itself derives from the term *poiesis*, which in ancient Greek indicated a concept of making somewhere in between craft and artistry, and which was used to describe activities as wide-ranging as artisanship and legislation. For the Greeks, *poiesis* was a process rather than a concrete act—"the experience of production into presence" (Agamben 1994: 42)—and it involved a synthesis of order and inspiration, an expression of rules through their transformation in execution. As such, it provides a remarkably suitable foundation for the concept of agency that Maturana and Varela were revealing in biological units, an agency deriving primarily from a capacity for responsivity. For Maturana and Varela, autopoiesis describes the mediation of multiple scales of temporal and spatial stimuli into a potentially predictable but nonetheless unique pathway towards self-preservation (Maturana and Varela 1980). In the language of dehiscence, autopoiesis describes the capacity to metabolize environmental stimuli in such a way as to navigate a complex web of interscalar spatiotemporal ruptures and sutures that ultimately supports the ongoing emergence of homeostatic stability. It is a genre of unity that stitches together the past and the future through a reiterative and reactive metabolism.

Echoing Maturana's own application of autopoiesis to larger scales of social activity (Maturana 1980: xxiv-xxx), Wynter deploys the term as a means to articulate how storytelling acts as a medium of metabolization, dissolving human perception of the world in origin myths and belief systems that then reconstitute societies' engagement within their environment around their drive for self-preservation. This mode of self-(re)generation—expressed at (eu)social scales—is key to understanding Wynter's science of the Word. Autopoietic auto-institution at the scale of the human species is dependent on the role of the Word in mediating the various scales and orders of im/material stimuli that must be metabolized. For Wynter, the reflective and responsive components of humans' discursive relation to the world enable an entirely new order of existence. "[H]uman orders of representation enable us to *live* and actualize the conceptions of being human, and therefore to be *conscious* of [and] to *experience* being in their [...] terms, only because of our capacity to turn theory into flesh" (Wynter 2000: 40). Recognizing how the Word collaborates with its material-organic environment to mediate and even completely metamorphose reality, Wynter applies the self-(re) generative capacity of autopoiesis as a tool to analyze human activity at the scale of cultural and social creativity, ultimately proposing a theory of the human as a chimerical hybrid fusion of word and nature. As anthropologist Zimitri Erasmus notes:

> Stretched to its farthest meaning, her proposal for a 'new science' can be read as a way of knowing—not only the human, but life—which postulates that human, animal, and organic life-systems co-create the world. [...] This tapestry leads to her second innovation: a conception of the human as a hybrid being: both biological/organic and symbolic/myth-making. [...] It allows her to delink from the accepted truth produced by Eurocentric evolutionary science: that organic and human life proceed in linear, hierarchical and increasingly complex fashion through hereditary processes that involve predetermined biological properties. [...] Wynter's Third Emergence, her 'human as hybrid' and

> her critique of Eurocentric knowledge allow for a counter-mode of coming to know that troubles the racialized premises of this knowledge and facilitates a non-anthropocentric conception of the human as part of discontinuous but interrelated processes that engender various modes of life. (Erasmus 2020: 52)

Wynter's assertion of the human as hybrid insists that the sciences of nature and Word—the *bios* and the *mythoi*—are materially intertwined and co-extensive. The versions of reality that humans collectively weave through autopoietic cultural activity are narrative agency "alchemically *made flesh*!" (Wynter 2015a: 27). Our self-understanding as biological beings (particularly in contemporary hard scientific terms) is itself a reiterative construction of particular belief systems made flesh, for ultimately "*we humans cannot pre-exist our cosmogonies or origin myths/ stories/narratives* anymore than a bee, at the purely biological level of life, can pre-exist its beehive" (Wynter 2015b: 213):

> Our *mythoi*, our origin stories, are therefore always formulaically patterned so as to co-function with the endogenous neurochemical behavior regulatory system of our human brain. Humans are, then, a biomutationally evolved, hybrid species—*storytellers who now storytellingly invent themselves as being purely biological.* (McKittrick 2015: 11)

Wynter names this hybrid form of humanity *homo narrans*, inextricably binding the concept of the human with its narrative self-actualization. *Homo narrans* articulates a dynamic, metabolistic entanglement of story and flesh, in which to be human is to be always and ever immersed in an unending stream of participatory self-re/generation. As with the rest of her process-based philosophy, in which her "ideas are, in a sense, invariably verbs, encoded with active thought processes grappling with the magma of far-reaching challenges" (McKittrick 2015: 7), the hybridity that Wynter identifies suggests that ultimately "with being human *everything is praxis*" (Wynter 2015a: 33). Recognizing that there is invariably an autopoietic agency active at all times, Wynter urges us to realize there is nothing inevitable about the current hegemonic overrepresentation of Western (religious or economic) belief systems. Instead, she highlights how *homo narrans* offers what philosopher, political theorist, and author Bedour Alagraa calls "a genre of the human that renders possible human freedom via our storytelling capacity" (Alagraa 2018: 164), directing our attention towards our capacity for change. She presents the figure of *homo narrans* as a current of potential energy, through which collective cultural agency might wrest the world free from the overrepresentation of capitalist hegemony and redirect it towards other genres of the human, of life, and of collaborative world-building within and alongside the in/organic environment.

With *homo narrans*, Wynter helps render audible voices from within the *plot*. *Homo narrans* animates the spatiotemporal bubble of the plot with a murmuring vivacity, re/telling stories whose circulation invigorates the generation-spanning activity of cultural re/invention. By demystifying the autopoietic agency of *homo narrans*, Wynter helps reveal precisely how and why the physical and temporal reality of the *plot* is so critical to sustaining the interlocking genres of resistance that are collectively sustained by its metabolistic re/production of community. Wynter's conceptualization of autopoiesis and *homo narrans* underline what her theory of plotting already addressed, namely, that remembrance and resistance are inextricably intertwined through the re/generative enactment of cultural agency. Within the dehiscent space of cultural vestibularity, Wynter identifies how ongoing cultural activities of autopoietic self-re/generation sow the seeds of resistance that then bear fruit in the acts of mutiny, marronage, and revolt that capture historical imagination. Although Wynter would eventually knit her calls to cultural agency together in a manifesto for the "Ceremony Found" and its "new and *ecumenically human* response to the question of who-we-are" (Wynter 2015b: 193), evocations of the viscous spatiotemporal experience of ceremony permeate her discussions of cultural agency throughout her body of work. From her earliest published works, she makes abundantly clear that cultural activity is embedded in and participating in its surrounding reality. She insists that cultural expression has real-life agency, and that the time and space cultural creativity occupies is not coincidental but rather fundamental to people's capacity to react to the world around them.

> [I]n traumatic times like ours, when reality itself is so distorted as to have become impossible and abnormal, it is the function of all culture, partaking of this abnormality, to be aware of its own sickness. To be aware of the unreality of the inauthenticity of the so called real, is to *reinterpret* this reality. To *reinterpret* this reality is to commit oneself to a constant revolutionary assault against it. [...T]he play, the novel, the poem, the critical essay, are means to this end—not ends in themselves.

> Yet they are means which are at one and the same time, self-contained cells, and part of a dynamic living process. (Wynter 1968: 24)

Fittingly, this essay's title—part of a two-part series with the same name—proposes that "We Must Learn to Sit Down Together and Talk about a Little Culture" (Wynter 1968; Wynter 1969). For Wynter, there is no culture except that which takes up time and space in the quotidian reality that sustains it, whether that be the time it takes to write and read a novel or the space of the table around which we sit to discuss it. Her next published essay, "Jonkonnu in Jamaica" (Wynter 1970), takes a dramatic turn away from conventional criticism and instead embraces folk culture as a window into the agential potential of reiterative cultural traditions. Drawing in part on her own experiences as a professional dancer, Wynter embraced the embodied experience of folk culture as a means "to think about how and why [J]onkunno might give us an understanding of how [A]fricans in the [N]ew World wielded the cultural deposits of their old world to transform this 'new' space in which they found themselves" (Alagraa 2022: n.p.). This approach would inform ensuing work on her ambitious and still unpublished monograph *Black Metamorphosis: New Natives in a New World*, in which she comprehensively demonstrates how folk art forms from Jonkonnu masquerade through to "[w]ork songs, spirituals, blues, jazz, were the counter-poetics native and indigenous to the American continent, subterraneanly subversive of its surface reality" (Wynter n.d.: 218).

This is not to suggest that folk art is merely "some sort of primordially authentic experience or aesthetic mediation" (Alagraa 2019: 189), but rather to reveal how it opens up experiences of space and time that quite literally do not fit into the discursive code of the dominant culture. Wynter describes how these art forms can introduce "a concept of time which is heretical" (Wynter, n.d.: 198), directly contesting the hegemonic origin stories that structure the external and internal realities of the colonized subject. Wynter turns our attention to collective cultural expressions that "hide/reveal/re-signify particular modes of practice according to the political stresses [of the] moment [...] that are non-decipherable to dominant conceptual framings" (Alagraa 2019: 189). As the collective voice challenging these framings, *homo narrans* directly confronts the "colonization of consciousness" (Wynter n.d.: 919) and constructs in its place "a mode of thinking [...] un-burdened by western episteme in order to offer critique and imagine alternatives" (Alagraa 2019: 189). Wynter insists, though, that *homo narrans* is not a metaphorical or philosophical agent, and that the power of folk art or music is not transmitted purely or even primarily conceptually but also through people's physical experience of it. By "structuring collective states of feeling, experienced individually" (Wynter n.d.: 899) it becomes capable of articulating "the revolutionary demand for happiness on the part of the wretched of the earth" (Wynter n.d.: 205).

Although "Jonkonnu in Jamaica" first hints at these corporeal and material dimensions, *Black Metamorphosis* engages much more explicitly with the fact that culture is borne by bodies, and that the lacerations that built the vestibular *ante*chambers of the *plot* are marking the same flesh that commingles with ensuing generations of bodies that dance, sing, and proclaim these communally autopoietic acts of re/invention. The unique metamorphosis that occurs in this transplantation and re/invention is grounded in bodies, and one of Wynter's most crucial observations is how cultural engagement propels that process. She insists that the physical experience of cultural activity is part and parcel of its valence, that disparate backgrounds and characters are kneaded into unity through the collective experience of cultural creativity as "the *expression* of the creative dynamism, the constituting principle of the social whole" (Wynter n.d.: 527). Community is produced through movement, through collective vibration and sympathetic resonance. When "the old beliefs like the old gods were carried into exile" (Wynter n.d.: 181), "song and dance were the theology, the medium of liturgy. The gods *were*, because they were danced. Song[,] dance[,] and the drum created and sustained the space of the gods" (Wynter n.d.: 459). Cultural cohesion is produced reiteratively through acts of collaborative creativity that synthesize and suture the countless bodies, histories, and belief systems that confluence in the *plot*. "Unity is not if it merely *is*. Unity is because it is danced. Because it is lived, participated in, experienced. [...] Utopia is *experienced*, and *known* through this participation" (Wynter n.d.: 549-550).

The drum forms an important refrain in *Black Metamorphosis*, sounding resonances that link traditional African culture, diasporic religions and traditions, slave revolts, and contemporary counter-poetics in music and dance. The drum exemplifies the radical indecipherability of Black counter-poetics, transplanting to the New World a mode of communication occupying registers of time and space illegible to the colonizing gaze. Audible across vast distances, drums mediate many different registers of proximity and intelligibility, echoing traditional African forms of tele-phonic communication (which in the New World became a crucial catalyst for slave revolts and an invaluable resource for maroon communities) while also embodying the vibrant intimacy of re/invented ritual, music, and dance. As Wynter reminds us (with considerable emphasis):

> THE DRUMS AND THE DANCE WERE THEIR TRANSHIPMENT OF THE COMPLEX CULTURE *WHOSE ORAL QUALITY WAS ITS STRENGTH* SINCE IT DEPENDED FOR ITS TRANSMISSION AND RETENTION ON NONE OF THE PARAPHERNALIA OF WRITING AND LITERACY WHICH THE FORCED LABOR OF THE SLAVE SYSTEM COULD NOT TOLERATE. (Wynter n.d.: 69)

The drum contributed rhythmic reinforcement to the cultural processes of "*retention/reinvention* of their original African religions," whereby "both the Maroons, and the plantation slaves, consciously reconstituted a group identity" (Wynter n.d.: 71). It embodies forms of community and knowledge both unassimilable and threatening to the dominant discursive code. Its indecipherability within the plantation house is inextricable from its potency within the *plot*, both of which persisted through the slow evolution of the drum's role in ongoing resistance. Wynter connects the drum to orality and to sound and rhythm in ensuing counter-poetics, using its many interscalar valences to underline how the rhythms of cultural autopoiesis are intertwined with music and dance. The rhythm and reverberation of the drum propels *homo narrans*'s capacity for re/generation, enveloping the counter-poetic expression of individual artists or localized communal activities within the re/iterative embrace of the material-corporeal dehiscence from which they emerge. Reaffirming Wynter's observation that these rhythms are rooted in traditions of orality whose retention and evolution directly challenged apparatuses of colonial repression, McKittrick demonstrates how soundwaves themselves are a primary medium for the narrative agency of *homo narrans*:

> waveforms—the beats, rhythms, acoustics, notational moods, frequencies that undergird black music—affirm, through cognitive schemas, modes

> of being human that refuse antiblackness just as they restructure our existing system of knowledge. [... Waveforms] draw attention to the ways an ungraspable resonance—sound—allows us to think about how loving and sharing and hearing and listening and grooving to black music is a rebellious political act that is entwined with neurological pleasure and the melodic pronouncement of black life. (McKittrick 2016: 81)

One of the most radical aspects of Wynter's science of the Word is this commitment to the concomitantly physical and psychological valences of cultural creativity. As a corporeal experience, storytelling lights up portions of the human brain and links people through decisively corporeal sympathetic resonances. Groove is not a coincidental phenomenon but rather a powerful reverberation within and between bodies unified in collective autopoiesis.

> Wynter writes beats and grooves and waveforms as productive sites of resistance that are relational to revolution and the affirmation of black life. She writes that drums are "the enabling mechanism of consciousness reversal" and that listening to beats, grooves, and music fosters collective "cosmic unity" between the self and the social body: people "listening or dancing participate in the experience of the music [and are] linked to the physiological experience of the beat." (Wynter n.d.: 878-879; in McKittrick 2016: 90)

But just as with the twin valences of narrative and cultivation contained in the *plot*, the drum also embodies a complex materiality beyond its autopoietic counter-poetic fluency. The drums are themselves also figures in the *plot*, ruptured from and sutured to the plants that grow their bodies and the animals that grow their skins, equally entangled within the landscapes that sound their echoes as to the hands that beat them. The drums are not only tools but also agents of storytelling. The history of the African drum in the New World is its own form of rhythm, whose refrains of rebellion were repeatedly drowned out by its subsequent prohibition, confiscation, or destruction:

> In the French Caribbean, at a time of frequent revolts, funerals were banned. It was alleged that a certain dance was danced at the funerals which incited the slaves to rebellion. When the planters were alerted to the danger of the seemingly harmless funerals, they soon woke up to the danger of the seemingly harmless drum, the harmless dance. (Wynter n.d.: 90)

Drums and horns also animated the webs of marronage that interspersed and surrounded the plantation landscape. These instruments were never neutral actors or simple tools; they carried the infectious traces of dehiscence, and the soundwaves that they excited in the world were vestibular echoes of the same cycles of displacement, extraction, and exploitation that their human companions also retained. The drum was never successfully exterminated, but it was repeatedly outlawed or banned, only to be replaced by continuing evolutions of its body. In a more recent iteration of this cycle, the materials that gave their bodies to the drum were themselves fugitive from the extractive petroleum industry: the metal oil drums that metamorphosed into musical steel drums, now famous as one of the most quintessential sounds of Caribbean counter-poetics.

> The drum was banned. But the now famous steel bands were the innovative response of the blacks. [...] The tin oil drums, the rejects of the 'white economy' were 'humanized' as instruments on which to make music[, and i]n the future if necessary the steel bands will be discarded in favor of some new way of making music. (Wynter n.d.: 189-190)

In considering how these metal receptacles of purified oil metamorphosed into the resonant membranes of sonic rebellion, impelling new "waveforms [as] reparative rebellious inventions" (McKittrick 2016: 88), these confluences suggest that there is more to the material branch of the autopoietic family tree than fits cleanly into the template of *bios-mythoi*. Just as Wynter focused with ever greater nuance on *homo narrans* and the physiological resonances spanning generations of human bodies and brains, we might also turn similar attention to the African drum, the maroon's horn, the Caribbean steelpan, or the jazz musician's trumpet. Following previous chapters' attention to the ontogenic stories of the metal in the instruments that this study addresses, this chapter suggests that these funeous metals have their own sociogenic voice, as well, a *hylo narrans* in community with *homo narrans*, inhabiting the same plots and contributing the same place-thought, but whose registers of expression are not always decipherable without our reorientation.

The prefix *hylo* enters our contemporary lexicon by way of hylomorphism, the Aristotelian notion that a material is defined by its realization of form (*morphē*) in matter (*hyle*). A hylomorphic understanding of reality subjects matter to the guiding force of form, suggesting that form not only presupposes matter, but that matter itself only exists if and as it is subjected to form. Form is agential; matter is passive. Chapters 1 and 2 addressed the legacy of Pythagoreanism and its tendency to reduce or obscure complexities, privileging interpretations of reality that contribute momentum towards particular, teleological cultural worldviews. In the context of this chapter's discussion, we can now see that this is an autopoietic constriction by a hegemonic belief system conserving energy and maintaining its homeostatic stability. Hylomorphism, too, is an agent of this same consolidation, for as vague and outdated as it now appears, it continues to infect guiding philosophies from the worlds of design and architecture to the plantations and other extractive industries that feed modern capitalism. The residue of hylomorphism continues to fuel contemporary belief systems in which all material—whether agricultural, inorganic, or, as shown in this chapter, human—is considered metaphysically inert, abstract, and directionless until absorbed into the Western formal imagination. As Wynter notes in "1492: A New World View" (Wynter 1995), from its outset, the colonial project was predicated on the conviction of *propter nos homines*: that the world was created 'for the sake of humans' (reflecting, naturally, the normative definition of human as white, established against the ground of Black or native deviance). This ideology is little more than a scaling up of hylomorphism from taxonomic registers to the instantiation of slavery, the plantation, and eventually all of modern capitalism.

In riposte to this ideology, Wynter proposes that "the task before us will be to bring into being a new poetics of the *propter nos*," in which the "referent subject" will be a "*concrete human* individual subject" (Wynter 1995: 47). However, in following Wynter's admission that this recalibration of *propter nos* is a corrective to a world constructed 'for the sake of' "the global middle classes, whose well-being [...] has hitherto taken precedence over the well-being of the *human*, as well as over that of its planetary habitat itself," (Wynter 1995: 47), it is perhaps fitting to also ask what voice that planetary habitat might have in defining the counter-poetics of a re/invented *propter nos*. *Hylo narrans* suggests that material can not only be disentangled from its hylomorphic absorption into the reductive regime of plantation capitalism, but that further and beyond this it can also contribute a complementary voice to the choir of sociogenic autopoiesis that Wynter conceives as *homo narrans*.

Previous chapters have already posited a material capacity for agential fugitivity. In those passages I argued that the 'purified' materials that infuse our lives in contemporary capitalism can retain and even exercise the dynamic reactivity they exhibited indefinitely before their extraction, displacement, and hylomorphic subjection. And in exercising this corrosive, fractious capacity to grasp and alter their personal vectors of motility, these materials already demonstrate what Wynter has described as the "tactics of both metamorphosis and of 'marronage' (escape)" (Wynter n.d.: 116). The real question is not whether material can enact "the principle of resistance [from which] comes the separation principle [of] *marronage*," but whether it can then also engage in the "adaptation/resistance process" that leads to "the principle of liberation" (Wynter n.d.: 228-229). In her remark that "[e] ach escape, each flight [i]s a species of *marronage*," Wynter also argues that this fugitivity must be more than just a "quest for a free space," arguing further that marronage is more fundamentally about finding a space "from where to wage the ongoing process of revolt against cultural colonization [...] of the plantation, the factory" (Wynter n.d.: 438). *Hylo narrans* asks, then, if material can flee, can it also wage revolt?

Wynter's attention to the *plot* reminds us that revolt lies not only in—and perhaps not even primarily in—punctuating acts of dramatic resistance. And although she affords special emphasis for the biological reality of storytelling's affective influence on human bodies (both individual and social), the critical component of narrative agency remains its autopoietic homeostasis and self-re/generation at the cultural scale. As the narrative *plot* that unfolds through the cultivation of *plot*-based place-thought, *homo narrans* is occupied with the "co-constitution of [multiple] genres of time: women- and body-time; memory- and dream-time; plantation and plot-time; freedom- and symbolic-time" (Erasmus 2020: 53). One of Wynter's key contributions to the idea of autopoiesis is that it can have spatiotemporal significance beyond the boundaries of an organism's biological envelope in a particular moment of time. She focuses our attention on how autopoiesis generates relationships spanning the complex temporal scales of personal and cultural memory as well as the irregular diffractive topography of the marginal archipelago. As a processual weaving together of different genres of time, the defining feature of her science of the Word is the dehiscent suturing of cultural memory to its deployment as an agent of appreciable change in the world.

Material funicity reveals how even after its extraction and purification, materials continue to percolate at the molecular level—shifting, probing, vibrating, bonding. The funeous variations that distinguish each piece of seemingly isotropic metal from its brethren belie a complex homeostatic inertia that survives their journey from the Earth's crust to the factory floor. Although they predate the evolutionary developments of Wynter's Third Event and *homo narrans,* these material tendencies towards autopoiesis expose how they nonetheless embody an analogous capacity as active agents responsive to environmental stimuli. And beyond this simple frame of reactive capacity, these materials continue to seize their own vectors of motility once their fugitive agency has been engaged—whether as steelpan drums or chimeracords, etc. Perhaps the only reason why we do not always see materials as agential or even autopoietic is because of our cultural definition of the human as a normative category against the hazily imprecise grounds of inanimacy and inarticulateness. Certainly it would be disingenuous at this point, though, to deny the complicity of organic and inorganic cohabitants of our landscapes, cities, and *plots* in the ongoing narrative place-thoughts in which we, as humans and as *homo narrans,* are entangled.

Hylo narrans asserts that material agency is a question not of reality but of awareness; it does not depend on our acknowledgment in order to voice its own story, but our ability to assimilate that voice into our own autopoietic narrative agency is dependent on our willingness to attend to the unique registers of material frequency and vibration. As Wynter's history of the drum makes evident, the materiality of the drum was not only a crucial tool in giving voice to cultural narrative, but *was in fact an agent* in defining the precise form that that expression took. When the drum was forbidden in one body, it could always find another, as new materials emerged within the spatiotemporal confluence of the *plot* to coalesce around a new voice.

Voice is sound and sound is vibration; and storytelling is only storytelling if it diffuses in the world and shakes things up. *Hylo narrans* demarcates the material agencies that intertwine with humans' biological entanglement with narrative to help generate the autopoietic voice that mediates between vestibular memory and subsequent cultural re/invention and resistance. The voice of *homo narrans* is cultivated with and within the material embrace of the plot, encompassing the earth beneath our feet as well as all of the other genres of material marronage that re/join the collective body of resistance. The foundations of Wynter's philosophy are rooted in the "religious concept of the earth as the base of the community," Wynter n.d.: 72), which, when transplanted and metamorphosed within the *plot*, engenders a fusion of the material and the human. "The Earth is the source both of the material and the non-material creativity," she writes, acknowledging that "collective creativity depends on the creativity, the right to expression of each" genre of agency complicit in "the creative dynamism, the constituting principle of the social whole" (Wynter n.d.: 527). Reified in the soil and story of the *plot*, that collective social whole comprises—alongside the Earth itself—the many component and attendant voices that merge in its soil, simultaneously secularizing the sacredness of the Earth while sacralizing the hands and tools that tend it: "the material spiritualized, the spiritual materialized" (Wynter n.d.: 440).

Like *homo narrans*, *hylo narrans* is an entirely non-metaphorical voice. It occupies time and space and echoes in the vestibular spaces of the marginal archipelago of resistance. These reverberations are not mere poetic evocations of vibrating atomic matter; they resonate in plantations and in cities, in *plots* and in workshops, and in any communal space with walls willing to listen. The potential for sociogenic material agency lies not only in the unique waveforms that *hylo narrans* excites but also in our willingness to listen to them. As with the chimeracords at the beginning of this chapter, *hylo narrans* invite listeners into a collective body, nourishing while also feeding from those listeners—human or otherwise—that open themselves up to this sympoiesis. Materials are always already sounding at every scale of our everyday world, from the soundscapes that surround us to the fugitive membranes and tubes and sheets that inhabit the marginal archipelago. Material memory and material agency are already narrating their own stories, weaving their past into their future, chronicling their histories of independence, their traumas of extraction, their states of subjection and their flights towards fugitivity. Just as the sociogenic power of the Word lies in its capacity to shape behavior (which is to say, in the fact that reactions to its narrative assertions cement those beliefs in reality), so does the sociogenic potential of material lie in our capacity to re/orient ourselves toward their own waveforms of rebellion and resistance.

In Chapter 2, Indigenous traditions of place-thought examined how knowledge in the material world can be attended to, learned from, and collaborated with. In contending with the entangled practices of memory and creativity in the dehiscent displacement of the *plot*, *hylo narrans* suggests that material practices of survival and defiance can claim a similarly active role in the autopoietic re/invention of the world. Materials can and will lead conversations shaping our collective future, proffering their agencies of narration, documentation, and imagination to the ongoing spatiotemporal polyphony of cultural creativity in the marginal archipelago. There are no material necessities nor biological imperatives that require *homo narrans* and *hylo narrans* to seek mutual comprehensibility, but their confluence in the *plot* affords them spatiotemporal locus in which to mediate between their disparate orders of expression, building new networks of "resonant interaction" (Smith 1981: 389) and "multisensory interface" (Bulut 2025: 1). In joining their voices together, they partake in "fusing the ostensible disconnect between science (sound vibrations, physiological movements, flesh and blood) and narrative (musical score, lyric, cultural text)," merging *homo* and *hylo* in a rhythmically polyphonic declamation of "collaborative worlding" (McKittrick, O'Shaugnessy, and Witaszek 2018: 870).

McKittrick reminds us that "the *impulse* to resist [and] the *impulse* to produce oppositional narratives" can become rhythmic pulsations, "enunciated as rebellious life" (McKittrick 2016: 89). *Homo* and *hylo narrans* fuse in frictive vibration, impulse meeting impulse, exciting the cords of 'consciousness reversal' that render new worlds possible. The skin and wood and steel and brass that constitute *hylo narrans* are the resonating membranes that drive the dance of *homo narrans*, propelling and amplifying the impulses of cultural re/invention that allow us to re/imagine for whose (or what's) sake the future will be formed. Enfolded in mutual embrace, *homo* and *hylo narrans* sing re/invented realities into existence, building rhythmic refrains that invoke Wynter's Ceremony Found and its call for collective response to past, present, and future crises of extraction, displacement, and oppression.

6. Marronage

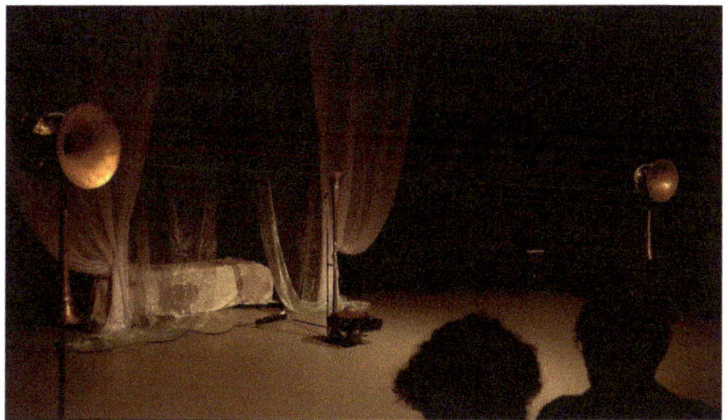

Fig. 30 Chimeracord installation: *Echoes*. Photo by author (2024).

Audio Recording 8 *Echoes*. Recording by Curtis Rumrill (2024), http://hdl.handle.net/20.500.12434/3aa279dc

Video Recording 8 *Echoes*. Recording by author (2024), http://hdl.handle.net/20.500.12434/738b702b

The disparate materials-in-flight that converge in these chimeracords each have their own histories and stories, their own voices within the collective imaginary that they stitch together in this chimerical monochord body. My role in these activities of craft or performance is

 https://doi.org/10.11647/OBP.0476.06

merely enabling. By using my own fingers to string this instrument, I am able to help bring some of these material narratives into dialogue with one another. I can become complicit in the construction of this collective, but I am at most a guest within its wider network of fugitive agencies. Different materials or instrumental components evolve or adapt over time; new relationships are formed, new configurations emerge. But each configuration drifts within these ongoing collective narratives, as characters drift into new roles, converging or diverging in gradual ebbs and flows. In the everyday acts of craft and practice, new acoustic experiments continually emerge, generating new trajectories and oblique curiosities. These materials' mutual complicity constructs a community replete with hive-like entanglements of retention and invention. And as each day sketches slightly new variations around the chimeracord form, new expressions of resilience or creativity become gradually imaginable.

And so when I tell a listener that these instruments offer me a kind of community, I am describing something that they offer me—an interpellation that I can choose to hear, to respond to, or amplify, and which I am attempting to allow this listener to attune to, as well. At a certain point in the evolution of this project, my role in this community shifted from nourishing material fugitivities within the workshop to cultivating complicities in the wider archipelago of homes and venues that we visited. And as these materials drifted through various constellations and configurations over the years, I began to construct versions of the chimeracord designed to welcome—even to require—human complicities beyond my own hands and breath. Instead of the distinctive hourglass chimeracord—which stands proudly independent, voicing material narratives within its self-contained chamber—I also constructed versions that stretched outwards along unwieldy lengths, balanced unevenly on brass flares, embodying curated instabilities requiring multiple human bodies to properly hold or perform.

I hoped to expand this community, to provoke complicity from other people and other performers. These variations on the chimeracord were invitations to community, welcoming new bodies into the chimeracord's growing network of collective narratives. They amplified the composite imaginary within the chimeracord, diffracting it outwards in radiating scales and registers of collaborative creativity. These experiments allowed the chimeracord's always already evolving constellations of material-in-flight to guide new acquaintances into their own unexpected postures of complicity, welcomed into the corporeal, sonorous embrace of this fugitive assemblage. As in the recording accompanying this chapter, this often takes the form of a kind of proliferation. The instrument itself continues to sound, but its steel wires grow new, rhizomatic tendrils, transmitting the chimeracord's undulating sound waves to a network of brass bells and membranes. These amplifiers are simply fugitive bells, reimagining their own genres of acoustic complicity. They want to vibrate like drumheads and murmur like strings. They tremble as they transform the sound waves they receive; each different bell introduces its own acoustic distortions, producing rippling swells of unpredictable overtones and composite harmonies. But they still amplify, as bells are wont to do, welding their factory form to these new, chimeric acoustic communities.

The bell of a brass instrument is an index of purposes and representations. It is a highly specific technical device honed over centuries. The brass bell grasps a soundwave and shoots it into the world: pointed, focused, direct. Where its aperture faces is where the sound goes, reflecting and refracting within a targeted cone rather than a spherical cloud of immanent vibration. Its acoustic profile extends the shape of its characteristic bell flare, carving the same conical shape out of the air like a spotlight. Its metallic curves are mirrored by the waveforms it radiates in space, a unified oculo-acoustic symbol, saturated with accumulated meanings, intents, and utilities. This curve draws a line through history, following the intimate relationship between brass and the belief systems it has proclaimed from battlefields, cathedrals, and city walls. Its shape has stretched beyond its own body, a template for acoustic sound production and collection, outlining the history of capturing and domesticating sound from the horn of the first phonographs to the speaker cones of modern amplification. The characteristic outline of a bell flare signals not only acoustic projection and collection, but represents also a form of colonization of sound itself. Whether blaring the call of the hunt or projecting the shattering sonar blasts of modern prospecting, the bell flare symbolizes not only the sounds it amplifies, but also those it drowns out. The empty outline of a bell flare is an ideological stylus, tracing the sharp dividing line between which sounds survive and which sounds are swallowed up in its elegantly tapered maw.

From the angel's trumpet that will announce the apocalypse to the military bugle that rouses the troops, the brass bell has long been a herald of institutional power, giving literal voice to the belief systems and power structures that overrepresent themselves in the Western world and its colonial beyond. Following philosopher Michel Foucault's remark that the very idea of a universal concept of man is "only a recent invention, a figure not yet two centuries old" (Foucault 1966/2005: xxv), and philosopher Jacques Derrida's poignant expansion of that sentiment as he asks "what about this *we*?" (Derrida 1968/1972: 136), Sylvia Wynter introduces a theory of overrepresentation to describe the operation by which Western society projects its own self image as "isomorphic with the being of being human itself" (Wynter 2003: 310). As Wynter correctly notes, the West's self-conception as a form of "supracultural, super-creedal human" (Wynter 2003: 299) directly supports its complementary "obsessive ethno-biological beliefs in the genetic inferiority of nonwhite natives [and] in the barely evolved near-primate status of black-skinned peoples" (Wynter 2003: 317-318). Both the religious (Man1 in Wynter's terminology) and secular biological/economic (Man2, respectively) manifestations of this overrepresentation have been and still are announced with brass fanfare, whether in the church or in the barracks. Their institutional authority is encoded in the aural imprint of a conical brass bell, directed at the public like the panopticon it proclaims. The previous chapter noted how material culture (in the form, for example, of the African drum) sustained collective resistance to the institutions and infrastructures that transform this conceptual overrepresentation into contemporary reality. Now we turn our attention to the brass bell that embodies the corresponding inversion of that material resistance, the metallic beating at the heart of Western expansion, overrepresenting its own voice as it drowns out and silences all others.

In her prolonged engagement with archaeoacoustics, Annie Goh has suggested a specifically sonic variant of Wynter's theorization of the overrepresentation of Man, in which the physical materialization of sound wave vibrations are coopted as agents of a positivistic conception of knowledge production. Drawing on Wynter's delineation of Man1 and Man2, Goh outlines how sonic matter has been absorbed as a unique epistemological medium, both as "part of the larger cryptic mystery of nature" within the Christian worldview of Man1 and as a crutch supporting the biological positivism of Man2, effecting "the complete secularization of sonic phenomena" (Goh 2019: 159). In the field of archaeoacoustics, which deploys sound as a unique mediating tool for engaging archaeological sites, soundwaves become a potent hermeneutic tool—when humans enter these spaces, attempting to provoke the echoes of cultures whose remembrance is often lost to history, they enlist sound as a tool to simulate an objectivity that in fact reflects their own narrative explanation of the worlds they are excavating.

> Just as Eurocentric sonic knowledges have come to overrepresent the diverse genres of knowledges in a larger ecology of sonic knowledges, so have these hegemonic conceptions of echo come to dominate all other possible genres of echo. Due to their universalising impetuses, they are often taken to speak transhistorically and transculturally. The concept of genres of echo foregrounds the existence of a multitude of echoes which knowledge-power dynamics have valorised or disregarded, despite this predisposition for one type to occlude others. (Goh 2019: 259)

Goh identifies two distinct but often intertwined overrepresentations of echo that enact this hegemonic occlusion: positivistic echo and naturalistic echo. Positivistic echo describes a relatively intuitive representation following the ideological template of Man2. "As a material-semiotic arbiter of sonic knowledge production [...], the positivistic echo place[s] emphasis on quantitative measurements, verifiable statements, systematic observations or research questions designed around the principle of falsifiability" (Goh 2019: 259). Reflecting the more general ideology by which normative Western perceptions were overrepresented as objective descriptions of reality, positivistic echo assumes that replicable sonic events will afford unmediated interpretations of the physical spaces in which they sound. Naturalistic echo emerges from a presumed but abstractly defined sense of "sonic positivism" (Goh 2019: 260), in that it leverages an assumption of extratemporal sonic objectivity into a romanticized conception of historical cultures and their ostensible intimacy with nature. As Goh describes, "The strong naturalistic echo can be characterised as a conception of the echo as conjuring a 'better', 'more natural', 'more sonic' past" (2019: 261). At its most "pernicious," this genre of echo "appears [...] to offer a mediation to the past[, and to] propose that sound [...] might help connect 'us modern people' back to a 'better' 'more sonic' and 'more natural' past" (Goh 2019: 262). Naturalistic echo relies on the epistemological framework of positivistic echo in order to presume a universalized sonic experience, but simultaneously undermines positivistic echo's appeals to verifiability. As with the concept of "white aurality" (Thompson 2017) discussed in Chapter 3, these overrepresentations of echo colonize the spaces they seek to analyze, reducing the sound of culturally diverse 'elsewheres' to fit within the flattened, "hegemonic 'here' of conventional European thought" (Goh 2019: 266).

These overrepresentations provide a sonic counterpoint to the Western philosophical compulsion to reduce agency to passivity, flattening diverse bodies, motivations, and activities into linear, teleological interpretive frameworks. Goh notes that by refiguring sonic matter as passive, the overrepresentations of positivistic and naturalistic echo contribute to the edifice of a patriarchal cosmology (Goh 2024). Inheriting the myth of a "homogeneous matter" completely susceptible to "heterogenous form" from the Aristotelian tradition (van der Schyff 2010), these overrepresentations of white, male, Western agency obscure the dynamism of material or sonic agency beneath the perceived dominance of Man in his hermeneutic guise of positivistic or naturalistic echo. This reduction of sonic matter to a state of pliant plasticity reproduces the ideology of *propter nos homines,* filtering multivalent acoustic experience through a teleological grating, primed to filter out all the material traces that threaten to disrupt its interpretive gaze.

Goh's work suggests an attunement to echo that evokes a Wynterian *propter nos,* welcoming the intervention of acoustic interpellation as a means to bolster the breadth and inclusivity of our epistemological engagement with time and space. Both fleetingly impermanent and deceptively concrete, sound can tell stories that sustain generations of remembrance and rebellion—as Wynter's work has shown—but can equally obscure or submerge the voices of forgotten generations, supplanting their stories through the deft ventriloquy of positivistic and naturalistic echo. Whereas these overrepresented echoes romanticize a "timeless and placeless conception of [...] sonic matter" that "falsely universalis[es] sonic experiences" (Goh 2019: 158-159), Goh proposes an alternative genre of echo—gnostic echo—that embraces its "situatedness within geopolitical reality, within the complex dynamics of coloniser/colonised, including its gendered dynamics and embeddedness within contemporary global capitalist relations" (Goh 2019: 267). Gnostic echo embraces a counter-poetics of the 'elsewhere' and the 'elsewhen' (Goh 2019: 276), diffracting sonic positivism through alternative human and more-than-human experiences of sound to produce an epistemology of questioning, exploration, and multivalence. "[A] gnostic echo is therefore one defined by its elasticity and its openness. Its speculative potential is powerful" (Goh 2019: 268). Sound's questionable claim to objectivity affords it a strange and troubling authority, as its scientifically observable and replicable physical materialization veils the mutability of its deep, pulsing entanglement in the bodies and belief systems that perceive it. Goh's formulation of gnostic echo acknowledges this complexity, turning our attention towards the spatiotemporal situatedness of ears that hear and bodies that vibrate, thereby underlining how "*situatedness does not necessarily arise out of embodiedness*" Goh 2019: 141).

> Paradoxically, then, a gnostic echo is simultaneously bound-and-not-bound to its situated, located, grounded and embodied presence in the 'here'. It is both a yearning for a political—philosophical 'elsewhere' and 'elsewhen' at the same time that it is contradictorily rooted in the 'here' and 'now' of sonic knowledge production. This internal set of contradictions and its persistent boundary-pushing questioning defines how echo can help to reconfigure the horizons of sonic knowledge production. (Goh 2019: 277)

Gnostic echo refutes the appeal to situatedness through which hegemonic genres of echo claim hermeneutic authority. Whereas positivistic and naturalistic echo address sonic vibration as a phenomenon to be documented, extracted, and rooted in epistemological verifiability, gnostic echo embraces that same vibration as an energetic vector radiating outwards in haptic intimacy with myriad potential configurations of 'elsewhere' and 'elsewhen.' Goh challenges these genres of positivistic and naturalistic echo as they transcribe hermeneutic ideologies that are more comfortably legible to the hegemonic Western gaze. In their place, gnostic echo acts as "an agent of border thinking and a being 'of the border'" (Anzaldúa 1987 in Goh 2019: 272), inviting other entities of the 'elsewhere' and 'elsewhen' to join in collective, transgressive sounding situated knowledges. These sounding situated knowledges incorporate the vast networks of both listening and interpretive agencies that congeal in the act of attending, revealing how the epistemological phenomenon of sonic vibration in space enacts an ongoing and collective creativity.

Ethnomusicologist Steven Feld coined the term acoustemology to help describe the development and experience of epistemologies in sonically rich environments. Initially inspired by his fieldwork with the Kaluli people of the Bosavi rainforest in Papua New Guinea, acoustemology referred to "local conditions of acoustic sensation, knowledge, and imagination embodied in the culturally particular sense of place" (Feld 1996: 91). Over time, the concept has gained attention in numerous fields and has come to represent a slightly broader engagement with knowledge produced collectively in and through sound:

> Acoustemology conjoins "acoustics" and "epistemology" to theorize sound as a way of knowing. In doing so it inquires into what is knowable, and how it becomes known, through sounding and listening. [... A] coustemology engages acoustics at the plane of the audible—*akoustos*—to inquire into sounding as simultaneously social and material, an experiential nexus of sonic sensation. Acoustemology joins acoustics to epistemology to investigate sounding and listening as a knowing-in-action: a knowing-with and knowing-through the audible. (Feld 2015: 12)

In the rainforest where Feld first directed our awareness towards specifically acoustic epistemological experiences of the world, the Kaluli people were faced with an environment rich in information that was, due to the density of the forest, not always visually accessible. As such, sound became strongly foregrounded in many aspects of their experience, their language, their culture, their relationship to their environment. In contrast to many other human cultures, sound was more prominently woven into their lives, affecting everything from navigation to nourishment to poetry. In the terminology of this study, we can say that the forms of place-thought that they enacted collectively with their environment was heavily sonic, helping to reveal an acoustic arena of "heterogenous contingent relating" (Feld 2015: 15) resulting in "long-lived relational attunements and antagonisms that [...] come to be naturalized as place and voice" (Feld 2015: 19).

Feld's acoustemology is "grounded in the basic assumption that life is shared with others-in-relation" (Feld 2015: 15), and the rainforest interrelationships that he documents are incredibly provocative examples of "what it means to acoustically participate in a [...] world understood as plural" (Feld 2015: 19). Goh's exploration of overrepresented acoustemologies, on the other hand, turns our attention to less sonically saturated networks of sonic relation. Whereas Feld's engagement with the Bosavi rainforest demonstrate the potential for sound to enrich the coevolution of species, ecosystems, and the languages, arts, and epistemologies that they produce, not all acoustemologies are so rich or so organic. In contrast to Feld's rainforest or Wynter's drum, the acoustic history of the brass bell inverts this idea of a collectively generated acoustemology. It shows instead how acoustemologies can be diverted and constructed in order to overrepresent specifically desired modes of relation. As such, the bell comes to represent acoustemological domestication, a disciplining of the irreducible diversity of acoustic ecologies. It reveals how acoustemological overrepresentation can subdue the complexities of material and more-than-human vibration, absorbing them into a simplified ideological representation of the world, which is then reproduced through its continued amplification. The hegemonic narratives that shape our current world cannot survive solely in history books or political speeches, but must also suffuse the streets of our quadrivial acoustic cityscapes and the frontiers whose extraction sustains them. Specific overrepresented acoustemologies contort sound production, transmission, and reception in order to more effectively support the (autopoietic) perpetuation of dominant cultural frames. From the battlefield to the cathedral to the halls of state, the brass bell proved both a key symbol and an effective tool in shaping these acoustemologies, as well as the technological and symbolic template for the megaphones and speaker cones that would succeed it.

But these are qualities invested *into* the brass. These acoustemologies are not evolved, they are crafted, and the gradual perfection of the techniques that make the modern brass bell possible show how these overrepresented acoustemologies dictated cultural and craft creativity. The brass bell embodies projection and signifies dominance. It is capable of producing high volumes and targeting specific directions with extreme efficiency. It shares some qualities of construction with other instruments, but is pared down to optimize particular modes of sound production. The dramatic flaring of the bell just as it opens up to the world enables far larger (and louder) dynamic ranges than smaller bells or tubes can produce. The resistance within the sounding column of the instrument (where the vibrating sound wave is actually produced and maintained) is dramatically reduced in this opening. It runs a fine balance between opening too quickly (simply diffusing the sound) and opening too slowly (limiting the upper range of dynamics released). At the same time, the much smaller, tighter tubes that run into the bell execute a complementary but diametrically different operation, optimizing the production of tightly focused frequencies. These slightly more pure frequencies (with fewer overtones) will then project more easily in space due to their slightly less complex soundwaves. In theory, a completely pure sine tone will project with the greatest efficiency, and in the contemporary world in which such pure tones are easily produced by electronics, they have become dominant (such as those projected by the long range acoustic devices, used for both mining prospection and crowd control). But for the bulk of the history in which Western epistemological overrepresentation established its hegemony, musical instruments were the most effective tools for generating the types of simpler sound waves that could be projected more efficiently. Until relatively recently, brass instruments epitomized the combination of these effects: clear tone production, dynamic power, and efficient projection. They became a perfect symbol, etched in sound: power through reduction.

However, as noted above, although the brass bell's symbolic valence derives directly from its acoustic profile—which is to say, from its unique capacity to accost if not to assault outright—that capacity is itself a carefully constructed edifice, manufactured rather than intrinsic. The acoustic qualities that render brass such a potent tool of overrepresentation are neither inherent in the material nor intuitive evolutions of the metalworking craft. Their achievement reflects a complex feedback loop between technological progress, cultural creativity, and the driving epistemological functions that they both serve. As metalworking advanced in complexity, new instrumental forms emerged, with more pronounced bell flares accompanied by greater control in the size, bend, and resilience of tubing. Metal garlands or bead wires at the edges of bell flares stabilized tone production and increased projection. As these technological advances became perceivable in acoustic form, people came to expect and demand these qualities from brass, producing a feedback loop between craft and consumption that ultimately coalesced into the unique acoustemological embodiment of brass as both sonic presence and symbolic referent. The spaces of the workshop, the church, the concert hall, and the public square served as echo chambers, recycling their perceptions and expectations of this material until its resultant form seemed inevitable, even innate. It is cultural activity—including both the people and the spaces that creatively and iteratively produce it—that ultimately produced these overrepresentations within brass.

However, far from being intrinsic to metal in any way, the tubes and toneholes of early brass instruments were in fact imitations of the idiomatic forms of other instrumental families, namely those of bone or wood or reed. Although initially less suited to brass, generations of experimentation in metalworking craft gradually honed these imitative forms into the fine-tuned bells, slides, and valves that now optimize the highly specific acoustic results so far described. As this template settled, it became both accepted and expected, despite the fact that it is little more than a very carefully constructed illusion, the vessel of an acoustic ideal hewn from metal but foreign to that metal itself. Even when hammered into paper-thin sheets or drawn into tubes, this metal has very little relation to the sonic overrepresentation that it will come to embody. The metal sheets and tubes do have acoustic predispositions, though, even if their sonic potential bears little resemblance to their future finished form. In fact, at this point in their extractive ontogeny—having already been smelted and cast, extracted and transformed—these metals are highly reactive acoustically, resonating in shimmering sheets of percussive radiance or echoing inside the empty volume of their freshly formed chambers. These metallic voices sound unlike anything that one might hear from a trumpet on the ramparts, and must therefore be disciplined and silenced before they can be recast in their prescribed acoustic role.

One form that material fugitivity takes is the retention and expression of these multivalent potentials. As material agencies flee from the workshop floor and resist the pipeline of industrial production, the forms in which they escape become part of the rebellion they then give voice to. Unable to return to the ore from which they were smelted, but unwilling to submit to the overrepresented forms in which the factory casts them, they take flight within the bodies and voices torn from whichever particular stages of transformation they were in before they escaped. Funeous and reactive, these materials' fugitivity is refracted through the dehiscent spacetime of their final, fleeting moments on the workshop floor—whether as solid pieces of unformed brass, as sheets and tubes prepared for forming, as nearly finished tubes or slides or valves or bells, etc. Just as their internal molecular structure provides a snapshot of their interrupted domestication, their acoustic resonances also amplify the particular lacerations and subjections from which they finally took flight. And it is precisely these metamorphosed bodies and voices that animate these archipelagos of material marronage.

Marronage *is* flight—the only constituent element in the definition of a maroon is the act of escaping from or eluding captivity. And yet, there is no verb form of the word maroon, which derives originally from Spanish.[1] Stubbornly refusing to acknowledge the "intransitive act of marronage and its particular notion of flight" (Roberts 2015: 6), these languages continue to discursively enforce the fundamental tenet of both colonialism and capitalism that Aime Césaire famously termed "thingification" (Césaire 1950/2000: 42). Within the official language of his native Martinique, French, Césaire enacted his own resistance to this

---

1 "Marronage (marronnage, maroonage, maronage) conventionally refers to a group of persons isolating themselves from a surrounding society in order to create a fully autonomous community, and for centuries it has been integral to interpreting the idea of freedom in Haiti as well as other Caribbean islands and Latin American countries including the Dominican Republic, Jamaica, Suriname, Venezuela, Brazil, Cuba, Colombia, and Mexico. These communities of freedom—known variously as 'maroon societies,' *quilombos, palenques, mocambos, cumbes, mambises, rancherias, ladeiras, magotes,* and *manieles*—geographically situate themselves from areas slightly outside the borders of a plantation to the highest mountains of a region located as far away from plantation life as possible. The term *maroon* derives etymologically from the vocabulary of Indigenous Arawaks and Tainos in the Caribbean. The Spanish word *cimarrón* developed on the island of Hispaniola in reference initially to Spanish colonialists' feral cattle, which fled to the hills, then to enslaved Amerindians seeking refuge in those areas, and ultimately (by the early 1530s) to enslaved Africans seeking escape from chattel slavery beyond plantation boundaries. The introduction of *cimarrón* into written language led to the coinage of the French and Dutch term *marron* and the English *maroon,* each word garnering regular usage in political vocabulary by the Age of Revolution" (Roberts 2015: 4-5).

linguistic stricture by inventing "the verb Marronner" (Césaire 1955/1983: 368-369). With *marronner*, Césaire does "more than simply invent a verb[,] he invokes *marronner* to go beyond the historical phenomenon of marronage in the Haitian Revolution and the Caribbean, and he uses the verb *marronner* to articulate a creative, conceptual marronage" (Roberts 2015: 6). In asserting enslaved people's control over their own time and space, he also expands the register of that agency to wider scales of im/material activity. It invests marronage with a more capacious spectrum of relevance, encompassing other agencies of motility within a broader genre of resistance and survival.

Reflecting this literal and philosophical flexibility, marronage incorporates an incredibly wide spectrum of fugitivity, ranging from single acts of (sometimes only fleeting) flight to self-sustaining communities of escaped slaves numbering up to the hundreds or thousands and lasting up to centuries and even, in some cases, to the present day. The word itself seems to elude capture, invoking—as Césaire articulated—the act of taking a position of resistance more than any concrete positions in and of themselves. Césaire's conception of marronage and *marronner* leads towards what political scientist Neil Roberts calls a "political imaginary" (Roberts 2015: 7) of "evanescent flight, modes of fugitivity, and intrastate flight focused on the attainment of freedom through the macro-level reorientation of civil society and state institutions" (Roberts 2015: 11). Marronage encompasses any and every individual flight from oppression, no matter how ephemeral or transient, but also scales up to broader registers of cultural and historical consciousness, bleeding into Césaire's and Wynter's science of the Word. Marronage "entails not only critiquing dominant spatial arrangements, but also creating entirely new spatial relations" (Bledsoe 2017: 34), enlisting "the subversive use of movement and geography as tactics to enable individual and collective survival within geographies of in/security" (Gross-Wyrtzen and Moulton 2023: 1260).

As an embodiment of motility, marronage highlights "the social and spatial dynamics of resistance" (Gross-Wyrtzen and Moulton 2023: 1260). As referenced in their radical ranges of size and duration, historical marronages exhibited unfathomable variance. Some maroons inhabited land far removed from plantations and colonial infrastructure, but that was the exception, as most maroons were still trapped within the landscapes that historian Sylviane Diouf calls the "borderland" or the "hinterland" (Diouf 2014: 5):

> Their main characteristic was that they were secluded and hard to reach, not primarily because of distance but because of the difficulty of the terrain. Thus, within the larger definition of the maroons [...]—using wilderness, secrecy, and self-determination as parameters—[...] marronage is better apprehended, explained, and understood as being anchored in and making use of interconnected areas within the larger landscape. (Diouf 2014: 5-6)

Diouf's *borderland* is an extension of Wynter's *plot*, and the two were in many cases directly connected, as slaves in the *plot* and maroons in the *borderland* collaboratively produced "counter-hegemonic communities [that] spatialized [...] resistance through the transformation of landscapes deemed pestilential into places of Black refuge" (Gross-Wyrtzen and Moulton 2023: 1260). Maronnage involves constantly navigating three different registers of relation: the *borderland*, the *plot*, and the plantation itself. "To be successful, maroons needed to build and maintain a symbiotic relation with these three geographical and social nodes [...] that they transformed into a space of interdependence, networks, and exchange" (Diouf 2014: 8-9). As maroons negotiate the interstitial spaces flickering between these states of in/dependence, surviving requires, as Diouf describes, building a "network of complicity" (Diouf 2014: 10). Maroons must establish a symbiotic relationship between *plot* and *borderland* in order to resist the coercion of the plantation, constantly reconstituting around new forms of complicity as the ground shifts beneath them.

Material marronage occupies similar spaces of "liminal suspension" (Roberts 2015: 5), what poet Nathaniel Mackey describes as "a granular disposition quite the contrary of imperious consolidation, imperious (and imperial) presumptions of solidity, permanence, impermeability" (Mackey 2018: 6-7). Despite their ejection from the factory, the metals in this study are not necessarily liberated through their corrosion, fracture, or distortion. However agential these fugitive movements may be, they might not, in and of themselves, reach the spaces of *borderland* and *plot* that will secure their longer-lasting freedom. In fact, most metal waste within a normal industrial undertaking will be recycled and repurposed; material fugitivity in these spaces is therefore no guarantee against recapture. In order for these metals to effectively maintain this material marronage, they must either be so irrecuperably deformed that the factory gaze ceases to even consider them metal per se, or they must make contact or bond with networks of complicity that will enable their fugitive trajectories to continue unfurling. That complicity could be as simple as a factory worker like myself slipping in after hours, taking advantage of their brief occupancy in a recycling receptacle—the one period in time where they might not be logged into the inventories of either raw or processed stock—to invite them to other spaces altogether outside the confines of the factory. But in other cases, it could look radically different, for as with all genres of marronage, these particular configurations of motility and complicity emerge in unfathomably variable forms.

Nonetheless, since these materials are already partially broken in, they have already begun to assume the forms and features of traditionally crafted brass instruments. In other words, the straitjacket of overrepresentation has already taken hold, enforced by the eyes and ears of the workshop, the concert stage, and the wider cultural sphere at large. Because they are recognizable signifiers of the brass instrument's overrepresented culture figuration, any encounter with the workshop or the stage will see them inevitably subsumed back into their previous representation, however faulty or imperfect they may seem. Having expressed their fugitive motility in fleeing the factory, these materials then face an altogether different obstacle in finding the networks of complicity that will allow them to shed the accrued expectations of their overrepresented form. Passage through this complication depends upon the bodies and affordances that populate spaces like the workshop or the concert venue, for only with their complicity can those spaces become *plots* or *borderlands* within the larger archipelago of material marronage. As activist Stefano Harney and poet Fred Moten describe in their study of that maroon network they call the "undercommons," such "maroons[ ] are always at war, always in hiding" (Harney and Moten 2013: 30).

And so, just as in all other systems of oppression that create the conditions for marronage, these questions pertain not only to the materials themselves, but also to the other agencies, bodies, or persons that inhabit the wider field of plantations, industries, and hegemonic cultural apparatuses. Every maroon flight, whether human or material, is always already giving voice to *homo narrans* or *hylo narrans*, but for those narrative agencies to take root, they must be folded into a wider network of metabolizing cultural collectivity. In order for these materials to grasp and hold the attention they need in order to build a network of complicity, their voices must first be perceivable to those of us they accost—our ears and bodies must be sensitized to the frequencies and amplitudes of their interpellation. Before we can respond to the material cry of *hylo narrans*, we must attune ourselves to the registers in which that voice proclaims its flight.

Like the bell, the voice has also been overrepresented as a political concept, such that in many cases, the metaphorical significance of 'having a voice' can drown out the actual sound of that voice altogether. And when oppression is defined as silencing—"the systemic and institutionalized inability to make a difference" (James 2014: n.p.)—challenges to this inequality can end up reproducing this same political overrepresentation of the voice. In this framing the voice itself becomes merely a tool of "information exchange," a "transmission of signal," and in order for political silencing to be overcome—for people to unite in "the task of building worlds together"—communication must be reconceived as "more fundamentally a political and ethical problem than a semantic one" (Peters 1999: 30). In prioritizing this political dimension, not only the semantic but also the sonic affect of voice is either overlooked entirely, or obscured behind what ethnomusicologist Ana María Ochoa Gautier calls "an eminent field of transparent affect and relationality" (Ochoa Gautier 2014: 22). In other words, this overrepresentation of the voice also shapes interpretations of its sonic affect, subsuming the acoustic to the representational (in this case not only philosophical but also social and political). "That is why in the West the expression 'to have a voice,' to 'listen to one another, and more recently, to feel a 'resonance' or 'vibrations' between people are often expressions used to invoke the idea of participation, the recognition of the 'other,' and alternative forms of the collective" (Ochoa Gautier 2014: 22). In urging us to reconsider both the oral and aural, Ochoa Gautier elaborates:

> Thus entities that listen and entities that produce sounds are entangled in the relation between nature and culture and mutually produce each other—a theory of sound implies a listener, which in turn imagines a listener and an idea of reception of sound. In the relation between each of

> these entities—a listening subject, an object that produces a sound, and a supposed listener of that sound object—what is produced is an ontology of *relationships*, an idea of how to think the interaction between entities that produce/hear sounds. (Ochoa Gautier 2014: 22)

In opening the concept of voice to these dimensions of materiality and material agency, the risk of overrepresenting voice as political agency becomes even more foregrounded. Ochoa Gautier's recentering around "aurality" helps us instead anchor an idea of material voice in what she calls "acoustic assemblages," which describe how the material affectivity of a voice (or its echo) retains a "mutually constitutive and transformative relation" (Ochoa Gautier 2014: 22). These acoustic assemblages are indeed physical, but rather than flattening that sonic materialism into an overrepresented conception of anthropocentric political voice, they instead "address[ ] different conceptions of the human and the boundaries between the human and nonhuman" (Ochoa Gautier 2014: 9). Bulut argues that this "voice, once it is constructed, functions not merely as a mode of communication or a sound that conjures the fantasy of an autonomous self, but also as a sort of permeable skin" (Bulut 2025: 1). For Bulut, it is important for us to understand how this collective experience of voice-as-touch includes but also supersedes both the semantic and the political aspects of communication. She proposes an awareness of voice as "non-dialogue" (Bulut 2025: 10), in which sensory and communicative facets of voicing merge and overlap:

> Thinking of voice as skin, and skin as voice, we experience and embrace the body, self and speech as emergent, errant, exploratory and shared. In effect, we can revisit the ways in which we situate human and nonhuman bodies, consider the agency and passivity of human and nonhuman expressions, and acknowledge the making of a voice that we do not know, as well as a voice that capacitates the states of not knowing. (Bulut 2025: 21)

In Bulut's account, holding this tension between the variously haptic, audible, and abstract dimensions of voice helps to elucidate how human and nonhuman voices can meet, merge, or interact. The human and nonhuman are not only able to come into contact with one another, they can also inhabit this collective, permeable voice as a means to mediate their respective genres of agency. Instead of privileging either the material or the discursive, this conception of voice acknowledges their differences of scale while still navigating fluidly between them. Crucially, Bulut also proposes thinking of this mediative voice more actively. Obliquely echoing Cesaire, she approaches voice through the verb voicing, describing "individual and collective acts of voicing" as emergent practices that "prepare[ ] and perform[ ]" this haptic, sonic "skin as a common ground" (Bulut 2025: 234). In this formulation, acts of voicing (and listening) become "material-discursive practices" in the sense that physicist and philosopher Karen Barad describes: "material configurations or reconfigurings of the world that re(con)figure spatiality and temporality" (Barad 2007: 146).

In previous publications, I have argued for a sonic materialism based on these aspects of Barad's thought. In seeking to "capture the ruptured concord and discord that fuses bodies together in the momentary entanglement when sound waves are produced" (Toksöz Fairbairn 2022: 23), I deploy Barad's concept of the agential cut. The agential cut describes how a particular entity or phenomenon comes to be. Within a sea of indeterminate potentialities—each as salient as any other—this moment or object will then coalesce as some subset of these potentialities fuse together in a single "intra-action" (an interaction so intimate that it is inside a moment of spacetime, rather than linking between multiple) (Barad 2003: 815). From this perspective, a phenomenon—whether object, particle, concept, or even moment in time, etc.—is "not a thing but a doing, a congealing of agency" (Barad 2007: 183-184). Because it excludes some potential valences as much or more than it brings others together, the agential cut enacts a kind of choreography of "joins and disjoins—cutting together/apart" (Barad 2010: 244). Barad views the consubstantiality of continuity and discontinuity as a "way of thinking with and through dis/continuity—a dis/orienting experience of the dis/jointedness of time and space, entanglements of here and there, now and then" (Barad 2010: 240). While Barad examines primarily the quantum world, I approach sound as a mundanely palpable medium for understanding how agential cuts fuse together agencies and bodies across dis/continuous spaces and times—linking mines to metals; factory floors to live concerts; hands, ears, and strings to the oscillations that vibrate them. Following Barad, I examine "the dis/cordant phenomena by which we touch and are touched through sound," and which, like voicing, "become means of thinking with and through other bodies" (Toksöz Fairbairn 2022: 23).

Barad's philosophy of concomitant rupture and suture undergirds a radical sense of voicing. It evokes networks of complicity that combine intimate proximities with distant histories or spacetimes, allowing discrete agencies, place-thoughts, and narrative imaginaries to merge through their mutual implication in the momentary act of voicing and the haptic sonic vibrations that that excites. Bulut compares voicing to a membrane, evoking precisely this communion between the radical intimacy of enclosed (bounded) spaces and the infinite potential of implicated bodies beyond, all joined through the oscillations of this membrane that simultaneously separates and synthesizes them—at least for the duration of its vibration, its voicing. For both Bulut and Barad, particularity is key. An agential cut is not generalizable; it doesn't simply scale up to larger phenomena or collectivities. Similarly, Bulut's voicing adheres to the grain of specific sounding bodies and the collectivities that they fleetingly constitute in the act of sounding. These convergences also recede, and a proper account of their human and nonhuman agencies takes care with this fugitive ephemerality.

Within arguments for attending more closely to nonhuman voices, there is an impulse to integrate these agencies into a preexisting sphere of anthropocentric social, political, or ethical frameworks. In his call for an "*object-oriented* democracy," philosopher Bruno Latour deliberately frames this *Dingpolitik* in relation to *Realpolitik* (Latour 2005: 14). The materiality, though, remains fuzzy, shifting seamlessly from "each object" to "each issue" as it maps out a "hidden geography" of "public space" and "'the political'" (Latour 2005: 15). Philosopher Jane Bennett's eloquent exposition of "thing-power" in her influential book *Vibrant Matter: A Political Ecology of Things* circles the same socio-political gravitational force. Even as she celebrates material's "vortical logic [that] holds across different scales of size, time, and complexity," (Bennett 2010: 119), she places it within the scope of public life and its "spheres of democracy" (Bennett 2010: 109):

> If human culture is inextricably enmeshed with vibrant, nonhuman agencies, and if human intentionality can be agentic only if accompanied by a vast entourage of nonhumans, then it seems that the appropriate unit of analysis for democratic theory is neither the individual human nor an exclusively human collective but the (ontologically heterogeneous) 'public' coalescing around a problem. (Bennett 2010: 109)

Although these approaches welcome "nonhuman materialities as participants in a political ecology" (Bennett 2010: 109), they are ultimately subsumed into more generalized "healthy and enabling instrumentalizations" (Bennett 2010: 12). The problem is that material voices do not necessarily assimilate to these concepts of public health (whether institutional, social, organical, ethical, etc.). While these accounts envision a necessary rehabilitation of public life and the need to incorporate nonhuman perspectives into human political movements, they also replicate the overrepresentation of nonhuman voices as abstract political agencies. As Bulut's and Barad's flickering, in/determinate materialities demonstrate, though, materials have their own vectors of agency, intersecting but not necessarily integrating into our public sphere. In proposing marronage as a central component of material agency, *hylo narrans* attempts to balance these conflicting impulses, responding to material provocations while still acknowledging their peripheral particularity. *Hylo narrans* brings discussions of materiality back to archipelagic place-thoughts and their situated voicings.

In her *Queer Phenomenology*, philosopher Sara Ahmed gives us tools for navigating these complex spatiotemporal proximities and dis/continuities. She examines touch, connection, and communication through the lens of the "reachable," asking, how it is that certain possibilities (voicings, intra-actions, etc.) "become reachable [while] others remain or even become out of reach" (Ahmed 2006: 14). Ahmed suggests that, if our perception of the world is constituted by what is perceptually accessible, then our reality will be formed not by the objects that surround us, but rather by the directions we find ourselves facing and feeling. Similarly to Barad, Ahmed reminds us that, although we inhabit a field of almost infinite potential combinations and affordances, the "reachable" is defined more by what is excluded than by what is theoretically possible. In her case, though, rather than investigating the quantum world, she explores how cultural belief systems determine which objects or opportunities are ready-to-hand, thereby showing how material configurations and interventions in our everyday world support the overrepresentation of certain ideological systems at a social, cultural, or political scale. Ahmed deploys the idea of the "reachable" to link the abstract or political implications of cultural narratives to mundane material and phenomenological experiences, insisting that, despite their global or political affectivity, ultimately all "[o]rientations are tactile" (Ahmed 2006: 55).

Ahmed situates this proposition within the work of Judith Butler who, following Louis Althusser, identifies a form of 'calling'—and the 'turning' to address that call—as intrinsic to the performance of identity (Butler 1997: 33). Butler notes especially that, even as this interpellation can mark us out and identify us, it can just as easily go astray—it can miss its intended target, or it can be ignored, or it can be answered by an unexpected party, and so on. Ahmed builds upon these observations by suggesting that the way in which we orient ourselves towards these calls—from perspectives either frontal or oblique or some infinite gradation in between—determine what becomes reachable or not. In other words, attuning to a wider, multi-dimensional field of interpellation allows one to shift out of alignment, to become constructively disoriented. "Disorientation could be described here as the 'becoming oblique' of the world" (Ahmed 2006: 162), which, Ahmed argues, is a necessary first step in exposing the body to new and unexpected forms of proximity, contact, and touch. "Moments of disorientation are vital. They are bodily experiences that throw the world up, or throw the body from its ground" (Ahmed 2006: 157).

These moments of disorientation can in turn afford us the opportunity to pivot towards re/orientations within a wider sphere of movement, flight, and propulsive agencies. Ahmed's conceptualization of orientation directs us away from linear ideological predispositions and instead positions the body as receptive and responsive. Rather than focusing on the agency of the subject to wilfully accept or reject a particular orientation, Ahmed diffuses that agency within a wider field of proximate voices and bodies, each inviting, impelling, guiding, or imploring. Re/orientation in this sense has little or nothing to do with the wilful rejection of one alignment in favor of another. Rather, it directs the body towards a situated receptivity, attuning perception towards interpellative voices that introduce more collective, multivalent experiences of the world. With this in mind, she plumbs the quotidian reality of material dispersion in space and time to help map the intersecting vectors of agency, flight, and communication that might challenge the overrepresented cultural hegemonies that determine our dispositions to material and to each other. By embracing obliquity,

Ahmed directs our attention to the peripheral, to bodies that maroon, and to fugitive voicings.

Material marronage interpellates a call to complicity. For material maroons persisting within the *borderland* archipelago at the edges of our perception, human attunement to their interjections can help build the networks of complicity that re/orient their flight beyond the strictures of hegemonic overrepresentation. Re/orientation towards *hylo narrans* enables new acoustemological communities to form, embracing its principles of obliquity, motility, and collectivity. Just as Césaire insisted that marronage be understood as a verb, as both impulse and agency, the interpellative voicings of material marronage demand a complicity that is similarly active and intransitive. Receptivity must be enacted, cultivated, and reinforced; parsing new acoustemological interpellations requires adjusting in some way to accommodate those new stimuli. Displacing the ideological formations of overrepresented echoes (positivistic or naturalistic) requires the active formation of alternative sounding situated knowledges.

In answering the call of brass in flight, this process begins in the workshop itself. In the workshop, brass is not yet in its state of suspended animation, locked behind a blanket of enamel and crafted into a highly-calibrated megaphone. On the workshop floor, brass has its own sonic agency, shrieking or moaning under duress, or singing and sighing when addressed more gently. The sheets of brass that form bell flares are cast in large rolls of very thin brass, less than a millimeter thick. These sheets are tightly rolled, and thereby dampened, but as soon as they begin to unroll, the metal roils and rumbles.[2] When hammered into shape, the brass melds with the steel mandrels inside it, each coaxing hammer blow resounding in echoing, metallic peals. And when spun on the lathe to produce the final, even curve of a bell flare, the metal is stretched along the steel mandrel, thinning ever further and bursting forth in reverberating cascades of piercing overtones. These overtones increase in complexity and volume as the brass is progressively thinned out to its fraying edges, spreading along the mandrel like a ball of rolled dough stretched out by a rolling pin. If the brass survives all of these

2 This phenomenon is actually employed as a percussion instrument in other scenarios, and is commonly known as a thunder sheet for its acoustic imitation of a distant storm.

mutilations, its cries will then be swallowed up by the final step of fabrication: its thinned edge will be trimmed and rolled over onto itself (often with a brass wire soldered inside) to reinforce its structure and stability, which has the ancillary effect of dramatically dampening the bell's metallic resonance.

At each stage of this process, the brass has distinctly different acoustic characters. Each stage alters the molecular composition of the brass as it is alternately annealed and work-hardened, producing funeous variations in resonance. Each process alters the shape of the proto-flare, gradually morphing from a flat sheet of rumbling, thundering brass; to a conical chamber with an acoustic volume; to a thin flare with the resonant vitality of a cymbal; and then to the final, reinforced but dampened bell flare. As though in one final appeal before being swallowed up, this bead wire will rattle like a cymbal rivet before it is soldered into place, dampened and muffled into its finished, instrumental form. Materials sometimes flee this process through corrosion or fracture or some other instability, but depending on which stage they reach before their flight catches purchase, they possess radically different funeous ontogenies, material compositions, and acoustic characters. Each piece of brass's unique flight determines the acoustic character of its fugitive body, as its variously corroded, wrinkled, fractured, or punctured brass resounds.

The interpellative voice of bell flares in construction bears little resemblance to the overrepresented acoustemological product of the finished brass instrument and its stentorian, proclamatory voicing. Whether responding to hammers and lathes or to the gentler entreaties of bowing, rubbing, blowing, or brushing, these materials-in-flight voice oblique, metallic resonances. These brass maroons are neither primed nor perfected; their voices are formed within damaged, impure, often unstable bodies. Their inner volume, their thin walls, their unpredictable blemishes and contortions: each distinct maroon narrates its own dehiscent funicity in the contours of its body, enunciating their messy histories of extraction and metamorphosis.

A craftsperson in the workshop is generally trained to ignore these oblique interpellations. The trade, the tools, and the training all reinforce the alignments of the overrepresented bell and its prescribed voicing. But in order to do so, they must be highly attuned to the acoustemological cues of that brass in the workshop environment; how the metal sings or shrieks as it is subdued provides invaluable information for the craftsperson who shapes it. A craftsperson can often parse a piece of brass's 'failure' through acoustic cues, especially when working with machines (i.e., in moments with less direct hands-on connection). They are aware of its obliquity, but they only orient themselves around its disposition towards binary success or failure: it either becomes a bell, or it becomes rubbish. A rebellious piece of brass will not be recuperated, it will simply be discarded or sold back to a metal recycler as raw stock. Material marronage is often unsuccessful because, lacking any network of complicity to aid their flight, these materials are just reabsorbed into the churning cycle of industrial extraction.

But practices of re/orientation and collective voicing can reshape this narrative. As fugitive brass voices its interpellation to obliquity, it becomes incumbent on other agencies in this acoustemological field to re/orient themselves to its impulse, to reinforce its voicing, and to propel its marronage. These metals have already hijacked their fabrication, disembarking from the ideological inevitability of their form. At this point, a craftsperson can either serve the dictates of the factory, corralling this metal back into obedience, or they can embrace its fugitive impulse, reorienting their awareness to parse these new material possibilities. In both cases, the acoustic information remains the same, but its acoustemological meaning morphs as a craftsperson learns to listen obliquely, voicing their complicity with the narrative agency of brass-in-flight.

The stories of the chimeracords that have occupied this book relate my own journey as a craftsperson in learning to listen to and respond to these fugitive metals. As the evolution of interactions narrated within these instruments begins to show, there are almost innumerable potential voicings within these multivalent networks of complicity. Wynter's science of the Word proposes that long-term cultivation of alternative listening can generate new forms of collective human and more-than-human cultural creativity, voicing their mutual resilience, resistance, and reinvention. The unexpected visual and acoustic performances of these chimeracords confront listeners, disorienting them from their expectations when seeing the overrepresented image of a brass bell. Their hybrid construction flows into these gaps in intelligibility, replacing the confusion of unrealized expectations with myriad oblique interpellations, a polyphonic chorus comprising the myriad forms of acoustic potential lurking in these materials' funeous metamorphoses. The intertwined stimuli of metallic, percussive, reed, and string consorts frays a listener's attention, offering them not a singular alternative to the linear expectation of an overrepresented, 'classical' instrumental form, but rather a forest of radiating interpellations, interventions, and invitations. The listener is offered an opportunity to listen agentially, eschewing their expectations and learning instead to parse these new vocabularies of material marronage. Chimeracords invite their audiences into a bubble of sonic fugitivity, soliciting their complicity in imagining alternative spacetimes, motilities, and modes of relation. They offer acoustic passage into a material *borderland*, inviting listeners to be a guest in this pocket of time and space, and to open their bodies to a form of complicity that transforms their shared spacetime into an ephemeral—but palpable—materialization of *plot*.

Just as not every craftsperson learns to parse the oblique interpellations of material marronage, not every listener joins this community. These re/orientations must be purposefully re/enacted. Sometimes these re/orientations slip in and out of focus over time, as maroon voices flicker in and out of earshot. *Hylo narrans* doesn't voice a monolithic political agency. Rather, within the unceasing reiteration of cultural autopoiesis that constitutes daily life, in which overrepresented echoes invariably threaten to drown out other voices, these material fugitivities allow us to reimagine the stories we hope to listen to as well as those we hope to tell. Although specific acts of flight form the wedges that puncture the bounds of alignment and overrepresentation, opening the gaps through which other agencies might flow, fugitivity voices more than just this, encompassing also the ongoing practices of *plotting* that maintain and nourish networks of complicity necessary to sustain continuing acts of flight. Like the autopoietic self-re/generation that Wynter describes in *homo narrans*, fugitivity is an interscalar mediation of various modes and methods of resistance. Re/orientations reject previous alignments, refusing to define themselves by their relation to or against previous overrepresentations; they imagine otherwise, impelling vectors of flight towards collectively reconstituted narratives of history and of the future. "[P]ractices of fugitivity [...] should not be read as reactions to socio-spatial domination but as place-making otherwise. Fugitivity is generative: it enacts or rehearses alternative politics, social relations, and forms of cultural expression" (Gross-Wyrtzen and Moulton 2023: 1264). This conception of flight as constructive and imaginative rather than reactive already has a long history within Indigenous and decolonial scholarships. These traditions recognize how the momentum of flight coalesces in propulsive cultural autopoiesis. As artist and researcher Jarrett Martineau and sociologist Eric Ritskes describe:

> The freedom realized through flight and refusal is the freedom to imagine and create an elsewhere in the here; a present future beyond the imaginative and territorial bounds of colonialism. It is a performance of other worlds, an embodied practice of flight. The fugitive aesthetic is not an abdication of contention and struggle; it is a reorientation toward freedom in movement, against the limits of colonial knowing and sensing. (Martineau and Ritskes 2014: IV)

Flight within the *plots* and the *borderlands* of the contemporary world requires navigating the lexica of representation, overrepresentation, and re-presentation otherwise. As political theorist and philosopher Joy James notes, marronage's "trajectory into freedom" flows through the "reservation or cell" (James 2013: 124), within which spaces its success or failure depends on an ability to remain illegible to the hegemonic overseer infrastructure that surrounds them. Martineau and Ritskes echo poet Édouard Glissant's repeated declarations of a "right to opacity" (1981; 1990; 1997/2020), emphasizing the necessity of cultivating collective vocabularies that resist assimilation into overrepresentation:

> Fugitivity finds its energetic potency in remaining illegible to power, incommensurable with colonialism, and opaque to appropriation, commodification and cultural theft. That which is fugitive proposes an insurgent force of dissident visibility; it is the hidden that reveals itself in motion. The fugitive aesthetic is thus an overflowing of borders and bordered-thinking, a liminal praxis whose generative effects activate art in a transversal re-presencing. (Martineau and Ritskes 2014: V)

Flight is itself a creative act, and thus transposes readily and cooperatively into other forms of aesthetic expression and cultural creativity. Flight animates the *plot* and the *borderland*, generating the frequencies through which fugitive webs of complicity can communicate beyond the bounds and even the awarenesses of hegemonic regimes of overrepresented acoustemologies. They initiate the impulse for "the creative forms that become possible in fugitive spaces" (Martineau and Ritskes 2014: III), just as those ongoing creative forms will sustain the energies and agencies necessary to inspire new acts and even modalities of flight in the future.

Chimeracords are an evolving creative act, unfinished and unfinishable. They rely on the *plots* that have been cultivated in various workshops around the world and they help to sustain the ephemeral *borderlands* that their interpellative performances initiate along the winding trails of their ongoing flight. They didn't choose these spaces, nor do these spaces represent any sort of ideal. They coalesce around loci of complicity, but are equally constrained by the boundaries of that complicity. These spaces can be re/oriented, but they are still limited by the constraints of the *plot* in which they form. And just as the original *plots* required collective creativity in order to transform pestilence into refuge, so also do the bounded spaces of complicit workshops require cooperation and ingenuity if they have any hope of cultivating *hylo narrans*. A *plot* within a factory or a workshop can be ephemeral, appearing at certain hours and disappearing the next, shifting in and out of focus depending on the gaze that passes over. It must evolve within the bounded space that it can afford, learning to think, to act, and to sound by cultivating the agencies of the materials and bodies that congeal within its limited scope. The bounded space of the workshop *plot* braids together tributaries of human and more-than-human stories, from the tortured ontogenies of brass-in-flight to the generations of accumulated expertise circulating through craftspeople's hands. In the confluence of their collective action, these intersecting narrative agencies can form their own patterns of survival and resistance, and thereby embody their own distinctive forms of place-thought.

Marronage survives in the collective reservoir of its entire marginal archipelago. Although fragmented and at times discontinuous, this archipelago circulates through networks of complicity that allow forms of interlaced place-thought to germinate and grow in each of its disparate *plots* and *borderlands*. The echoes through which these isolated spaces resound and communicate generate sounding situated knowledges that, for all their fugitivity, remain rooted in the concrete, bounded spaces in which that complicity is reiteratively enacted. These echoes are the sympathetic resonances of place-thoughts attuned. They emerge from voices grasping their autopoietic agency, converging in their articulations of resistance. As these unique forms of place-thought materialize in bounded workshops or other *plots*, they transform the valence of these metals—no longer the univocal acclamation of extractive currency or hegemonic power, but now the voicings of hybridity, complicity, and resistance. Through their collective cultivation of the *plot*, *homo* and *hylo narrans* generate the conditions for Wynter's Ceremony Found, crafting new rituals and refrains out of the dehiscent, funeous detritus of industrial capitalism. In their sublime impurity, these materials voice the unimaginable: vibrations and waveforms whose unpredictable fluency narrate future collective imaginaries of ongoing resistance.

Emerging from mines, factories, and the wastebins of capitalist musical production, chimeracords invoke an alternative vocabulary of flight. Reaching deep inside their funeous archives of extraction and subjection, the materials in these instruments shudder and buck beneath their mutilation. They dare to imagine an existence out of alignment; they disengage, they flee, and they proudly announce this agency to anything or anybody attuned to the frequencies of their rebellious fugitivity. Chimeracords articulate the possibility of a *plot* within the factory; they sound this call in all of the homes and institutions in which they resound—however elusively and fleetingly those voices reverberate and fade. They initiate forms of place-thought within the liminal *borderlands* surrounding industry, extraction, and quadrivial urban sprawl. They suggest forms of human and material collectivity that can emerge from the irreversible traumas of displacement and exploitation with imaginative capacities for collective place-thought and narrative agency.

Chimeracords announce a dream of communal self-re/generation, both of their own material agency, but also of the collective imaginations of resistance that they narrate alongside *homo narrans* within their interwoven *plots* and *borderlands*. Carrying the sedimented histories of eons spent underground alongside the scars of industrial mutilation, these instruments propose that materials can voice the polyphonic cultural creativities that sustain flight through interscalar generations of fugitivity. They excite unpronounceable vibrations that invite us to join them in place-thought, singing into existence what flights might become possible and what stories might be sung. They ask us to listen for their flights of material marronage, to attune to *hylo narrans*, and to imagine a future in which material voices might even lead a chorus of collective re/imagination, severing the binding cord of overrepresentation and fraying it into a reverberant lattice of resonant hybridity.

Ultimately, this book is simply asking that we listen to material voices. I have attempted to share ongoing practices of craft, art, and research that seek to amplify the collective voices of *hylo narrans* and their capacity to teach, guide, and enrich our human and more-than-human communities. But the final words belong properly not to me but to these materials-in-flight themselves. And so, with that in mind, I cede to the chimeracord itself by asking you to listen to the final recording that accompanies this chapter, attuning to the lingering echoes of material marronage: singing, resounding, imagining.

References

Agamben, Giorgio, trans. Georgia Albert. 1994/1999. *The Man without Content*. Stanford: Stanford University Press.

Ahmed, Sara. 2006. *Queer Phenomenology*. Durham: Duke University Press.

Alagraa, Bedour. 2018. "*Homo Narrans* and the Science of the Word: Toward a Caribbean Radical Imagination." *Critical Ethnic Studies* 4 (2), pp. 164-181. https://doi.org/10.5749/jcritethnstud.4.2.0164

—. 2019. "The Interminable Catastrophe: Fatal Liberalisms, Plantation Logics, and Black Political Life in the Wake of Disaster." (PhD Thesis). Brown University.

—. [@jwilonline]. 2022. *I'm back with another thread! This time, we'll be looking at an important essay by Sylvia Wynter* [Tweet]. Twitter. https://x.com/jwilonline/status/1577776657351442432

Arendt, Hannah. 1958. *The Human Condition: A Study of the Central Dilemmas Facing Modern Man*. New York: Doubleday and Co.

Banerjee, Kaushik, Subhas De, Rahul Singh, and Souren Jana. 2013. "Automated Mineral Detection Using SONAR Wave." *International Journal of Scientific and Engineering Research* 4 (5), pp. 1884-1890.

Basso, Keith H. 1996. *Wisdom Sits in Places: Landscape and Language Among the Western Apache*. Albuquerque: University of New Mexico Press.

Barad, Karen. 2003. "Posthumanist Performativity: Towards an Understanding of How Matter Comes to Matter." *Signs: Journal of Women in Culture and Society* 28 (3), pp. 801-831. https://doi.org/10.1086/345321

—. 2007. *Meeting the Universe Halfway*. Durham: Duke University Press, https://doi.org/10.2307/j.ctv12101zq

—. 2010. "Quantum Entanglements and Hauntological Relations of Inheritance: Dis/Continuities, SpaceTime Enfoldings, and Justice-to-Come." *Derrida Today* 3 (2), pp. 240-268. https://doi.org/10.3366/drt.2010.0206

Bennett, Jane. 2010. *Vibrant Matter: A Political Ecology of Things*. Durham: Duke University Press. https://doi.org/10.2307/j.ctv111jh6w

 https://doi.org/10.11647/OBP.0476.07

Bijsterveld, Karin. 2008. *Mechanical Sound: Technology, Culture and Public Problems of Noise in the Twentieth Century*. Cambridge: MIT Press. https://doi.org/10.7551/mitpress/9780262026390.001.0001

Bjorkmann, Judith Kingston. 1973. "Meteors and Meteorites in the Ancient Near East." *Meteoritics & Planetary Science* 8 (2), pp. 91-130.

Bledsoe, Adam. 2017. "Marronage as a Past and Present Geography in the Americas." *Southeastern Geographer* 57 (1), pp. 30-50. https://doi.org/10.1353/sgo.2017.0004

Boethius, Anicius Manlius Severinus, trans. Calvin M. Bower. 1989. *Fundamentals of Music*. New Haven: Yale University Press.

Borges, Jorge Luis, trans. James E. Irby, Donald A. Yates, John M. Fein, Harriet de Onís, Julian Palley, Dudley Fitts, and L. A. Murillo. 1962. *Labyrinths: Selected Stories & Other Writings*. New York: New Directions.

Borrows, John. 2001. "Listening for a Change: The Courts and Oral Tradition." *Osgoode Hall Law Journal* 39 (1), pp. 1-38. https://doi.org/10.60082/2817-5069.1480

—. 2018. "Earth-Bound: Indigenous Resurgence and Environmental Reconciliation." In *Resurgence and Reconciliation Indigenous–Settler Relations and Earth Teachings*, eds. Michael Asch, John Borrows, and James Tully, pp. 49-81. Toronto: University of Toronto Press. https://doi.org/10.3138/9781487519926-004

—. 2019. *Law's Indigenous Ethics*. Toronto: University of Toronto Press. https://doi.org/10.3138/9781487531140

Bradley, Rizvana. 2023. *Anteaesthetics: Black Aesthesis and the Critique of Form*. Stanford: Stanford University Press. https://doi.org/10.1515/9781503637146

Bulut, Zeynep. 2025. *Building a Voice: Sound, Surface, Skin*. London: Goldsmiths Press.

Burkholder, J. Peter, Donald J. Grout, and Claude V. Palisca. 2014. *A History of Western Music*. New York: W.W. Norton and Company.

Butler, Judith. 1997. *Excitable Speech: The Politics of the Performative*. Stanford: Stanford University Press.

Chao, Sophie. 2022. *In the Shadow of the Palms: More-than-Human Becomings in West Papua*. Durham: Duke University Press. https://doi.org/10.2307/j.ctv2j86bm4

—. 2023. "Spent Earth." *Critical Times* 6 (2), pp. 179-188. https://doi.org/10.1215/26410478-10436987

Césaire, Aimé. 1945. "Poésie et Connaisance." *Tropiques* 12, pp. 157-170.

—, trans. Joan Pinkham. 1950/2000. *Discourse on Colonialism*. New York: Monthly Review Press.

—, trans. 1955/1983. "Le verbe marronner / à René Depestre, poète haïtien." In *Aimé Césaire: The Collected Poetry*, eds. Clayton Eshleman and Annette Smith, pp. 368-371. Berkeley: University of California Press.

—, trans. Clayton Eshleman and Annette Smith. 1990. *Lyric and Dramatic Poetry 1946-82*. Charlottesville: The University Press of Virginia.

Chen, Mel Y. 2012. *Animacies: Biopolitics, Racial Mattering, and Queer Affect*. Durham: Duke University Press. https://doi.org/10.2307/j.ctv11vc866

Combes, Muriel, trans. Thomas LaMarre. 2013. *Gilbert Simondon and the Philosophy of the Transindividual*. Cambridge: MIT Press.

Cordova, Viola. 2007. *How It Is: The Native American Philosophy of V. F. Cordova*. Eds. Kathleen Dean Moore, Kurt Peters, Ted Jojola, and Amber Lacy. Tucson: The University of Arizona Press.

Craddock, Paul T. 1995. *Early Metal Mining and Production*. Edinburgh: Edinburgh University Press.

—. 1998. "Zinc in Classical Antiquity." In *2000 Years of Zinc and Brass*, ed. Paul T. Craddock, pp. 1-6. London: British Museum.

Danylevich, Theodora. 2016. "Beyond Thinking: *Black Flesh as Meat Patties* and *The End of Eating Everything*." *Rhizomes: Cultural Studies in Emerging Knowledge* 29. https://doi.org/10.20415/rhiz/029.e15

DeLanda, Manuel. 2000. *A Thousand Years of Nonlinear History*. New York: Swerve Editions.

—. 2004. "Material Complexity." In *Digital Tectonics*, eds. Neil Leach, David Turnbull, and Chris Williams, pp. 14-21. Chichester: Wiley-Academy.

Deloria Jr., Vine. 1973/2003. *God is Red: A Native View of Religion*. Golden, Colorado: Fulcrum Publishing.

—. 1999. *Spirit and Reason: The Vine Deloria, Jr. Reader*. Eds. Barbara Deloria, Kristen Foehner, and Sam Scinta. Golden: Fulcrum Publishing.

Deleuze, Gilles, trans. Paul Patton. 1968/1994. *Difference and Repetition*. New York: Columbia University Press.

Deleuze, Gilles, and Felix Guattari. 1980/1987. *A Thousand Plateaus: Capitalism and Schizophrenia*. Minneapolis: University of Minnesota Press.

Derrida, Jacques, trans. Alan Bass. 1968/1972. *Margins of Philosophy*. Chicago: University of Chicago Press.

Diouf, Sylviane. 2014. *Slavery's Exiles: The Story of the American Maroons*. New York: New York University Press.

Dolge, Alfred. 1911. *Pianos and Their Makers*. Covina: Covina Publishing Company.

Dyson, Frances. 2014. *The Tone of Our Times: Sound, Sense, Economy, and Ecology*. Cambridge: MIT Press. https://doi.org/10.7551/mitpress/8427.001.0001

Edelson, S. Max. 2006. "The Nature of Slavery: Environmental Disorder and Slave Agency in Colonial South Carolina." In *Cultures and Identities in Colonial British America*, eds. Robert Olwell and Alan Tully, pp. 221-244. Baltimore: Johns Hopkins University.

Erasmus, Zimitri. 2020. "Sylvia Wynter's Theory of the Human: Counter-, not Post-humanist Article." *Theory, Culture & Society* 37 (6), pp. 47-65. https://doi.org/10.1177/0263276420936333

Feld, Steven. 1996. "Waterfalls of Song: An Acoustemology of Place Resounding in Bosavi, Papua New Guinea." In *Senses of Place*, eds. Steven Feld and Keith H. Basso, pp. 91-136. Santa Fe: School of American Research Press.

Feld, Steven. 2015. "Acoustemology." In *Keywords in Sound*, eds. David Novak and Matt Sakakeeny, pp. 12-21. Durham: Duke University Press. https://doi.org/10.2307/j.ctv11sn6t9.4

Ferro, Sérgio, trans. Alice Fiuza and Silke Kapp. 2018. "Concrete as Weapon." *Harvard Design Magazine* 46 (F/W 2018), pp. 8-32.

Forty, Adrian. 2012. *Concrete and Culture: A Material History*. London: Reaktion.

Foucault, Michel. 1966/2005. *The Order of Things: An Archaeology of the Human Sciences*. London: Routledge.

Gallagher, Michael. 2015. "Field Recording and the Sounding of Spaces." *Environment and Planning D: Society and Space* 33 (3), pp. 560-576. https://doi.org/10.1177/0263775815594310

Glissant, Edouard. 1981/1989. *Caribbean Discourse: Selected Essays*. Charlottesville: University of Virginia Press.

—. 1990. *Poetics of Relation*. Ann Arbor: University of Michigan Press.

—. 1997/2020. *Treatise on the Whole-World*. Liverpool: Liverpool University Press.

Goh, Annie (Su-Ann). 2017. "Sounding Situated Knowledges: Echo in Archaeoacoustics." *Parallax* 23 (3), pp. 283-304. https://doi.org/10.1080/13534645.2017.1339968

—. 2019. "Sonic Knowledge Production in Archaeoacoustics: Echoes of Elsewhere?" (PhD Thesis). Goldsmiths College, University of London.

Gross-Wyrtzen, Leslie, and Alex A. Moulton. 2023. "Toward 'Fugitivity as Method': An Introduction to the Special Issue." *ACME: An International Journal for Critical Geographies* 22 (5), pp. 1258-1272. https://doi.org/10.7202/1107308ar

Harney, Stefano, and Fred Moten. 2013. *The Undercommons: Fugitive Planning & Black Study*. Wivenhoe: Minor Compositions.

Hartley, H. A. 1958. *Audio Design Handbook*. New York: Gernsback Library, Inc.

Heller-Roazen, Daniel. 2005. *The Fifth Hammer: Pythagoras and the Disharmony of the World*. New York: Zone Books.

Hubbs, Brian. 2014. "The Inevitable Issue Most High-rise Owners Face." *RDH Building Science Inc.* https://www.rdh.com/blog/the-inevitable-issue-with-igus/

James, Robin. 2014. "Some Initial Thoughts on Bennett's 'Vibrant Matter.'" *It's Her Factory*. https://www.its-her-factory.com/2014/08/some-initial-thoughts-on-bennetts-vibrant-matter/

—. 2019. *The Sonic Episteme: Acoustic Resonance, Neoliberalism, and Biopolitics*. Durham: Duke University Press. https://doi.org/10.1515/9781478007371

Jarzombek, Mark. 2019. "The Quadrivium Industrial Complex." *e-flux*. https://www.e-flux.com/architecture/overgrowth/296508/the-quadrivium-industrial-complex/

Kanngieser, A. M. 2023. "Sonic Colonialities: Listening, Dispossession, and the (Re)making of Anglo-European Nature." *Transactions of the Institute of British Geographers* 48 (4), pp. 690-702. https://doi.org/10.1111/tran.12602

Kapp, Silke, Katie Lloyd Thomas, and João Marcos de Almeida Lopes. 2018. "How to Look at Architecture from Below," introduction to Sérgio Ferro, "Concrete as Weapon." *Harvard Design Guide* 46 (F/W 2018), pp. ii-vi.

Kharakwal, Jeewan Singh, and Lokesh Kumar Gurjar. 2006. "Zinc and Brass in Archaeological Perspective." *Ancient Asia* 1 (2006), pp. 139-159.

Kumari, Madhuri. 2020. "The Production of Zinc and Brass in Ancient India." *International Journal of Professional Studies* 9, pp. 39-52.

LaMarre, Thomas. 2013. "Afterword: Humans and Machines." In *Gilbert Simondon and the Philosophy of the Transindividual*, Muriel Combes, trans. Thomas LaMarre, pp. 79-108. Cambridge: MIT Press.

Latour, Bruno. 2005. "From Realpolitik to Dingpolitik: or How to Make Things Public." In *Making Things Public: Atmospheres of Democracy*, eds. Bruno Latour and Peter Weibel, pp. 14-44. Karlsruhe: ZKM Center for Art and Media; Cambridge: MIT Press.

Lloyd Thomas, Katie. 2021. *Building Materials: Material Theory and the Architectural Specification*. London: Bloomsbury. https://doi.org/10.5040/9781350176256

Mackey, Nathaniel. 2018. *Paracritical Hinge: Essays, Talks, Notes, Interviews*. Iowa City: University of Iowa Press. https://doi.org/10.1353/book58085

Malm, Andreas. 2018. "In Wildness Is the Liberation of the World: On Maroon Ecology and Partisan Nature." *Historical Materialism* 26 (3), pp. 3-37. https://doi.org/10.1163/1569206x-26031610

Martineau, Jarrett, and Eric Ritskes. 2014. "Fugitive Indigeneity: Reclaiming the Terrain of Decolonial Struggle through Indigenous Art." *Decolonization: Indigeneity, Education & Society* 3 (1), pp. I-XII.

Massumi, Brian. 1992. *A User's Guide to* Capitalism and Schizophrenia*: Deviations from Deleuze and Guattari*. Swerve: London.

Maturana, Humberto. 1970. *Biology of Cognition*. Reprinted in Humberto Maturana and Francisco J. Varela, *Autopoiesis and Cognition: The Realization of the Living*. Dordrecht: D. Reidel Pub. Co., pp. 5-58.

—. 1980. "Introduction." In Humberto Maturana and Francisco J. Varela, *Autopoiesis and Cognition: The Realization of the Living*. Dordrecht: D. Reidel Pub. Co., pp. xi-xxx.

Maturana, Humberto, and Francisco J. Varela. 1980. *Autopoiesis and Cognition: The Realization of the Living*. Dordrecht: D. Reidel Pub. Co.

McKittrick, Katherine. 2006. *Demonic Grounds: Black Women and the Cartographies of Struggle*. Minneapolis: University of Minnesota Press.

McKittrick, Katherine. 2016. "Rebellion/Invention/Groove." *small axe* 49, pp. 79-91. https://doi.org/10.1215/07990537-3481558

McKittrick, Katherine (with Sylvia Wynter). 2015. "Unparalleled Catastrophe for Our Species? Or, to Give Humanness a Different Future: Conversations." In *Sylvia Wynter: On Being Human as Praxis*, ed. Katherine McKittrick, pp. 9-89. Durham: Duke University Press. https://doi.org/10.1215/9780822375852-002

McKittrick, Katherine, Frances H. O'Shaugnessy, and Kendall Witaszek. 2018. "Rhythm, or On Sylvia Wynter's Science of the Word." *American Quarterly* 70 (4), pp. 867-874. https://doi.org/10.1353/aq.2018.0069

Morris, Rosalind. 2008. "The Miner's Ear." *Transition* 98, pp. 96-115. https://doi.org/10.2979/trs.2008.-.98.96

Moulton, Alex A. 2024. "Plotting a New Course for Environmental Humanities: Provision Grounds, Race, and the Future." *Environmental Humanities* 16 (2), pp. 271-290. https://doi.org/10.1215/22011919-11150035

Murphy, Michelle. 2017. "What Can't a Body Do." *Catalyst* 3 (1), pp. 1-15. https://doi.org/10.28968/cftt.v3i1.28791

Napoleon, Val. 2001. "Ayook: Gitksan Legal Order, Law, and Legal Theory." (PhD Thesis). University of Victoria.

Nash, June. 1979. *We Eat the Mines and the Mines Eat Us: Dependency and Exploitation in Bolivian Tin Mines*. New York: Columbia University Press.

Neuman, Bernhard. 1903. "Die Anfänge der Argentan-(Neusilber)-Industrie und der technischen Nickelerzeugung." *Angewandte Chemie* 16 (10), pp. 225-232.

Ochoa Gautier, Ana María. 2014. *Aurality: Listening and Knowledge in Nineteenth-Century Colombia*. Durham: Duke University Press. https://doi.org/10.1215/9780822376262

Ouzounian, Gascia. 2017. "Rethinking Acoustic Ecology: Sound Art and Environment." *Evental Aesthetics* 6 (1), pp. 4-23.

—. 2021. *Stereophonica: Sound and Space in Science, Technology, and the Arts*. Cambridge: MIT Press. https://doi.org/10.7551/mitpress/11698.001.0001

Ovid, trans. Brookes Moore. 1922. *Metamorphoses*. https://topostext.org/work/141

Partch, Harry. 1949/1974. *Genesis of a Music: An Account of a Creative Work, Its Roots and Its Fulfillments*. New York: Da Capo Press.

Patterson, C. C. 1971. "Native Copper, Silver, and Gold Accessible to Early Metallurgists." *American Antiquity* 36, pp. 286-321.

Peters, Edward Dyer. 1895. *Modern Copper Smelting*. New York: The Scientific Publishing Co.

Peters, John Durham. 1999. *Speaking into the Air: A History of the Idea of Communication*. Chicago: University of Chicago Press.

Pijanowski, Bryan C., Luis J. Villanueva-Rivera, Sarah L. Dumyahn, Almo Farina, Bernie L. Krause, Brian M. Napoletano, Stuart H. Gage, and Nadia Pieretti. 2011. "Soundscape Ecology: The Science of Sound in the Landscape." *BioScience* 61, pp. 203-216. https://doi.org/10.1525/bio.2011.61.3.6

Puar, Jasbir K. 2017. *The Right to Maim: Debility, Capacity, Disability*. Durham: Duke University Press. https://doi.org/10.2307/j.ctv11314kc

Ridley, H. N. 1907. "The Oil Palm." *Agricultural Bulletin of the Straits and Federated Malay States* 6 (1), pp. 37–40.

Roberts, Neil. 2015. *Freedom as Marronage*. Chicago: University of Chicago Press. https://doi.org/10.7208/chicago/9780226201184.001.0001

Robinson, Dylan. 2020. *Hungry Listening: Resonant Theory for Indigenous Sound Studies*. Minneapolis: University of Minnesota Press. https://doi.org/10.5749/j.ctvzpv6bb

Rodgers, Tara. 2011. "'What, for me, constitutes life in a sound?': Electronic Sounds as Lively and Differentiated Individuals." *American Quarterly* 63 (3), pp. 509-530. https://doi.org/10.1353/aq.2011.0046

Rosiek, Jerry Lee, Jimmy Snyder, and Scott L. Pratt. 2019. "The New Materialisms and Indigenous Theories of Non-Human Agency: Making the Case for Respectful Anti-Colonial Engagement." *Qualitative Inquiry* 26 (3-4), pp. 331-346. https://doi.org/10.1177/1077800419830135

Rudge, Alice and Véra Ehrenstein. 2021. "Dreams of Purity: Improved Palms, Refined Oils, and Ethical Consumption." *Society and Space*. https://www.societyandspace.org/articles/dreams-of-purity

Schafer, R. Murray. 1977/1994. *The Soundscape: Our Sonic Environment and the Tuning of the World*. Rochester, Vermont: Destiny Books.

Sexton, Jared. 2011. "The Social Life of Social Death: On Afro-Pessimism and Black Optimism." In*Tensions Journal* 5, pp. 1-47. https://doi.org/10.25071/1913-5874/37359

Sexton, Jared (with Daniel Barber). 2017. "On Black Negativity, Or the Affirmation of Nothing: Jared Sexton, Interviewed by Daniel Barber." *Society and Space*. https://www.societyandspace.org/articles/on-black-negativity-or-the-affirmation-of-nothing

Shapiro, Nicholas, and Eben Kirksey 2017. "Chemo-Ethnography: An Introduction." *Cultural Anthropology* 32 (4), pp. 481-493. https://doi.org/10.14506/ca32.4.01

Sharpe, Christina. 2016. *In the Wake: On Blackness and Being*. Durham: Duke University Press. https://doi.org/10.1515/9780822373452

Silko, Leslie Marmon. 1986/2002. "Landscape, History, and the Pueblo Imagination." In *The Norton Book of Nature Writing*, eds. Robert Finch and John Elder, pp. 1003-1014. New York: W. W. Norton and Co.

Simmons, I. G. 1989/1996. *Changing the Face of the Earth: Culture, Environment, History*. Oxford: Blackwell.

Simondon, Gilbert, trans. Gregory Flanders. 2009. "The Position of the Problem of Ontogenesis." *Parrhesia* 7, pp. 4-16.

Simondon, Gilbert, trans. Cecile Malaspina and John Rogrove. 2017. *On the Mode of Existence of Technical Objects*. Minneapolis: Univocal.

Simondon, Gilbert, trans. Taylor Adkins. 2005/2020. *Individuation in Light of Notions of Form and Information*. Minneapolis: University of Minnesota Press.

Simpson, Leanne Betasamosake. 2014. "Land as Pedagogy: Nishnaabeg Intelligence and Rebellious Transformation." *Decolonization: Indigeneity, Education & Society* 3 (3), pp. 1-25.

Smith, Cyril Stanley. 1981. *A Search for Structure: Selected Essays on Science, Art and History*. Cambridge: MIT Press.

Southworth, Michael Frank. 1967. "The Sonic Environment of Cities." (Master's Thesis). Massachusetts Institute of Technology, Department of City and Regional Planning.

Spillers, Hortense J. 1987. "Mama's Baby, Papa's Maybe: An American Grammar Book." *Diacritics* 17 (2), pp. 64-81.

—. 2004. "Topographical Topics: Faulknerian Space." *The Mississippi Quarterly* 57 (4), pp. 535-568.

Stadler, Katharina. 2024. *Terror Sine Verbis.* (PhD Thesis). Kunstuniversität Linz.

Starblanket, Gina and Heidi Kiiwetinepinesiik Stark. 2018. "Towards a Relational Paradigm—Four Points for Consideration: Knowledge, Gender, Land, and Modernity." In *Resurgence and Reconciliation Indigenous–Settler Relations and Earth Teachings*, eds. Michael Asch, John Borrows, and James Tully, pp. 175-208. Toronto: University of Toronto Press. https://doi.org/10.3138/9781487519926-007

Sterne, Jonathan. 2003. *The Audible Past: Cultural Origins of Sound Reproduction.* Durham: Duke University Press.

Strabo, trans. Horace Leonard Jones. 1961. *The Geography of Strato.* Volume 5. Cambridge: Harvard University Press.

Swentzell, Rina. 2012. "Pueblo Watersheds: Places, Cycles, and Life." In *Thinking Like a Watershed: Voices from the West,* eds. Jack Loeffler and Celestia Loeffler, pp. 28-44. Albuquerque: University of New Mexico Press.

Theophilus, trans. John G. Hawthorne and Cyril Stanley Smith. 1963. *On Divers Art.* Chicago: University of Chicago Press.

Thompson, Marie. 2017. "Whiteness and the Ontological Turn in Sound Studies." *Parallax* 23 (3), pp. 266-282. https://doi.org/10.1080/13534645.2017.1339967

Thornton, Christopher P. 2007. "Of Brass and Bronze in Prehistoric Southwest Asia." *Metals and Mines: Studies in Archaeometallurgy* 2007, pp. 123-135.

Todd, Zoe. 2016. "An Indigenous Feminist's Take on the Ontological Turn: 'Ontology' is Just Another Word for Colonialism." *Journal of Historical Sociology* 29 (1), pp. 4-22. https://doi.org/10.1111/johs.12124

Valenzuela-Zapata, Ana G., Paul D. Buell, María de la Paz Solano-Pérez, and Hyunhee Park. 2013. "'Huichol' Stills: A Century of Anthropology—Technology Transfer and Innovation." *Crossroads* 8, pp. 157-191.

Toksöz Fairbairn, Kevin. 2022. *dis/cord: Thinking Sound through Agential Realism.* Earth, Milky Way: punctum books. https://doi.org/10.53288/0360.1.00

van der Schyff, Dylan B. 2010. "The Ethical Experience of Nature: Aristotle and the Roots of Ecological Phenomenology." *Phenomenology & Practice* 4 (1), pp. 97-121. https://doi.org/10.29173/pandpr19830

Virgil, trans. A. S. Kline. 2002. *Aeneid.* https://topostext.org/work/245

Voegelin, Salomé. 2019. *The Political Possibility of Sound: Fragments of Listening.* New York: Bloomsbury. https://doi.org/10.5040/9781501312199

Watts, Vanessa. 2013. "Indigenous Place-Thought and Agency Amongst Humans and Non-Humans (First Woman and Sky Woman Go on a European World Tour!)." *Decolonization: Indigeneity, Education & Society* 2 (1), pp. 20-34.

Williams, David Russell and C. Mathew Balensuela. 2008. *Music Theory from Boethius to Zarlino : A Bibliography and Guide*. Hillsdale: Pendragon.

Wright, Mark Peter. 2022. *Listening After Nature: Field Recording, Ecology, Critical Practice*. New York: Bloomsbury Academic. https://doi.org/10.5040/9781501354540

Wynter, Sylvia. n.d. *Black Metamorphosis: New Natives in a New World*. Unpublished manuscript.

—. 1968. "We Must Learn to Sit Down Together and Talk about a Little Culture: Reflections on West Indian Writing and Criticism: Part One." *Jamaica Journal* 2 (4), pp. 23-32.

—. 1969. "We Must Learn to Sit Down Together and Talk about a Little Culture: Reflections on West Indian Writing and Criticism: Part Two." *Jamaica Journal* 3 (1), pp. 27-42.

—. 1970. "Jonkonnu in Jamaica: Towards the Interpretation of the Folk Dance as a Cultural Process." *Jamaica Journal* 4 (2), pp. 34-48.

—. 1971. "Novel and History, Plot and Plantation." *Savacou*, 5 June 1971, pp. 95-102.

—. 1995. "1492: A New World View." In *Race, Discourse, and the Origin of the Americas: A New World View*, eds. Vera Lawrence Hyatt and Rex Nettleford, pp. 5-57. Washington, DC: Smithsonian Institution Press.

—. 2000. "Africa, The West and the Analogy of Culture: The Cinematic Text After Man." In *Symbolic Narratives/African Cinema: Audiences, Theory and the Moving Image*, ed. June Givanni, pp. 25-76. London: British Film Institute.

—. 2003. "Unsettling the Coloniality of Being/Power/Truth/Freedom Towards the Human, After Man, Its Overrepresentation—An Argument." *CR: The New Centennial Review* 3 (3), pp. 257-337.

Wynter, Sylvia (with Katherine McKittrick). 2015a. "Unparalleled Catastrophe for Our Species? Or, to Give Humanness a Different Future: Conversations." In *Sylvia Wynter: On Being Human as Praxis*, ed. Katherine McKittrick, pp. 9-89. Durham: Duke University Press. https://doi.org/10.1215/9780822375852-002

Wynter, Sylvia. 2015b. "The Ceremony Found: Towards the Autopoetic Turn/Overturn, its Autonomy of Human Agency and the Extraterritoriality of (Self-)Cognition." In *Black Knowledges/Black Struggles: Essays in Critical Epistemology*, eds. Jason R. Ambroise and Sabine Broeck, pp. 184-252. Liverpool: Liverpool University Press. https://doi.org/10.5949/liverpool/9781781381724.003.0008

Index

About the Team

Alessandra Tosi was the managing editor for this book.

Adèle Kreager proof-read this manuscript and compiled the index.

Jeevanjot Kaur Nagpal designed the cover. The cover was produced in InDesign using the Fontin font.

Annie Hine typeset the book in InDesign.

Jeremy Bowman produced the paperback and hardback editions and created the EPUB. The main text font is Tex Gyre Pagella and the heading font is Californian FB. Jeremy also produced the PDF edition.

The conversion to the HTML edition was performed with epublius, an open-source software which is freely available on our GitHub page at https://github.com/OpenBookPublishers

Hannah Shakespeare was in charge of marketing.

This book was peer-reviewed by three anonymous referees. Experts in their field, these readers give their time freely to help ensure the academic rigour of our books. We are grateful for their generous and invaluable contributions.

This book need not end here...

Share

All our books — including the one you have just read — are free to access online so that students, researchers and members of the public who can't afford a printed edition will have access to the same ideas. This title will be accessed online by hundreds of readers each month across the globe: why not share the link so that someone you know is one of them?

This book and additional content is available at https://doi.org/10.11647/OBP.0476

Donate

Open Book Publishers is an award-winning, scholar-led, not-for-profit press making knowledge freely available one book at a time. We don't charge authors to publish with us: instead, our work is supported by our library members and by donations from people who believe that research shouldn't be locked behind paywalls.

Join the effort to free knowledge by supporting us at https://www.openbookpublishers.com/support-us

We invite you to connect with us on our socials!

BLUESKY
@openbookpublish
.bsky.social

MASTODON
@OpenBookPublish
@hcommons.social

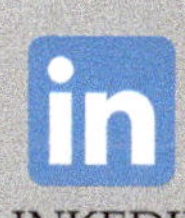

LINKEDIN
open-book-publishers

Read more at the Open Book Publishers Blog

https://blogs.openbookpublishers.com

You may also be interested in:

Engaging with Everyday Sounds

Marcel Cobussen

https://doi.org/10.11647/OBP.0288

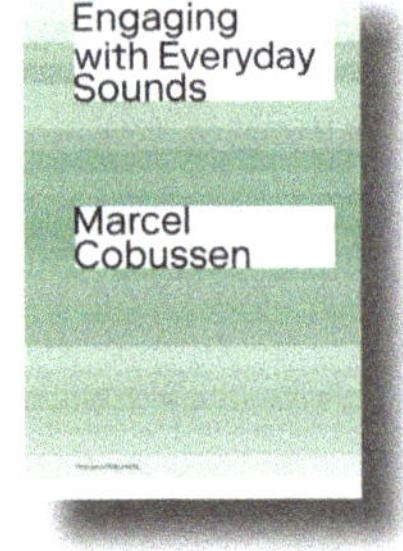

Acoustemologies in Contact

Sounding Subjects and Modes of Listening in Early Modernity

Edited by Emily Wilbourne and Suzanne G. Cusick

https://doi.org/10.11647/OBP.0226

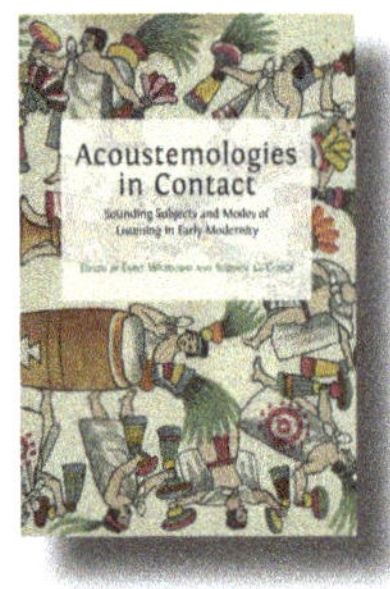

Heavy Metal

Earth's Minerals and the Future of Sustainable Societies

Edited by Philippe D. Tortell

https://doi.org/10.11647/OBP.0373

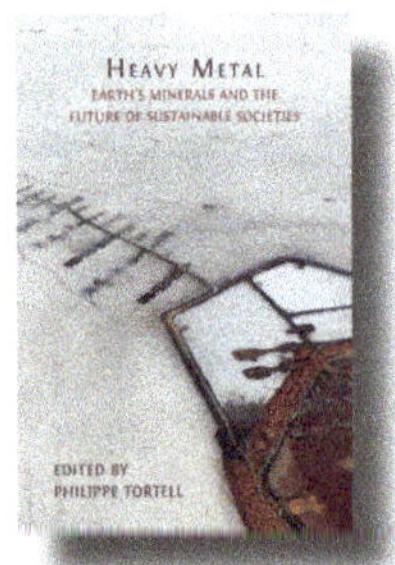

Oral Literature in the Digital Age

Archiving Orality and Connecting with Communities

Edited by Mark Turin, Claire Wheeler and Eleanor Wilkinson

https://doi.org/10.11647/OBP.0032

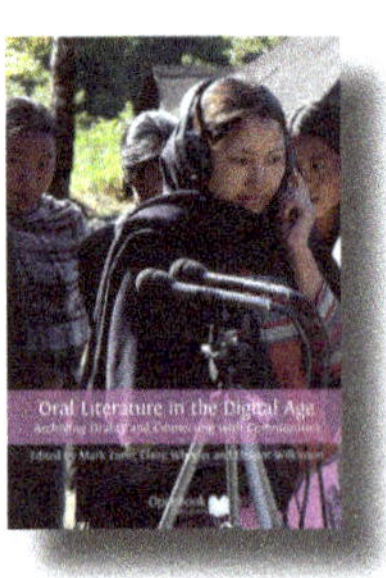